SKUSE'S COMPLETE CONFECTIONER

This is the classic text on the art of sugar boiling and all its branches, covering the manufacture of fondants, creams, chocolates, pastilles, jujubes (jelly babies) comfits, lozenges (plain and medicated), caramels, noyeaus, nougats, jap nuggets and pralines.

There are also discussions on the practicalities of ice creams, ices, jams, jellies and marmalades, table jellies, preserved and crystallized fruits, candied peel and English and Scotch pastry.

SKUSE'S COMPLETE CONFECTIONER

E. SKUSE

LONDON AND NEW YORK

First published in 2004 by
Kegan Paul International

This edition first published in 2010 by
Routledge
2 Park Square, Milton Park, Abingdon, Oxfordshire OX14 4RN

Simultaneously published in the USA and Canada
by Routledge
711 Third Avenue, New York, NY 10017

First issued in paperback 2016

Routledge is an imprint of the Taylor & Francis Group, an informa business
© Kegan Paul, 2004

All rights reserved. No part of this book may be reprinted or reproduced or
utilised in any form or by any electronic, mechanical, or other means, now
known or hereafter invented, including photocopying and recording, or in
any information storage or retrieval system, without permission in writing
from the publishers.

British Library Cataloguing in Publication Data
A catalogue record for this book is available from the British Library

ISBN 13: 978-1-138-98206-2 (pbk)
ISBN 13: 978-0-7103-0903-7 (hbk)

Publisher's Note
The publisher has gone to great lengths to ensure the quality of this reprint
but points out that some imperfections in the original copies may be
apparent. The publisher has made every effort to contact original copyright
holders and would welcome correspondence from those they have been
unable to trace.

PREFACE

An author is usually expected to make an excuse or apology for every new venture : this is mine :

The "Complete Confectioner" has now been out of print for several months while the demand and enquiries continue.

The Publishers have decided to issue a new and enlarged edition from the same pen.

With every passing year the realm of the confectioner gets wider, new methods are adopted while variety is ever changing and increasing.

The Engineer, the Artist, and the Chemist compel us to alter our systems and provide ourselves with their new contrivances, if we would keep in the front, and, even to have a fairly good knowledge of what is going on, we must make ourselves acquainted with the ideas and achievements of men of science outside as well as inside our own Kingdom.

It is therefore difficult, if not impossible, to make oneself conversant with all that has happened which would be of interest and value to the trade.

I have used my best endeavours in this direction with what result I must leave the reader to find in the pages.

The present will make the 10th edition (21,000 copies in all) since the original "Confectioner's Hand Book."

This is evidence that my efforts have been helpful and appreciated ; but for such encouragement I certainly would not have undertaken the responsibility of revising and practically re-writing the present edition.

Wishing my readers, every success,

E. SKUSE.

Ashmore Works,
  Harrow Road, London, W.

SUGAR BOILING.

THIS branch of the trade or business of a confectioner is perhaps the most important. Many manufacturers are more or less interested in it, and certainly no retail shop could be considered orthodox which did not display a tempting variety of this class of goods. So inclusive is the term "boiled goods" that it embraces drops, rocks, candies, toffees, caramels, creams and a number of different sorts of hand-made, machine and moulded goods. It is the most ancient method of which we have any knowledge, and perhaps the most popular process of modern times; the evidence of our every day experience convinces us that, notwithstanding the boom which heralds from time to time a new sweet, cooked in a different manner, composed of ingredients hitherto unused in the business, it is the exception when such goods hold the front rank for more than a few months, however pretty, tasty, or tempting they may be, the public palate seems to fall back on those made on the old lines which, though capable of improvement, seem not to be superseded. Of the entire make of confectionery in the United Kingdom, at least two-thirds of it may be written down under the name of boiled sugar. They are undoubtedly the chief feature with both manufacturers and retailers, embracing, as they do endless facilities for fertile brains and deft fingers for intending novelties in design, manipulation, combination, and finish. Notwithstanding the already great variety, there is always something new in this department brought into the market. Many of the most successful houses owe their success more to their heads than to their hands, hence the importance of studying this branch in all its ramifications. The endless assortment requiring different methods for preparing and manipulating make it necessary to subdivide this branch into sections, order and arrangement being so necessary to be thoroughly understood. When we consider the few inexpensive tools required to make so many kinds of saleable goods, it is not to be wondered at that so many retailers have a fancy to make their own toffees and such like. There is no reason why any man or woman with an ordinary amount of patience, a willing and energetic disposition, and favoured with a fair amount of intelligence should not become a good sugar-boiler, with the aid of this book and a small outlay for tools, after a few months' practice.

There are many reasons why a retail confectioner should study sugar boiling. It gives a character to the business, a fascinating odour to the premises, and a general at-homeness to the surroundings. The goods when freshly made look more attractive and tempting to the sweet eating public than those of any other description. A bright window can only be so kept by makers. Grainy or sticky drops may be reboiled; scraps and what would otherwise be almost waste (at least unsightly) may be redressed in another shape, and become not only salcable, but profitable. A manufacturer possesses many advantages over one who buys all; for instance, clear boiled goods should be kept air-tight, and are therefore delivered to the shopkeeper in bottles, jars, or tins, on which a charge is made. These have to be re-packed and returned. Breakages are an important item, so is carriage—the cost of the latter is saved and the former reduced to a minimum.

The writer's former efforts to instruct the uninitiated were looked upon by some in the trade as giving away the business to the injury of those who served their time to the art.

It is not so. Whatever means are adopted to benefit the retailer and advertise the business by brighter windows, cleaner shops, less faded goods, and healthier financial conditions must contribute to the general prosperity of the trade.

It should be the aim of all amateurs to study quality rather than price. Goods well made, carefully flavoured, and nicely packed will always command a ready sale at a fair price, giving satisfaction to the customer and credit to the maker. Give your customers something to please the eye as well as the palate, and every sale may then be looked upon as an advertisement. Cheap, bulky, insipid stuff is unprofitable and damaging to the trade as well as the seller. The writer ventures to assert that more would-be makers have come to grief trying to cut out each other in price for rubbishy sweets than through any other cause. Look at the hundreds of firms of repute whose names command trade at good prices, and who year after year increase their turn-over. What is the talisman? Look at their goods. There is, perhaps, nothing very striking in them, but they are always of uniform appearance, and in busy or slack times are manufactured carefully, packed with taste, and delivered neatly in a business-like fashion. Compare this to the many makers whose existence proves only to be ephemeral. They obtain orders, sell at unprofitable prices, frequently at a loss, and try to make up the difference by resorting to various methods of increasing the bulk, the ultimate result being ruin to themselves, loss to their creditors, and injury to everyone concerned. Many who read these lines will later on verify all that is stated. The writer's advice has always been to keep up a high degree of excellence, to endeavour to improve in every direction, and his success has been the reward of patience and energy. This work is written to initiate those who have a desire to know the mysteries of the confectioner's art. The instructions are plain, simple, and should be easily understood ; only that which is necessary is stated : the repetition of processes, which may apply to many recipes, is avoided as far as possible. We have no space to spare for long rambling descriptive details, which bewilder and confuse a beginner. Short, crisp, essential instructions are given at the commencement of every section, and apply to all the formulæ which follow ; these should be carefully read and re-read. When a particular recipe is required, the reader is referred to the special instructions.

Difficult processes in any branch should not be attempted until the more simple ones are mastered. Success depends, not only on genuine information, but also on the faithful working out of it.

It is not pretended to give a complete list of all kinds known in the trade, that would be absurd and impossible, but all the different branches are given, consequently any article of confectionery may be imitated by careful comparison and reference to the class or section to which the sample belongs. To be able to tell this will require knowledge only to be gained by experience, so that much depends on the thoughtful endeavour of the beginner.

THE WORKSHOP.

SUGAR BOILING REQUISITES.

SUGAR boiling, like every other craft, requires a place to do it, and fitted accordingly. The requisites and requirements can be easily suited to the accommodation and the purse of the would-be confectioner. A work to be useful for all must cater for all, and include information for the smaller shopkeeper as well as the larger maker. To begin at the bottom, one can easily imagine a person whose only ambition is to make a little toffee and hardbake for the window fit for children. This can be done at a very small outlay for utensils. Where circumstances compel us to be very economical, we can manage with a saucepan, a clean clay pipe, a few toffee tins, a large pair of scissors, and an ordinary kitchen fire. This is rather a primitive arrangement, but it will answer the purpose. The tins should be made of stout tinned iron, about 15 inches long and 8 or 10 inches wide and 1 inch deep, wired round the top for strength. A copper saucepan would be much preferable to an iron one. We can make with these appliances Everton toffee, cocoanut candy, and such like, and at a pinch clove stick and hand cut balls. The next tool to be added should be a small cast-iron pouring plate, say 3 feet long by 1 foot 8 inches wide, costing about £1. Fix this to a rough bench about 2 feet 4½ inches high,

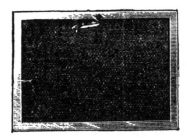

Pouring Plate.

letting the pouring plate form as it were the top of a table. This will be very useful, and will enable us to extend our operations to sticks,—striped and plain,—also creams of various kinds. A pouring plate of this size will allow 12 or 14 lbs. of sugar to cool at a time. The next move is an important one, viz., the erection of a sugar boiler's furnace. It is not very costly but is certainly indispensable where quality and variety are required. A great economy in time and money will be effected; the boiled sugar will be a much better colour, so that cheaper sugar may be used for brown or yellow goods, while one can make acid drops and other white goods from granulated, Dutch crushed, or loaf sugar, which otherwise would be impossible on an ordinary kitchen fire. The furnace may be erected in a back kitchen, cellar, or outhouse, of ordinary size, while the requisites are few. Here is a drawing, cut from a photograph, which will form a guide to any bricklayer or handy man,

Confectioner's Furnace.

and shows almost every brick and where to place it. To build this, 100 common bricks, 12 fire bricks, a cast-iron furnace top, a 13 inch flat grate or furnace bottom, a piece of iron bar 12 inches long, 6 inches wide, and a $\frac{1}{4}$ inch thick would be required. If the floor is stone, you could commence to build; if of wood, either take the wood up and put down concrete, or lay a thick stone slab over the floor, the ash pit thus is well protected against fire. In commencing to build, first form your ash pit (A) by raising the two pillars (BB) four bricks high and three bricks from back to front, or, in other words, 2 feet 3 inches. Leave a space of 9 inches across for the ashes; the stove will then be 2 feet 3 inches square. When the pillars are four bricks high, lay the piece of 12 inch iron between the two pillars to carry the top course of bricks; let the ash pit be 18 inches from the front; build in the back solid. Now place the square grate between the two pillars, $4\frac{1}{2}$ inches from the front of the stove. Now form a circle 9 inches in diameter, by placing the fire-bricks on their ends round the grate, then build up the sides of the stove to the level of the top of the fire-bricks; pack the fire-bricks well up with rubble, cementing the whole firmly with fire-clay. The furnace must be built near a chimney; when the flue is being formed, half one of the fire-bricks, which stand upright and form a small flue, having the iron stove top for a covering, letting it run into the chimney. Build up the chimney all round the flue, so that it might have a good draught. When the furnace has been built and the top surface levelled, the furnace top should be placed on damp mortar or fire-clay, so that it will adhere firmly. In this case, the cast-iron plate should be 2 feet 3 inches square, with a nine inch hole in the centre. It will then match the brick-work built as per instructions, but a stove-top can be had any size with larger or smaller hole and the brick-work built accordingly. Reducing rings are also made to fit the stove top, which will make the hole smaller. These are very useful for boiling smaller quantities of sugar for stripes and other purposes. The cost of plate and necessary iron work—about £1 10s—from any machine maker.

Having got the furnace fixed, it is now absolutely necessary to have a copper-pan,—the size, according to trade requirements,—but as some sugars foam a great deal, it is just as well to have a large one. We must expect to do big things when we have a furnace to work with.

Copper Sugar Boiling Pan.

COPPER SUGAR BOILING PAN.

A pan something of the above shape, say 12 inches across the top and 6 inches deep, would be sufficient to boil from 14 to 20 lbs. of sugar at a time. With these simple appliances (but more slab room) we could make 2 cwt. of various sorts of boiled sugars per diem. There is no need to go further with these directions, as when additional work is required, the experience already gained with these appliances will show the beginner what he requires much better than books; besides which machine makers will give him any information respecting their various, ever-changing, and augmenting labour-saving appliances.

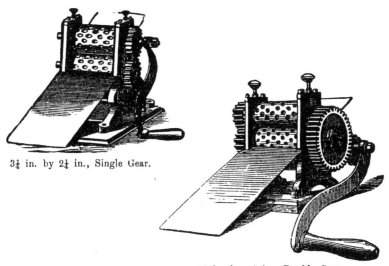

3¼ in. by 2¼ in., Single Gear.

4¾ in. by 2¼ in., Double Gear.
Drop Machines.

I cannot go any further into the mysteries of this art successfully, unless we provide ourselves with something like the above machine to enable us to make drops. They are indispensable, and if we are to go on, we must have them. They enable us to make drops, and as every confectioner sells drops, these machines are constructed to suit all classes of trade, big and little. The small ones make just as nice drops as the large ones, and the smallest will turn out in the course of a day 2 to 3 cwt., so that for retail purposes a small machine would generally suffice. A description of the machines may not be out of place, and will guide the reader in his selection. Here are 2 illustrations, showing what is known as the smaller sizes in common use—the first block showing 3¼ inches long by 2¼ in diameter, with cog wheels at one end only; the other block shows a 4¾ inches long by 2¼ inches in diameter, double gear, *i.e.*, having cog wheels at each end, the latter being larger are more easily turned by having 2 sets of cogs, the former being smaller 2 sets are unnecessary.

The frame or stand in which the rollers are fitted is made to a standard gauge, and it admits of any number of rollers being placed in the same frame; one pair of rollers may be taken out and replaced by another pair in one minute, so that one frame is all that is necessary for any number of rollers.

The rollers are made to cut and mould almost any shape or pattern—*i.e.* raspberries, pears, grapes, horses, dogs, leaves, in endless variety.

The smallest frame costs 16/-, and each pair of rollers to fit about 30/- The larger sizes are considerably dearer. For latest prices, apply to the makers. Beginners, in selecting machines, should have the rollers as useful as possible, and not buy fancy shapes to begin with, because the rollers will simply cut or print the pattern they were intended for, and nothing else can be made out of them. For example, suppose you buy a pair of rollers to cut elephants, you may stripe your sugar, case your sugar, or put it through plain, they would still be elephants. On the other hand if you bought a pair of ball rollers, see what a variety you could make out of a single pair. With a little judgment and manipulation, you could make acid balls, brandy balls, rose-buds, or striped balls of various sorts. Another useful pair are acorn rollers. You could, at a pinch, make pears, grapes, pine-apples, ripe pears, acorns, &c. To do this only requires a little arrangement of colours and flavours—there is not much difference in the shape. Two pairs of rollers more useful to a beginner it would be difficult to name.

Where a wholesale trade is the aim, $4\frac{3}{4}$ double gear rollers are the most useful, as they are as large as can be conveniently turned by hand, and are capable of doing an immense amount of work; whereas, if $3\frac{1}{4}$ size are bought in the first place and afterwards found too small, the whole lot would require to be replaced, very little money being allowed for second hand rollers. The larger rollers can be bought a pair or two at a time, and those in hand would always be worth their cost, while increased trade would simply necessitate a few more extra pairs, the saving in labour when an extra quantity is required would soon pay the difference and show a profit. These machines should be fixed on a corner of a table, from 7 to 10 feet long and about $2\frac{3}{4}$ to 3 feet wide. The table should have a cast iron top, or better still, the top may be made of a smooth stone slab, "not slate." Of course, the size of the table would be determined according to the accommodation of space, extent of trade, and size of machine. Another table covered with wood at the opposite side of machine bench, would be useful for mixing, weighing, bottling, labelling, and packing. On one side of the furnace a shelf or small table should be provided for holding the bottles of flavours, acids, etc.; the other side may be used for storing sugar and other heavy and bulky materials. Arrangements for coke should be made close to the stove on either side. The following drawing will give a rough idea of what is meant.

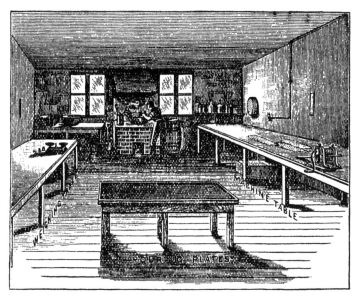

Confectioner's Boiling Room.

ORDER AND METHOD IN WORKSHOP.

HAVING so far got our workshop arranged the next thing is to keep it in order. Sugar boiling is a dirty, sticky business, especially on wet days, unless every part of the workshop is kept scrupulously clean and dry. Slabs and tables should be washed, no trace of sifting, scraps, or boiled goods should be left exposed to the atmosphere during the night; the floor should be well swept, and a little clean sawdust put down every night.

The comfort and ease in working in a clean place amply repays the trouble and time it takes to keep it in order, besides, the goods are much drier, brighter, and easier to bottle or pack. Nothing is more unpleasant than to work with sticky slabs, slimy machines, and dirty scales; the boil adheres to the slabs, sticks to the rollers and spoil the shapes, and becomes cloudy and spotty in weighing. Any one who has worked in or visited small workshops, can endorse these remarks, and too much importance cannot be attached to these apparently unnecessary points.

Of course our boiling shop is but a small primitive affair. It is almost superfluous to state that large manufacturers have big rollers in steam power benches.

Power Bench.

Six, eight, or ten pairs of rollers in a row, all or some ready to be put in motion by a touch of the lever; besides cold water pouring plates, and many other labour and time saving appliances.

Since the publication of the last edition of this work, steam has come to the front, as a means of cooking sugar for boiled goods, a process not previously attempted. The merits of vacuum pans have been tried and tested not only in the workshop but in the law courts, a somewhat costly experiment. Machine manufacturers have vied with each other in producing large and expensive plant, some claiming to be capable of making clear, bright drops from dark and inferior sugar, leaving it to the imagination what they could do with good and white sugar. While writing this page I have turned over the advertisement columns of a trade paper wherein vacuum and open boiling steam plant are advertised. The maker of the vacuum plant says, "it will turn out glucose and sugar boilings superior in every way to fire work. The maker of the open boiling plant says "the sugar is cooked quicker than by any other process, and better results are obtained than is possible to get in vacuo." Both makers have many of their plant in use, giving great satisfaction, as is testified by the users who are among the largest manufacturing confectioners in the trade. Readers who require a plant of this magnitude will have sufficient experience to select one suitable. Makers are always pleased to supply particulars and show the advantages of their latest productions. Improvements being constantly made, the best of to-day may be antiquated next year so that the best guide is to study the latest catalogues of the best manufacturers.

METHOD OF SUGAR BOILING.

In sugar boiling, as in everything else, science has had a look in and systematised, that which was formerly a crude rule of thumb. A pair of scissors was the weapon, *par excellence*, with which the confectioner cut his drops, while his fingers were the only tool for moulding, shaping, pinching, striping, rolling and twisting the variety then known as the goodies of the day.

The process was tedious, laborious, and costly, but it must be admitted, in many cases, the results are unmatched by anything we have yet produced by machinery. However, by many years' practice, and then only by clever workmen, such results could be obtained. The art has now been reduced to a system thoroughly understood and easily acquired, various appliances having been introduced, the assistance of which will enable an aspirant to learn the business correctly and quickly. Of course, practice alone will make an expert, at the same time no goods need be wasted to gain this practice. With very little experience plain drops and toffees might be made equal to those of the best houses, the ornamental and artistic kinds would only be a question of degree and appearance; they would still be sweet and go with the "all sorts" or "mixtures," and bring a price at least to cover cost, if not a profit. If the learner will study the following instructions, the author guarantees to place him in a position to boil sugar as correctly as the most experienced workman. To accomplish this, the reader should provide himself with a sugar boiler's thermometer, which may be had from any of the machine makers or from the publishers, price 7/6. The cost of this is very soon repaid by the saving of material and time, as well as anxiety. While the sugar is undergoing the process of boiling, it is impossible for a learner to determine the exact degree of temperature which the sugar has attained without the aid of a thermometer, and even the journeyman finds it so useful that you will find very few indeed who boil sugar without it; in fact, many of the large houses will not allow a sugar boiler to work without one. For almost any purpose the following degrees will be found all that is necessary. For example: put into the pan in which you intend to boil, 7 lbs. of loaf sugar, (broken into small pieces), or white crystallized sugar will answer the same purpose, together with one quart of water, and place same on the fire and allow to boil. When boiling point is reached (if lump sugar) lift it off and see if the sugar is all dissolved; if not use your spatula (a stick about two inches wide and a couple of feet long), and crush any remaining lumps against the side of the pan; replace again on the fire, put a cover over the

pan, and allow to boil for ten minutes; then take off the cover and insert the thermometer into the pan, immersing the bottom part of it in the boiling sugar, and let it remain there until the sugar is boiled to the degree you require. The following degrees are those used by confectioners for the different purposes, viz. :—

1st. The Smooth, 215° to 220° by the thermometer. When the mercury registers these figures the sugars may then be used for crystallizing creams, gum goods, or liqueurs.

2nd. The Thread, generally 230° to 235° is the degree which is used for making liqueurs.

3rd. The Feather or Soft Ball, 240° to 245°. Only a very few minutes elapses between these degrees, and the sugar must be watched closely during the boiling at this point. This degree may be used for making fondants, rich creams, cream for chocolates and fruit candying.

4th. The Ball, 250° to 255°. The sugar at this point is used for making cocoanut and other candies, cocoanut ice, and almost every description of grain sugar generally.

5th. The Crack, viz., 310° to 315°. This is the degree which is used, with little variation, for all kinds of drops, rocks, toffees, and all clear goods, whether for the purpose of passing through machines or manipulating with the hands.

These degrees can be tested by an experienced hand without the aid of the thermometer, and the learner may accustom himself by trying them in the following manner :—Take the stem of a clay pipe and dip into the sugar as it boils, draw out again and pass through the forefinger and thumb; if the pipe stem feels oily you will find by looking at your thermometer that the sugar has reached the degree of smooth, 215° to 220°.

The next degree, or thread, may be tried by taking a little of the sugar off the pipe stem between your finger and thumb and part them gently; if you see small threads hanging between your finger and thumb, the temperature will be about 230° to 235°.

For the degree of the ball,—250° to 255°,—you must have by your hand a small jug of cold water; when you draw the pipe stem out of the sugar dip it in the water, and on taking it out of the water, if you can work the sugar up like a piece of putty, you have got the degree of ball.

The degree of crack must be tested in the same way, but the sugar must leave the pipe stem clean; dip again into cold water; when off the pipe break a piece of sugar with your teeth, if it snaps clean in your teeth, pour the sugar on the slab at once.

NOTE.—This last degree must be tried sharply in giving the process for trying it without the thermometer. We caution all beginners to get a thermometer. It may be necessary to state that thermometers differ a little, and should be tested.

During hot weather, it is necessary to bring the sugars up to the full degree; during the winter months, the lower degrees marked will answer the purpose.

CUTTING THE GRAIN, LOWERING OR GREASING.

ALMOST all sugars, especially refined, whether loaf, crystallized, or granulated, and most sugars known to the trade as "pieces" will, if boiled beyond the degree of ball (250° by thermometer), when turned out of the pan, become cloudy, then grainy, and ultimately a solid lump of hard opaque sugar. To prevent this candying,—as it is called,— several agents are used, such as glucose, cream of tartar, pyroligneous acid, vinegar, &c., the action of which will cause the sugar to boil clear, be pliable while hot, and transparent when cold. It is therefore necessary to use some lowering agent for all boilings intended for clear goods, such as drops, toffees, rocks, &c.

Experience has taught most of the old hands that two of these agents—cream of tartar and glucose—possess all the merits necessary for the purpose, and are to be preferred to the others for reasons it is unnecessary to state. A great deal could be said in favour of either or both; cream of tartar is handier and cleaner to use, as well as more exact in its action; goods boiled with it will be a better colour, and, some assert, more crisp; for acids and all best and export goods it is to be recommended—use a proportion of $\frac{1}{2}$ an ounce to every 14 lbs. of sugar—we say about, as some strong sugars require a little more; this is generally measured in a teaspoon, 2 teaspoonfuls to every 14 lbs.

Glucose may be bought in either solid or liquid form, the latter is generally used by the trade. It is a thick heavy syrup, best qualities being water white, odourless, and flavourless. Being cheaper than sugar, it is valuable to the confectioner, not only for its lowering qualities, but also as a bulk producer, reducing the cost of the product. On this account, there is a tendency to over do it by using too much the result causing goods to become sticky and turn soft immediately they are exposed to the atmosphere, not only so, but we have seen drops in bottles run in to a solid lump through being overdosed. If glucose is used in proper proportions, it makes an excellent lowering agent, and will answer the purpose first rate for ordinary drops and the like. Use 3 lb. of glucose to every 14 lb. of sugar; keep a panful on the furnace top, so that it will be always hot and may be easily measured by means of a saucepan or ladle holding the exact quantity; add the glucose when the sugar begins to boil.

HINTS TO BEGINNERS.

The information contained in this book, although chiefly intended for beginners, is not written exclusively for them. To the many confectioners who have only had an opportunity of learning one or more branches, and are often anxious to learn others, this work affords an opportunity of doing so. We have included new goods to date of going to press—these no doubt will be useful to most readers. The work has been so arranged that the most simple and easiest recipes come first under each section. These we advise beginners to try first and often. The book is not large, and will not take long to read through. It is very advisable to do this, especially is it important to novices, as here and there additional instructions are gleaned, which are not only applicable to the class of goods under which they are given, but may apply generally.

It is absolutely necessary to at least read carefully the whole of the section, from which an odd recipe is required, to be able to thoroughly understand it, because so many different kinds are made in exactly the same way that a volume might be written reiterating the same line over and over again under each recipe. This has been avoided as much as possible, as it would be unnecessary and tedious. Enough and just enough has been said to be thoroughly understood to make the recipes workable and successful. There is no space to spare for redundancy on any subject. It is presumed that the reader has already read the remarks on cleanliness in the workshop, now just a word about the pan used for boiling. In making all clear goods, keep the sides of the pan above the level of the liquid sugar perfectly clean, some of the previous boil may adhere to the side of the pan after it was poured out; it has a tendency to granulate by the heat of the furnace during the cooking process of the next. It may be easily seen, and should be removed by means of a wet rag or sponge, or it may cause the whole boil to grain and be therefore spoiled for clear goods. When boiling candies or creams, this precaution is unnecessary. Learners should first try their hand with toffee, then candies, then clear plain drops, and then have a turn with stripes. The practice obtained in the first will be useful in experiments with the second, besides hot sugar requires quick handling, but that will soon be found out. No doubt the result of a good many attempts will have to be consigned to the "All sorts," but the only talisman is practice. Carefully follow instructions, put up with hot hands until you get used to it, "don't be beat," it is to be done.

FLAVOURS AND COLOURS.

These form almost as important a part of the trade as sugar itself, and it should be the chief object of every workman to try and excel in these two important features; if you do not use good flavours, it is a moral certainty you cannot produce good sweets. Flavours for boiled sugars should be specially prepared, those bought at an ordinary chemist's shop may do very well for flavouring custards and pastry, but are of no use for boiled sugars, in fact, better use no essence at all, as they are so weak that, to give the drops, &c., even a slight taste, the quantity required reduces the degree to which the sugar has been boiled so much that it works like putty, and sticks to the machine while being pressed through; the drops when finished look dull, dragged and stick together when bottled; tons of drops are weekly spoiled by small makers using such flavours, while a little trouble and less expense would put them out of their misery, besides giving to the goods that clear, bright, dry appearance to be found in the drops of a respectable house.

It must be remembered that the flavour is the very life of the sweet. Colour may please the eye, but excellence in that alone is not all that is required. A buyer may be attracted by the eye, but he does not eat with it. Neither old nor young would knowingly eat only coloured sugar. A sweet taste may be satisfied from sugar alone.

It is the variety of pleasant flavours that is desired, and it is the business of the confectioner to supply it. Flavours for sugar boiling should be as concentrated as it is possible for them to be. Several large houses who have confined their attention to the wants and requirements of the confectionery and mineral water trades, have succeeded in producing fruit essences of a quality, which it is a pleasure to work with, being very powerful, only a very small quantity is required to give the boil a rich flavour, consequently it passes through the machine easily forming a perfect drop on which is a clear imprint of the engraving characteristic of the machine used. Essential oils used by confectioners are those having an agreeable aromatic flavour, and should be used in their original strength, without being adulterated or reduced. It is absolutely necessary that they should be pure and fresh, more particularly the oils of lemon and orange, as when not fresh and pure they partake of the flavour of turpentine, and are particularly unpleasant to the taste.

Small makers would do well to buy carefully from a good house not more than would be used up in two or three months, especially the two before mentioned. Some oils, on the contrary, improve by keeping, such as peppermint and lavender. All essences and oils are best kept in a cool dark place, well corked.

Essential oils being powerful, popular, and expensive, they are frequently adulterated. Cream of tartar and tartaric acid on account of the price, is often increased, the former with different cheap white powders, the latter usually with alum. Many people fail in the process through no fault of their own, but simply through being supplied with inferior ingredients, it is therefore of great importance, that colours, flavours, &c., should be purchased at some respectable house.

The colours, consisting of several very nice shades of yellow and red ; also coffee brown, jetoline black, damson blue, and apple green, etc., are generally prepared in paste form and ready for use; being vegetable, they are wholesome, and may be used with confidence. There are, however, several colours which confectioners may prepare for themselves, both on the ground of economy and convenience, viz. :—

COCHINEAL.—For extracting the colour from this insect this is a good recipe :—grind in a small mill, or crush with a large rolling pin or heavy bottle (or it may be obtained already ground), 4 ozs. of cochineal, put into a large pan with three pints of water, place on your fire or stove, when boiling add 4 ozs. of pearlash (or salts of tartar will do), 4 ozs. of ground alum, and 4 ozs. of cream of tartar, allow to continue to boil for fifteen minutes, then add 2 lbs. of sugar ; when the sugar has dissolved strain the mixture through a fine hair sieve or flannel. Stir occasionally while on the fire and see that it does not flow over the pan while boiling. Should this colour be wanted in a paste, allow to boil five or six minutes after it has been strained. Cochineal makes a pretty red and is a harmless colour.

SAFFRON.—This decidedly makes the prettiest yellow colour. The colour may be extracted almost in the same manner as you would get an infusion from tea. For example : take one eighth of an ounce of saffron and put it into a jam pot about three parts full of boiling water, allow to stand on the stove or by a fire for one or two hours ; when ready, strain a sufficient quantity into your boiling sugar, until the desired shade is obtained.

18

Turmeric.—This is a cheap yellow colour. It simply requires mixing with a little cold water, and should be added either while the sugar is boiling on the fire, or used as a paste and mixed in after the sugar has been poured on the slab ; this colour is also used by pastry cooks, to represent the use of eggs ; a little of it improves the colour and gives cakes a rich appearance ; being harmless, it may be used with freedom—an objection to it is that it possesses a taste and smell.

Blue.—Use powdered Prussian blue (soluble) or ultra-marine blue of the best quality ; if these colours can be had genuine and of good quality they are harmless, but the high price frequently tempts adulteration, which is anything but wholesome ; therefore, taking into consideration the very small quantity of the colour which is required, I should advise the readers to use W. J. Bush & Co.'s vegetable blues, which can always be relied upon.

Green.—There are few greens which are non-poisonous, therefore either use W. J. Bush & Co.'s vegetable green or mix a blue and yellow together.

Purple.—Purple colours may be produced by combining a blue with red.

Orange.—A mixture of red with yellow will produce an orange ; vary the proportions of each according to the shade you require.

Red.—Cochineal, carmine, Brazil wood, or cherry red.

Aniline Colours.—The so-called Aniline colours from coal tar have worked their way to the front for all sugar boiling purposes, the improvement in the manufacture of these lovely tints has abolished all fear of their being in any degree deleterious, while for beauty and strength they are unequalled. The quantity necessary to colour a boil being so small the consistence of the bulk is not lowered, and by exercising a little care, the slab and hands of the worker may be kept clean and free from stain (which was not possible when weak vegetable colours were used for this purpose.) This is a consideration where slabs are few and variety required.

The preparation of these colours for use is simplicity itself. Procure half a dozen small jelly pots, into each put about one ounce of a colour, cover the powder over with boiling water, add one ounce of glycerine, stir well and put aside. It is ready for use and will keep good for a long time.

POISONOUS COLOURS.

1 deem it necessary to add the following list of poisonous colours, and to state that they should under no circumstances be used even in a stripe, as they are highly dangerous to health. I give this list that people may not get into trouble innocently.

I know sugar boilers who are very partial to use a little chrome yellow for stripes; it should not be done, as, although a nice colour, it is a deadly poison.

YELLOW.—Chrome yellow, sulphate of arsenic, iodide of lead, in fact, no preparation of lead or arsenic.

RED.—Vermillion (Vermillionite), red lead, sulphate of mercury, oxide of lead.

BLUE.—Blue verditer, carbonate or sulphate of copper.

GREEN.—Emerald green, arsenite of copper, green verditer, carbonate of copper, Scheel's green, Emerald substitute, &c.

WRINKLES ON SUGAR BOILING.

Experience teaches daily and without a desire to be dogmatic or savour of pedantry, the writer might be allowed to suggest little improvements and alterations, which, he can assure the reader, might, with advantage, be adopted in more workshops than one with which he is familiar, both in the interest of employer and the credit of the workman.

It is or should be the aim of every workman to do the best he can with the tools and materials he has at his disposal. We do not expect to get white acids out of yellow crystals, or bright colours out of pieces, but in many cases we have seen yellow acids made from white loaf sugar and dull colours of good Dutch crushed. The former is impossible, the latter the result of carelessness. I have known workmen, and good workmen too, who could not, or did not, make a first class acid drop, no matter what sugar they had to work with, they were too big to be told, anything was put down as the cause—bad fire, pan too thick or too thin, or not the proper water.

To make an acid drop to perfection, the pan must not only be clean, but bright; use best white sugar, and just enough water to melt it, with a little extra cream of tartar (no glucose); boil on a sharp fire to 310°; after passing through machine, well dust with icing sugar and bottle. Beginners should not try to work with less water, as the boil is more liable to grain, which can be seen by an expert and avoided. Before putting on the boil, see that there is sufficient fuel on the furnace to carry through the operation—to make up a fire during the process spoils the colour and quality—the sharper the sugar is boiled the better the appearance and durability. When boiling common sugars, have the pan large enough—some throw up a deal of foam when they reach the boiling point and are liable to throw over; watch closely, and if unable to beat the foam down, lift the pan on to the side of the fire a few minutes until boiled through. Many weak sugars burn on a clear fire before they come to a degree of crack. In this case, sprinkle a little fresh fuel or ashes over the fire and replace the pan. Should it again catch, repeat the operation, nursing it up to the desired degree. Bad boiling sugar is very troublesome. A good plan is to make a rule of straining the whole batch just after it boils, through a very fine copper wire or hair sieve; this prevents foreign matter such as grit, sawdust, or even nails, which is often mixed with the sugar, getting into the goods. Keep thermometer when not in use in a jar of water standing on the furnace plate by the side of the pan, wash out the jar and fill it with cold water every morning; keep the thermometer clean, especially the top part, as the sugar which adheres to it becomes grainy, and might spoil a whole boil. After making dark sweets, thoroughly wash the thermometer before putting it into a light boil.

In using colours for drops and clear goods, mix them in when the boil is on the slab, thus saving your pan; keep the colours damp in jars, look over occasionally and, where necessary, add a little cold water to keep them moist or the top may get dry and hard which would make the goods specky. Use a separate piece of stick for each colour to rub in with, and be very careful not to use too much colour; a very little goes a long way with a clear boil; goods are more often spoilt by using too much than too little; more can always be added if shades are too light, but there is no remedy if you have added too much. When colouring toffees, this must be done in the pan; liquid colours are best; trouble will be saved if used in the following order. Suppose Raspberry, Everton, and Lemon Toffee were wanted, make the lemon toffee first, add the saffron just before the boil is ready then the lemon and pour out; make the Everton toffee next in the same way adding the butter before the lemon; then make the raspberry. In this arrangement there is no necessity of steaming out the pan. Had the raspberry toffee been made first the pan would have to be cleaned again before the lemon or Everton toffee could have been made because it would have been red.

Measure the flavours in a graduated glass; wash out the glass frequently or it will get rancid; weigh the acid and see that it is well ground; if it has become dry and lumpy rub it down to a powder wlth a rolling pin or heavy bottle on a sheet of paper before using. In using fruit essences a little powdered tartaric acid throws up the flavour. Mix the acid into the boil after it has been poured on the slab in a little heap and then add the essence thoroughly incorporating the whole.

For the slabs use the best oil with a clean flannel cloth; keep the cloth in a saucer; if it lies about it is liable to fall on the floor and pick up dirt which gets carried to the pouring plate. When the flannel gets hard or gritty burn it at once and get a new one or it may be used by mistake and make a mess. I have seen the beauty of a boil spoilt scores of times by using dirty rags and rancid oil. A sugar boiler cannot be too careful in these little details, the success of his work largely depends upon it. It is easy to inaugurate a good system and much more comfortable to work to it than a slovenly "what shall I do next sort of a method." Know where to find and put your hand on everything; when the boil is hot there is no time to look for what you require. "A place for everything and everything in its place" should be a practical feature in every boiling shop.

STICKY SWEETS.

Perhaps there is nothing more annoying to the trade than sticky boiled sugars; all clear goods when exposed to the atmosphere will turn damp, especially in wet weather. It is a question of degree, some get slightly damp while others will run almost to syrup; it is impossible to obviate the former, but the latter can be prevented. Great care should be used in adding the lowering, whether cream of tartar or glucose, too much of either will cause the goods to run immediately they are turned out. Weak or inferior sugars, or not sufficient boiling, also have this effect. I know of no reliable agent which will altogether prevent this result but I know that a careful arrangement of the different proportions, using good sugar and well boiling greatly mitigate if not altogether prevent the grievance. Goods intended for exposure should contain just sufficient lowering to prevent the boil from going grainy, and boiled right up to the standard. Of course different sugars will carry more or less lowering but this can be easily tested by the workman. A few experiments will determine the exact quantities for each boil. There is no excuse for drops sticking in bottles when well corked ; this should not occur, if it does, the fault is in the making ; the water has a great deal to do with causing sweets to be sticky. The writer has experienced this in several country places where the only supply of this indispensable ingredient was drawn from artesian wells. To look at it it was all that could be desired—a beautiful cold, clear and wholesome beverage. Of its chemical constituents I do not pretend to give an opinion but the drops and other clear boils for which it was used got damp directly they were exposed, and would have run to a syrup had they not been covered up. The goods keep all right in bottles but it is very annoying, not to speak of the injury and loss to a business, when this is the position with regard to the water supply. The only remedy I could suggest and which was very successful was powdered borax. I used this in the proportion of a teaspoonful to every 14-lb. of sugar, adding it just as the sugar began to boil. Borax has been found useful with any water when making goods such as toffees, rocks and clear boiled sugars generally, which were likely to be exposed in the window or on the counters. Where the supply of water is suitable, as in most large towns, given good sugar, cream of tartar or glucose in proper proportions, and careful boiling up to the standard, the addition of borax is unnecessary and should only be resorted to under special circumstances.

PLAIN TOFFEE.

14-lbs. White Sugar.
½-oz. Cream of Tartar.
2 Quarts Water.

Process.—This is an easy and capital recipe to begin with. The process is practically the same as for all other clear goods but the ingredients being few there is little chance of their getting complicated. If the reader has a thermometer it is hardly possible to make a mistake, besides it will make the instructions more intelligible ; should he not possess this appliance, we must ask that the instructions, "How to Boil Sugar," should be committed to memory as it would be tedious and a great waste of time and space to keep explaining how to tell the different degrees through which the sugar passes before it comes to the point required for the different goods given in this book. For this and other reasons I will assume the learner to be working with one.

Put the sugar and water in a clean pan, place on the fire and stir occasionally till melted; when it comes to the boil, add the cream of tartar and put a lid on the pan; allow to boil in this way for ten minutes, remove the lid and immerse the bottom part of the thermometer in the boiling liquid and allow it to remain in this position until it records 310 degrees, then quickly take out the thermometer, lift off the pan and pour contents into frames, tins, or on a pouring plate, which have been previously oiled. If on pouring plate, mark the boil into bars or squares while warm with a knife or toffee cutter; when quite cold, it is ready for sale.

LEMON TOFFEE.

14-lbs. White Sugar.   2 Quarts Water.
½-oz. Cream of Tartar.   Lemon Flavouring.
Saffron Colouring to fancy.

PROCESS.—Proceed as directed for plain toffee. When the sugar reaches 305° degrees, add the saffron colour; when it reaches 310 degrees, add a few drops of oil of lemon and pour out immediately into frames or tins; or if on pouring plate mark out into bars or squares before it gets cold. The pouring plate should be level, so that the sheet be all the same thickness.

IMPROVED FRAME AND CUTTER FOR EVERTON TOFFEE OR BUTTER SCOTCH.

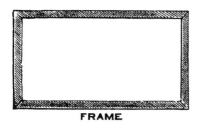
FRAME

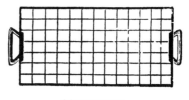
CUTTER

BUTTER SCOTCH.

8-lbs. White Sugar.	¼-oz. Cream of Tartar.
1-lb. Fresh Butter.	1 Quart Water.
Lemon Flavouring.	

PROCESS.—Melt the sugar in the water by an occasional stir when the pan is on the fire, then add the cream of tartar and boil up to 300; lift the pan on to the side of the furnace and add butter in small pieces broken off by the hand; slip the pan on the fire again, adding the lemon flavour and let it boil through, so that all the butter is boiled in, then pour into frames; when partly cold mark with cutter into small squares; when quite cold, divide the squares; wrap each in wax paper, then tinfoil. It is sold generally in ½d, 1d, and 3d packets, the latter containing 6 halfpenny pieces. N.B.—There is good butter scotch and better butter scotch, but no bad butter scotch; this quality may be improved by the addition of a larger proportion of butter; some makers would put 2-lb. or even 3-lb. to this quantity, but that would be regulated by the class of trade and the size of the halfpenny squares. These frames are made to hold 144 squares; a boil this size will make each square weigh 1-oz, but any weight of square may be arranged by adding or deducting from the boil.

EVERTON TOFFEE.

12-lbs. White Sugar.	½-oz. Cream of Tartar.
2-lbs. Dark Sugar.	2 Quarts Water.
2-lbs. Fresh Butter.	Lemon Flavouring.

PROCESS.—Melt the sugar in the water, add the cream of tartar, and boil the whole to the degree of 300°; lift the pan on to the side of the fire, put in the butter in small pieces, place the pan again on the fire and let it boil through; add the lemon and give it time to just mix in, then pour out the contents into frame, or on pouring plate, to cut up into bars. Everton toffee and butter scotch are similar, except in colour; same remarks as to quality will apply in both cases; if the fire is very fierce, do not put the pan down flat on it after butter is added; nurse it gently to prevent burning; a little fresh coke shaken over the fire would assist.

RASPBERRY TOFFEE.

14-lbs. White Sugar.
½-oz. Cream of Tartar.
Raspberry Flavour.

2 Quarts Water.
Carmine Colour.

PROCESS.—Bring the sugar and water to the boil, add the cream of tartar, put on the lid for ten minutes. then uncover and immerse the thermometer ; continue to boil to 300° ; tinge to a bright red with liquid carmine, and add raspberry essence ; pour out on to frame or pouring plate and mark into bars or squares of convenient size ; when cold, the toffee is ready for packing and sale. N.B.—Cream of Tartar is given as lowering for these toffees, but glucose can be used if preferred.

FIG TOFFEE.

6-lbs. Good Yellow Sugar.
2-lbs. Glucose.

4-lbs. Figs, Chopped Fine.
3 Pints Water.

PROCESS.—Boil the sugar, glucose, and water to a weak crack, 295° ; lift the pan partly off the fire, putting a piece of iron under it to prevent burning ; add the figs gently letting the whole thoroughly boil through and mix ; pour in oiled tins or on slab and mark into squares. When adding the figs let them drop in through the fingers, not in a heap.

WALNUT TOFFEE.

5-lbs. Brown Sugar.
5-lbs. Crystal Sugar.
2½-lbs. Glucose.

3-lbs. Walnuts.
Quarts Water.
Lemon Flavouring.

PROCESS.—Shell the walnuts, peel off the skin, chop very fine. Boil the glucose, sugar, and water as before directed to the degree of weak crack, 300°. Lift the pan a little from the fire ; add the prepared nuts by letting them run through the fingers gently ; let the whole boil through, then add a few drops of the oil of lemon ; when thoroughly mixed in pour out the boil and mark into bars before too cold. The flavour is improved by roasting the walnuts a little before putting in the boil.

BARCELONA TOFFEE.

5-lbs. Brown Sugar.
5-lbs. Crystal Sugar.
3-lbs. Barcelona Nuts.

2-lbs. Glucose.
2 Quarts Water.
Lemon Flavouring.

PROCESS.—Prepare the Barcelona nuts by chopping them fine. Boil the sugar, glucose and water to the degree 300°. Remove the pan a little way from the fire, add the nuts carefully; when thoroughly boiled through and amalgamated add a few drops of lemon and pour out contents into frame or on pouring plate, and mark into bars.

COCOANUT TOFFEE.

6-lbs. Granulated Sugar.	3-lbs. Desiccated Cocoanut, Unsweetened.
4-lbs. Brown Sugar.	3 Pints Water.
2-lbs. Glucose.	Lemon Flavouring.

PROCESS.—Dissolve the sugars in the water, bring to the boil, add the glucose and continue to boil to the degree of 300°; lift the pan a little way from the fire; let the desiccated cocoanut run gently in the boil; continue to boil until the lot is well mixed through; add a few drops of oil of lemon and pour out in frames; use the lemon cautiously, too much spoils the flavour.

COCOANUT TOFFEE, or STICK JAW.

6-lbs. Granulated Sugar.	2-lbs. Glucose.
4-lbs. Brown Sugar.	4 Large Cocoanuts, Sliced.
	3 Pints Water.

PROCESS.—Boil to crack, 310° by thermometer, the sugars, glucose, and water; have the cocoanuts freshly peeled and sliced ready; raise the pan two or three inches from the fire; slide in the nut, stirring gently with spatula to keep them off the bottom till well boiled through; then pour out in tins or frames. N.B.—Stir gently only the one way or you may grain the boil; desiccated cocoanut may be used, but if so, boil only to 285.

EGGS AND BACON.

10-lbs. White Sugar.	1-lb. Nonpareils.
2½-lbs. Glucose.	1 Cocoanut.
3 Pints Water.	Cochineal Colouring.

PROCESS.—Cut a large cocoanut into slices, dry them and lay them on the pouring plate in rows about half inch apart; sprinkle between them thickly some nonpareils of various colours (hundreds and thousands). Boil to crack the sugar, glucose, and water; tinge with cochineal, and carefully and evenly pour the contents over the pouring plate, disturbing the nut and nonpareils as little as possible. A good plan is to have a small shallow ladle with an open spout, into which pour a little of the boil, run over the plate a small stream from the ladle first, this will bind the nut, &c., and keep them in their places while the bulk is being poured out.

ALMOND HARDBAKE.

10-lbs. Good Brown Sugar.   3-lbs.   Valencia Almonds.
2-lbs. Glucose.   3 Pints Water.
Lemon Flavouring if desired.

PROCESS.—Split the almonds with a sharp knife, lay them face downwards on an oiled plate, cover the plate as closely as possible ; boil the glucose, sugar, and water to the crack, 305 ; remove the pan from the fire and pour contents carefully and evenly over the almonds ; the addition of a little lemon or almond flavouring will improve it. N.B.—See remarks *re* ladle in previous recipe.

ALMOND ROCK.

10-lbs. Brown Sugar.   7-lbs.   Sweet Barbary Almonds.
3-lbs. Glucose.   3 Pints Water.

PROCESS.—Clean your almonds by blowing out all dust and grit, pick out the shells ; dissolve the sugar, water, and glucose ; boil the lot up to crack ; pour the contents on oiled plate ; sprinkle the almonds all over the boil ; shake over the lot a few drops oil of lemon ; turn up the edges first, then the whole boil ; mix and knead it up like dough until all the almonds are well mixed in ; no time must be lost in this process, or the sugar will get too hard ; when firm, make a long roll of the entire boil, place it on a hard wooden board, and cut it up into thin slices ; it will have to be kept in shape while cutting, by turning over and pressing the sides as it becomes flat ; a special large sharp knife is used for this purpose. A smaller boil than the above had better be tried by beginners, say half the quantity. This can be done by halving the ingredients. Needless to state these remarks apply to other recipes.

FRENCH ALMOND ROCK.

12-lbs. White Sugar.   6-lbs.   Sweet Almonds, Blanched.
3-lbs. Glucose.   4 Pints Water.

PROCESS.—Boil the sugar, water, and glucose in the usual way to the degree of weak crack, 305 by thermometer, then ease the pan a little way off the fire, and let the almonds gently slide into the mass ; use the spatula a little just to keep the almonds from sticking to the bottom, stirring lightly only the one way, then watch the boil carefully till it turns a light golden colour; lift off the pan and pour the contents into the frames. The almonds will come to the top better in tins than on pouring plates.

Of course, a better quality is made by adding more almonds, or *vice versa*. The almonds after being blanched should be spread on a tin and dried, either on the stove top or in the oven,

ALMOND PEELER.

TO BLANCH ALMONDS.

Put any quantity of almonds into a pan or other vessel; pour over them sufficient boiling water to well cover; stir carefully; in a few minutes the skins will peel off easily by squeezing the almonds between finger and thumb. Machines are made for this purpose, or the almonds can be purchased already blanched.

AMERICAN FRUIT TOFFEE.

½-lb. Shelled Walnuts.
½-lb. Shelled Brazil Nuts.
½-lb. Almonds, blanched and slightly roasted.
½-lb. Glacé Cherries.
¼-lb. Sliced Cocoanut.
4-lbs. Sugar.
2½-lbs. Glucose.
Water.
¼-lb. Citron Peel, cut in pieces.

PROCESS.—Dissolve the sugar and glucose in water, boil to 290° by thermometer, remove the pan from the fire, stir in the mixed fruits then place the pan again on the fire to warm through and pour out on oiled pouring plate, mark while warm into bars, break up when cold. This is a very attractive toffee for the retail shop.

AMERICAN HASH.

1½-lb. Shelled Walnuts.	4-lbs. Sugar.
1-lb. Seedless Raisins.	3-lbs. Glucose.
Dessicated Cocoanut, fine.	1 Quart Water.

PROCESS.—Dissolve the sugar and glucose with water, add the raisins and boil the batch to 250°. Stand the pan off the fire, add the walnuts, and stir in all the dessicated cocoanut possible, turn the lot on slab, flatten out with rolling pin to the thickness of a caramel. Cut up into pieces with caramel or toffee cutter.

TOFFEE APPLES.

Brown Sugar.	Apples.

PROCESS.—Procure any quantity of small apples, into each apple force a small stick about the size of a match. Boil up some brown sugar with a pinch of cream of tartar to 280°, then stand the pan off the fire and dip each apple in the boil until covered. Stand on sieve to drip, when cold they are ready for sale. Suitable for retailer, sells well in season amongst children.

CANDIES.

LEMON CANDY.

12-lbs. White Sugar.	2 Qrts. Water.
3-lbs. Glucose.	Saffron or other yellow colouring.
Lemon Flavouring.	

PROCESS.—Melt the sugar in the water, add the glucose and boil the whole to the degree of ball, 250° by thermometer; tinge to a light yellow by adding a little saffron; lift the pan off the fire, then with the spatula commence to rub the syrup against the side of the pan gently, not to agitate the whole boil; in a few minutes it will become opaque and thick; now add the lemon and stir the whole together until the entire boil becomes cloudy and grainy; pour out the contents carefully on to an oiled slab; when set, mark into squares with a sharp knife; when cold, break it up. N.B.—It is unnecessary to put a cover on the pan when making candies of any kind; the boils may be run into tins; if the pouring plate is cold, cover it with a sheet of waxed paper. Candies grain better and work cleaner with less waste when poured on paper.

COUGH CANDY.

7-lbs. Brown Sugar.
2-oz. Horehound Herb or Essence ¼-oz.

¼-oz. Oil of Aniseed.
3-pints. Water.

PROCESS —If the herb horehound be used, boil it in the water on a slow fire for 15 minutes, then strain through a fine sieve; add the sugar to the liquid and boil to a stiff ball, 255°; remove the pan from the fire and rub part of the syrup against the side of the pan with spatula until it becomes cloudy and opaque; add the aniseed and the essence horehound, if herb is not employed, and stir the whole together until it becomes a uniform dark thick cloudy mass; pour out this boil into tins or frames; when cold, it is ready for sale. N.B.—This formula is only a guide to the process. These ingredients will make a very good candy, but most makers have a mixture of their own which they use to flavour cough candy as well as cough drops. The herbs horehound, coltsfoot, and marshmallow are often boiled together in more or less equal proportions; add the liquid used with or without the addition of oil of aniseed, clove, cassia, or capsicine. A cough drop essence is also made for this purpose by W. J. Bush & Co. A volume might be made up of the different recipes for this class of goods alone. However, I will leave the reader to mix his own remedies, as opinion differs as much on the virtues of drugs as it does on politics.

RASPBERRY CANDY.

12-lbs. White Sugar.
3-lbs. Raspberry Jam.

2 Quarts Water.
Cochineal Colouring.

PROCESS.—Melt the sugar in the water and boil to ball, 250°; add the raspberry jam and stir it well in; remove the pan from the fire; add sufficient colouring to make a bright raspberry; rub part of the mixture with spatula against side of pan until it changes a heavy opaque, then stir the whole mass until uniform; pour the contents carefully on a slab, covered with greased paper; make the sheet about ½-inch thick, mark into bars with a sharp knife, and break up when cold.

APRICOT CANDY.

7-lbs. White Sugar.
2-lbs. Apricot Jam or Pulp.

2 Pints Water.
Saffron Colouring.

PROCESS.—Melt the sugar in the water and boil up to ball, 250°; add the jam or pulp; stir well till thoroughly mixed in; remove the pan;

rub part of the contents against the side of the pan with spatula until cloudy and opaque; colour to a bright yellow with saffron, then stir the whole together until uniformly cloudy; pour out in frames or on slab covered with oiled paper. A pinch of tartaric acid would improve the flavour, but often prevents candying unless in the hands of an expert. In any case, the acid should be added in a fine powder after the whole has been thoroughly grained. A palette knife is very useful for rubbing the sugar against the sides of the pan.

COCOANUT MACHINE.

BROWN COCOANUT CANDY.

14-lbs Brown Sugar.   3 Pints Water.
6 Large Cocoanuts Sliced.

PROCESS.—Dissolve the sugar in the water and boil to degree of ball, then add the sliced cocoanuts, stir in; remove the pan from the fire and rub the sugar against the side until cloudy; stir the whole together until all the sugar becomes cloudy and thick; turn out the batch into tins or on slabs; mark with sharp knife into squares or bars; when cold break up at marks. Prepare the cocoanuts by cutting them up into thin slices with a spokeshave or machine. The brown skin is seldom peeled off for this dark candy.

WHITE COCOANUT CANDY.

14-lbs White Sugar   3 Pints Water.
6 Large Cocoanuts, peeled and sliced.

PROCESS.—Peel off all the brown skin from the nuts with a sharp knife; wash them and cut into thin slices; dissolve the sugar in the water and boil to ball, 250°; add the sliced nuts, keeping the boil well stirred; when thoroughly mixed remove the pan from the fire and commence to grain with palette knife or spatula until the whole mass turns an opaque white; now turn out the batch into frames or on slab, which has been covered with paper; mark into convenient size bars; break up when set hard.

CHOCOLATE COCOANUT CANDY.

10-lbs. Brown Sugar.   4   Cocoanuts shreded.
1-lb.   Pure Block Cocoa.   3 Pints Water.

PROCESS.—When cracking the nuts, do so over a basin and save the milk; peel all brown skin off and cut the nut into fine shreds with machine; dissolve the sugar in the pan with the water and cocoanut milk; boil up to ball; remove the pan a little off the fire, then add the nut together with the pure block cocoa; stir the whole together; grain on side of pan as before directed; stir the whole well up and turn out into frames or on pouring plates. N.B.—The pure cocoa should be broken up into small pieces; and the heat of the sugar will soon melt it.

FRUIT CANDY.

7-lbs. White or Brown Sugar.   ¼-lb.   Sweet Almonds.
1-lb. Currants, cleaned and dried. 2 Pints Water.
¼-lb. Sultanas.   Saffron Colouring.

PROCESS.—Mix together the fruits, which should have been freed from grit and dust; boil the sugar and water to the degree of ball, 250°; remove the pan from the fire; gently grain the boil by rubbing a little of the syrup against the side of the pan until cloudy, then slide in the fruit and stir the whole together, adding a little saffron to colour a bright yellow. See that the mass has changed to an opaque, then turn the lot out into frames or on pouring slab.

LEMON SPONGE CANDY.

4-lbs. White Sugar.   1 Large Egg.
1 Pint Water.   Lemon Flavour.
            Powdered Sugar.

PROCESS.—Mix two teaspoonsful of finely powdered sugar with the white of the egg, beat up to a stiff paste; dissolve the sugar in the water and boil to weak crack, 305°; remove the pan from the fire, drop in the egg paste together with flavour and colour; commence immediately to well stir the whole with spatula; the boil will rise in a minute or two, but allow it to drop again and keep stirring until it commences to rise for the second time, then quickly pick up the pan and pour out contents into a wooden frame, say 8 inches square, or form a square frame on pouring plate with four loose bars (wood or iron) 8 inches long, 2 inches deep, having greased paper at the bottom.

ROSE SPONGE CANDY.

4-lbs. White Sugar.	1 Large Egg.
1 Pint Water.	Rose Flavouring.

Cochineal Colouring.

PROCESS.—Exactly as described in last, flavour and colour alone differing. This sponge candy process requires expertness, everything must be ready at hand. When the boil commences to rise for the second time, the pan must be lifted at once and emptied or the boil will not run out. It must not be poured out at the first rise or it will become flat on the slab. A beginner should not attempt sponge candies until he has had experience.

CREAM CANDIES.

There are at the time of writing a new species (if I might use the term) of candies known in the trade as cream candies which are very popular and sell in quantities. They are something between a fondant and a grained sugar or candy. When well made and carefully cut up, they make a nice show, eat rich and are much enquired for. The variety which may be brought out is unlimited; the store from which we may select our ingredients is almost inexhaustible. Fruits-green, dried or preserved almonds and nuts of almost every description, as well as flavours and colours of pleasant taste and pretty tint are adaptable, for this class of goods and many of them specially so. Thought and taste in the arrangement and manipulation are equally important to the ingredients used to make a new article. Although the following are but a sample of the formulas I have used for some time for this class, still they contain the process I have adopted for the whole.

WALNUT CREAM.

16-lbs. White Sugar.	4-lbs. Shelled Walnuts.
6-lbs. Glucose.	4-lbs. Desiccated Cocoanut Medium.
Vanilla Flavour.	2-qts. Water.

PROCESS.—Boil the sugar, glucose and water 240° by thermometer, then lift the pan off the fire and stand it aside until the syrup gets quite cold. Now place the pan again on a slow fire and with a spatula commence to move about this now thick heavy syrup until it thins a little and gets as warm as you can bear your finger in it (not hotter) then lift the pan again off the fire and work up the whole with spatula until you see it commences to get white and creamy. Now add the desiccated Cocoanut and sufficient essence of Vanilla to flavour, still working up until the whole of the nut is well amalgamated, then stir in the walnuts and beat up till quite stiff. Now remove with the hands one-third of the whole into another pan or dish and colour this portion red. When the colour is well mixed in, have a frame of suitable size, (about four inches deep) lined with wax paper. Lift out the boil and fill the frame, mixing alternately, two parts white and one part red not in layers, but the red portion promiscuously; let it stand all night. Next morning cut it into bars with wire, as you would a cheese. It should look very nice, the red showing in streaks. This sweet is a great favourite.

BARCELONA CREAM.

16 lbs. White Sugar.	4 lbs. Shelled Barcelona Nuts.
6-lbs. Glucose.	4-lbs. Desiccated Cocoanut Medium.
Essence of Vanilla.	2 Quarts Water.

PROCESS.—Exactly the same as last but colour the third portion brown and streak it in with the white. Where a lot of this cream is made, a quantity of boiling pans are necessary, so that the syrup may be cooling in some, while others are being used for boiling. A large tank full of water with frame on top to fix the pans so that they rest in the water, hastens the process of cooling, and is absolutely necessary where the process of commencing and finishing must be done in one day. However, under any circumstances the finished boil must remain in frame for 8 or 10 hours at least, to set firm before cutting into bars.

This cream also looks very nice and sells well. A retailer making for his own window may improve the batch by using more nuts. Wholesalers must study cost.

CHERRY CREAM.

16-lbs. Sugar.	4-lbs. Desiccated Cocoanut Medium.
6-lbs. Glucose.	3-lbs. Glace Cherries.
Red Colour.	2-Quarts Water.
	Vanilla Flavour.

PROCESS.—Same as for Walnut Cream. When the boil has been creamed add the cocoanut, mix well in, then add the cherries and vanilla flavour mixing and beating the whole well up. Now remove half the boil into prepared frame and colour the remaining half to a bright pink, put it on top of the white portion already in frame and cut into bars next morning.

INDIAN CREAM.

16-lbs. Sugar.	4 lbs. Desiccated Cocoanut Medium.
6-lbs. Glucose.	2-qts. Water.
Red Colouring	Vanilla Flavour.

PROCESS.—Exactly as before, boil to 240°; remove the pan from fire and let the syrup stand till quite cold then replace the pan on fire and stir till it gets thin and as warm as new milk, now add the cocoanut and vanilla flavour and cream with spatula, beating up the whole well until creamy and stiff. Now divide the boil by removing one half to a table covered with wax paper, and colour the half left in the pan to a bright red, turn this lot also on to the table, but apart from the white heap. Let both lots stand one hour or so, then with the hands take, say, half a pound of the white cream, mould and shape it like an egg, then take sufficient of the red cream, mould it out and cover the whole portion over with it. Continue this process till the boil is worked up, let the blocks stand to set for some hours. They will then be ready for packing in boxes for sale. When moulding the cream, keep the hands well dusted with flour.

DEVONSHIRE CREAM.

16-lbs. Sugar.	4-lbs. Desiccated Cocoanut Medium.
6-lbs. Glucose.	2-qts. Water.
Vanilla Flavour.	Red Colouring.

PROCESS.—Exactly as before. When the cream is finished run it into a frame at least six inches deep, two-thirds white cream at bottom, and one-third pink on top. Cut it next morning into slices about 1½ inches thick. Have the frame, of course, lined with wax paper. These slices look rich and tempting.

CREAM CHIPS.

16-lbs. Sugar.	7-lbs. Desiccated Cocoanut slices.
6-lbs. Glucose.	2-qts. Water.
Vanilla Flavour.	Colouring.

PROCESS.—Same as for Walnut Cream. When the cold syrup is placed on fire the second time, be careful not to over-heat it or you do not get a nice cream. When the cocoanut slices are added stand the pan in a secure place, say, on the top of an empty acid barrel, and beat up the cream well rubbing it now and then against the side of the pan until it turns white and creamy. Now stir the whole batch together and turn out into frame. Then proceed again in the same way with a boil half this size in every ingredient, when cocoanut slices have been added, colour to a bright pink, flavour with vanilla and cream well, then pour this boil on top of the white batch. Let it stop in frame for twelve hours and cut up into convenient size for show or for packing in boxes.

CHOCOLATE CREAM CANDY.

12-lbs. White Sugar.	7-lbs. Desiccated Cocoa Slices.
4-lbs. Raw Sugar.	1-lb. Pure Chocolate.
6-lbs. Gluoose.	Brown Colouring.
2-quarts Water.	

PROCESS.— Proceed as before. When the boil has been warmed add to the cocoanut the pure chocolate broken up in small pieces with sufficient brown colouring to make the boil a rich chocolate colour, a little vanilla flavour will improve, well beat up the boil in the pan and be sure that the sugar has turned creamy before you throw out the boil into the frame.

These goods want some elbow grease with the spatula, but more so when the boils are larger.

CREAM CANDY (WHITE).

16-lbs. Sugar.
6-lbs. Glucose.

7-lbs. Dessicated Cocoanut Slices.
Vanilla Flavour.
2-quarts Water.

PROCESS.—As before. A pinch of blue will improve the colour.

CREAM PATS.

16-lbs. Sugar.
6-lbs. Glucose.
Red and Brown Colouring.

7-lbs. Dessicated Cocoanut slices.
Vanilla, Raspberry, and Chocolate
Flavour.
2-quarts Water.

PROCESS.—Prepare the batch in exactly the same way as for Walnut Cream but do not boil higher than 240°, when creamed, and the cocoanut has been well stirred in, divide boil into three parts (or make three separate small boils) colour one part to a bright red and flavour with raspberry colour, another to a brown, and flavour with pure chocolate, leaving the third and the largest part white, and flavour with vanilla. Take small portions, about half-a-pound from the pan and put them in little heaps on a wax papered table ; when set they are ready for packing.

COCOANUT CREAM ICE.

16-lbs. Sugar.
6-lbs. Glucose.
2-qts. Water.

4-lbs. Dessicated Cocoanut.
Pink Colouring.
Vanilla Flavouring.

PROCESS.—Prepare batch as already instructed, when the boil has been creamed, flavoured, and the cocoanut well mixed in, divide boil into two parts, colouring one part red. You can either pour the white portion first into the frame, then the red or vice versa. When set cut up with wire into bars and pack. Raspberry and many other kinds worked with cocoanut are all boiled and creamed in this way, but flavoured, coloured and finished to fancy.

VANILLA CREAM.

16-lbs. Sugar.
6-lbs. Glucose.
Vanilla Flavour.

Pure Chocolate.
2-qts. Water.

PROCESS.—Boil the sugar, glucose and water as before to 239°. Then remove pan from fire and stand aside till syrup is cold. Replace pan on to fire and move the sugar with spatula until just warm, (not hotter than new milk), now remove the pan from fire and place it in secure position. Flavour with vanilla and cream with spatula well working the sugar and rubbing well against side of pan. When the batch commences to cream stir well together and turn out into frame lined with wax paper, let it set all night. Next morning cut into bars and paint the top of each bar over with pure chocolate using a camel's hair brush for the purpose. N.B.—Raspberry Cream with chocolate top is made in the same way. only colour the boil to a red and flavour with raspberry.

DROPS.

MACHINE MADE

BARLEY SUGAR DROPS.

14-lbs. White Sugar. $\frac{1}{4}$-oz. Oil of Lemon.
3-lbs. Glucose. Saffron Colouring.
2 Quarts Water.

PROCESS.—Put the sugar and water in the pan, place on the fire, stirring occasionally till sugar is dissolved, then add the glucose or $\frac{1}{2}$-oz. cream of tartar—either will do, but do not use *both*; place the cover on the pan and let boil for 10 minutes or so (the cover is put on to steam the sides of the pan and keep it clean and free from granulation); take off the cover and put in the thermometer, immersing the bottom part in the boiling liquid; let the whole boil until it reaches the degree of crack, 310°; tinge with saffron; then pour the contents on pouring plate, which has been previously oiled; sprinkle a few drops oil of lemon over it; turn in the edges as it begins to cool; then turn it over; knead it up as soon as you can handle it; if it is on a cold slab, you must be pretty smart or it will get too hard; as soon as it gets stiff enough, cut off small convenient pieces and pass through barley sugar drop machine; when cold, break up; give them a good shake in a rough sieve to free them from machine scraps; the drops are then ready for bottling. Powdered sugar is not usually mixed with these drops.

PEAR DROPS.

14-lbs. White Sugar.	1-oz. Tartaric Acid.
3-lbs. Glucose.	2-qts. Water.
¼-oz. Essence of Pear.	Red Colouring.

PROCESS.—Dissolve the sugar in the water, add the glucose, and bring the whole to the degree of crack, 310°; pour the contents on the slab; rub in a little red colouring in one corner of the boil to colour light pink; turn up the edges; add the powdered acid in a little heap; pour over the acid the pear essence, and thoroughly mix through the entire mass by kneading; when the batch is stiff enough cut off in small pieces and pass through the pear drop rollers; when cold, sift and mix some icing sugar amongst them, weigh, and bottle.

RASPBERRY DROPS.

14-lbs. White Sugar.	½-oz. Essence Raspberry.
2 qts. Water	1-oz. Tartaric Acid.
3-lbs. Glucose.	Cherry Paste or Carmine.

PROCESS.—Dissolve the sugar in the water; add the glucose and boil the whole up to crack; pour the boil on to a cold slab; rub in a little of the cherry paste to colour; turn up the edges; put in the powdered acid in a little heap; pour over the acid the raspberry flavour, and knead up the batch till thoroughly mixed and fit for machine; cut off in pieces and pass through raspberry rollers; sift, dust, and bottle when cold.

CHOCOLATE NIBS.

14-lbs. Sugar.	1-lb. Pure Cocoa.
3-lbs. Glucose.	2 qts. Water.
Chocolate Colouring.	

PROCESS.—Dissolve the sugar in the water and bring the syrup to the boil; add glucose, then put cover on for ten minutes; now put in thermometer and boil to crack; pour out on oiled slab; spread the pure cocoa in small pieces over the boil: add a little colour; mix and knead the whole till stiff; cut off in small pieces and pass through machine; break up and sift when cold.

40.

ALMOND TABLETS.

14-lbs. Brown Sugar.   2-lbs. Sicily Almonds, chopped.
3-lbs. Glucose.   4 pts. Water.
Lemon Flavouring.

PROCESS.—Boil the sugar, glucose, and water as directed to the degree of crack; pour the boil on oiled plate, sprinkle the almonds over it with a few drops of oil of lemon; knead the whole together till stiff; cut off small pieces and pass through tablet rollers.

PINE APPLE DROPS.

14-lbs. White Sugar.   1-oz. Acid Tartaric.
3-lbs. Glucose.   Saffron Colouring.
4 pts, Water.   ¼-oz. Essence Pine Apple.

PROCESS.—Boil the sugar, glucose, and water as before directed to the degree of crack, 310°; liquid saffron may be added to the boil in pan, or saffron paste, after it has been poured out on slab—when on the slab put in the acid and essence of pine-apple; knead the whole to gether; when stiff enough, cut off in pieces and pass through Pine apple rollers.

COCOANUT TABLETS.

14-lbs. White Sugar.   1-lb. Desiccated Cocoanut.
3-lbs. Glucose.   4 pts. Water.

PROCESS.—Boil the sugar, water, and glucose to the degree of crack; pour on slab and sprinkle the desiccated cocoanut over the boil; flavour with lemon; mix up and pass through tablet rollers.

ACID DROPS AND TABLETS.

14-lbs. Best White Sugar.   4-pts. Water.
¾-oz. Cream of Tartar.   4-oz. Tartaric Acid.
Lemon Flavouring.

PROCESS.—Put the sugar and water into a clean bright pan and bring to the boil; add the cream of tartar; place the lid on the pan and boil for ten minutes; remove the cover and put in thermometer, boiling quickly on sharp fire to the degree of crack; pour out at once on to a clean greased slab; when cool enough, turn up the edges and fold the boil over, then add the acid, which has been finely powdered, together with a few drops of oil of lemon; knead up the whole until stiff and pass through drop or tablet rollers; break up when cold, dust with powdered sugar, weigh, and bottle. N.B.—We mean the term "white sugar" to include loaf, Dutch crush, granulated or crystal, any of these of best quality will answer the purpose.

BROWN COUGH DROPS.

14-lbs.	Good Brown Sugar.	$\frac{1}{4}$-oz.	Oil Cloves.
3-lbs.	Glucose.	$\frac{1}{4}$-oz.	Oil of Peppermint.
3-oz.	Acid, Tartaric.	2-oz.	Herb Horehound.
$\frac{1}{2}$-oz.	Oil of Aniseed.	5 Pints Water.	

PROCESS.—First boil the herb horehound in the water for 10 minutes, then strain; add the liquor to the sugar and glucose, and boil as for other drops to crack, 310; pour on oiled slab; turn up edges and fold in the boil, then put the tartaric acid in a little heap on the boil, and pour over it the aniseed, clove, and peppermint; knead up the whole, thoroughly mixing the flavours until stiff enough to pass through machine cough drop rollers. N.B.—The Brown sugar should be of good boiling quality.

LIGHT COUGH DROPS.

14-lbs.	White Sugar.	$\frac{1}{2}$-oz.	Cough Drop Essence.
3-lbs.	Glucose.	$\frac{1}{2}$-oz.	Oil of Aniseed.
3-oz.	Acid, Tartaric.	4-pts.	Water.

PROCESS.—Boil the sugar, glucose, and water as before directed to the degree of crack, 310°; pour on greased slab; first turn up the boil, then add powdered acid, cough drop essence, and oil of aniseed; mix thoroughly until ready for machine, and pass through cough drop rollers; break up, sift, and dust with powdered sugar. N.B. Enough has now been said about plain machine drops; they are practically all made alike, the colour, flavour, and shape alone differing. See list for colours and flavours, and the machine-maker's list for the different shapes in rollers.

PULLED SUGARS.

THERE are a great variety of drops, rocks, &c., which look exceedingly pretty when well made, known as striped goods; they are by no means difficult to make. Nevertheless they require practice and discretion to make a good job of them. The beginner must accustom himself first with making the plain toffees and drops before trying his hand with these goods, because they require greater expertness, more judgment, and some experience with boiled sugar for all kinds of striped work. It is necessary that some part of the boiling at least must be "pulled, that is, by cutting off a part of the boil while hot, throwing it over a hook, pulling it out and throwing it over and over again, taking a fresh hold of it every time. The sugar by this action will gradually assume a white satin-like appearance, and become light and porous. The hook on which the sugar is pulled should be fixed firmly against the wall about five feet from the ground and near the pouring plate; it should be large, taking a sweep of 10 or 12 inches. Where only a small trade is done, a good 10 in. nail may answer the purpose. The fine colour and appearance of the sugar, after pulling, depends upon the quickness of the operator. Should the worker have not previously handled hot sugar, the process of pulling will make his hands very warm; however, he must get used to that. Do not leave the sugar, simply dust a little dry flour on the hands and stick to the work until finished, the hands very soon get accustomed to the heat. Should the worker not be successful the first few times, he must not be discouraged, as only practice and perseverance can make him overcome this difficulty. When he has succeeded, he may almost say he is master of the situation. In making the first experiment in striping, he should do so with drops, as, if they are not striped in an artistic manner after being passed through the machine, they will not show the defects. After a little practice with the drops, he may then commence rock making in variety, always keeping in mind—"Rome wasn't built in a day." Perhaps it would be as well for me to note here that customers in the different parts must not always expect to find the same names applied to the same goods as they are in the habit of seeing or selling; every district has got its speciality. Nevertheless, the different recipes for the sweets given in this work are those usually known in London by their respective names, and customers residing in different parts may re-christen them to suit the locality they are to be sold in. N.B.—Many American confectioners don chamois leather gloves to pull sugar, they say it saves the hands and finishes the pulled work with a better gloss.

PEPPERMINT ROCK.

8-lbs. White Sugar.	3 Pints Water.
2-lbs. Glucose.	Peppermint Flavouring.

Process.—Mix the sugar with the water, place the pan on the fire, add glucose and boil to weak crack, 300; pour the batch on oiled slab, add the flavouring, turn up the edges and mix in, then commence to draw the boil out; double it up and pull out again, repeating this process on the slab a few times till the sugar gets a little tough, then throw the lot over the hook and pull until it becomes white and spongy; a tinge of blue before pulling will improve the colour; remove the the boil to slab and roll out into sticks 1½ inch thick; when cold, chop in lengths to fit size of bottles or tins in which it is to be packed.

PINE APPLE ROCK.

8-lbs. White Sugar.	1 oz. Powdered Acid, Tartaric.
2-lbs. Glucose.	Pine Apple Flavouring.
3 pts. Water.	Yellow Colouring.

Process.—Boil the sugar, glucose, and water to a weak crack, 300°; pour on slab; add the acid, flavouring and colouring; mix up the whole, then cut off about one third and pull it over the hook until a bright yellow and spongy; now remove it to the slab; spread out the other part of the boil; lay the pulled portion in the centre, casing it all round with the clear sugar and roll the whole round on the slab, pulling it out lengthways until the desired thickness. In some places this rock is pressed into iron moulds, the shape of a pine apple, in others left in round or oval sticks, two or three inches thick, to be chopped up and sold by weight.

SHERBET STICKS.

8 lbs. White Sugar.	3 pts. Water.
2-lbs. Glucose.	1½-oz. Powdered Acid, Tartaric.
	1-oz. Bicarbonate of Soda.

Process.—Boil the sugar, glucose, and water to a weak crack, 300°; pour on oiled slab; turn up the edges; fold in the boil, then add the acid and soda with a pinch of blue; thoroughly incorporate the whole together; when tough enough to handle, throw the batch over the hook and pull until white and spongy; remove the mass to the slab, roll out into sticks the required thickness; when cold, snip into required lengths.

ROSE ROCK.

8-lbs. White Sugar.
2-lbs. Glucose.
3 pts. Water.

2-oz. Acid, Tartaric.
6 Drops Otto of Roses.
Red Colouring.

PROCESS.—Dissolve the sugar in the water, add the glucose and boil to weak crack, 300°: pour out on oiled slab; rub in sufficient colour to give a deep rose tint; add the acid and otto of roses; thoroughly mix the whole, then cut off one third of the boil and pull it over the hook till it becomes a light satiny pink, now spread out the clear portion on the slab, put the pulled in the centre and case it nicely round, rolling the whole down to desired thickness; when cold snip with scissors into required lengths.

PLAITED ROCK.

8-lbs. White Sugar.
2-lbs. Glucose.

3 pts. Water.
$\frac{1}{4}$ oz. Essence of Peppermint.

PROCESS.—Boil the sugar, water, and glucose in the usual way, to the weak crack 300°; pour on an oiled slab; add the flavour and mix up till stiffish, then pull the mass over the hook until it becomes spongy; remove it to the slab, roll and pull out in rods about $\frac{1}{2}$-inch thick; cut into equal lengths; take hold of three and plait with the fingers, while the sugar is still pliable. It is advisable to keep the bulk of the boil on a piece of hard wood during the process, unless assistance is at hand to do the plaiting, the sugar keeps soft and pliable for a longer time on wood.

IMITATION CHOCOLATE CREAM STICKS.

8-lbs White Sugar.
2-lbs. Glucose.
Vanilla Flavouring.

3 pts. Water.
1 oz. Tartaric Acid.

PROCESS.—Place the pan containing the sugar and water on the fire, stir in the glucose and bring the lot to the degree of weak crack, 300°; pour on the slab, turn up the edges, fold over the boil, and add the acid and vanilla; when thoroughly mixed and stiff enough to handle, pull over the hook until glossy white; remove it to the slab and roll out into rods about $\frac{1}{2}$-inch thick; when cold, snip off into short equal lengths and dip them into melted chocolate paste, taking them out immediately and laying them on wire frames to dry. The chocolate paste is prepared as follows :—$\frac{1}{2}$-lb. pure block cocoa, $\frac{1}{2}$-lb. ground sugar, and

3 oz. of lard or cocoa butter (no water).   Mix these ingredients in a vessel standing on the hot furnace plate (not too near the fire), stir until all is melted and incorporated, then dip in the sticks into this. mixture singly.

CHOCOLATE COCOANUT STICKS.

8-lbs. White Sugar.	3 pts. Water.
2-lbs. Glucose.	4-oz. Pure Cocoa.
Desiccated Cocoanut.	

PROCESS.—Boil the sugar, water, and glucose as directed, to the degree of weak crack, 300°; pour on oiled slab; cut off one third for pulling;. add to the other two thirds the pure cocoa and mix it in; pull the smaller piece over the hook until white and glossy; spread out the solid sugar and lay the pulled in centre, casing it round evenly, then roll into sticks 1-inch thick; when cold, snip off into lengths.   Now make a thin solution of gum or gelatine, brush over each stick with the solution and then roll it in desiccated cocoanut; when dry, the sticks are ready for sale.

IMITATION ALMONDS.

10-lbs. White Sugar.	3 pts. Water.
2-lbs. Glucose.	Cocoa Powder.
Almond Flavouring.	

PROCESS.—Boil the sugar and water and glucose in the usual way to a weak crack, pour it on an oiled slab, add the flavouring, and mix up the batch until it gets stiffish, then pull over the hook until white and spongy, return it to the slab, cut up into convenient pieces, and pass through almond rollers; when sifted, damp them slightly with a thin solution of gum or gelatine and mix them up amongst cocoa powder until they take a thin brown coating; sift again; they will dry in a short time and will then be ready for packing.   Ground cocoa husks may be used for coating and are much cheaper than cocoa powder.

FARTHING AND HALFPENNY STICKS.

THESE goods are made in a great variety of styles, colours and flavours, and look very pretty indeed when done by a clever workman, but there are many kinds which are simple enough to be attempted by a learner; the more artistic can be tried later on.   I do not here attempt to even enumerate a tithe of the different samples which are on show, nor is it necessary for my purpose.

I select the more general and saleable kinds met with, which will be sufficient to give all the knowledge and practice necessary to enable the pupil to imitate all he sees or fancies; at the same time I would suggest the exercise of a little of the inventive faculty, knowing what ample scope there is for it—anything between the modest looking acid stick to the elaborate tartan plaid arrangement will answer the purpose.

Beginners are generally fond of colours. This is a mistake. Care and discretion should be exercised even in handling the ordinary reds and yellows; the slightest tinge, in many cases, has the best effect, and no solid sugars should be deeply coloured, except, perhaps, little pieces for stripes, blues, and greens. However harmless they may be, they are never very popular. In making striped goods, some part of the boil must be pulled over the hook; if the body is to be composed of plain sugar, then a small portion must be pulled to stripe with; if the body is to be of pulled sugar, then a small portion or portions must be cut from the boil and coloured rather deeply to give contrast. Machines can be had for making sticks in various shapes, but the majority of shapes, especially with small makers are produced by hand somewhat in the way already described.

ACID STICKS.

CLEAR WHITE.

10-lbs. White Sugar.	½-oz. Cream of Tartar.
2-oz. Tartaric Acid.	3 pts. Water.
Lemon Flavouring.	

PROCESS.—Put the sugar and water in a clear bright pan, add the cream of tartar, and boil up sharply to weak crack, 300°: pour the batch on oiled slab; turn in the edges, fold the boil over, then put in the powdered acid with a few drops of oil of lemon; knead the whole together; when it begins to get stiff commence to roll the boil round on the slab, working one end down to a point: draw it out to the required thickness, the full length of the plate, cut it off, then do another length likewise, repeating the operation till the boil is worked up; keep the first pieces in shape by occasionally rolling them while the remainder of the boil is being pulled out and shaped. When the boil is finished and the sticks are cold, snip off in desired lengths with scissors. An assistant is very useful to keep the sticks in motion to prevent them becoming flat while the boil is being worked off.

PEPPERMINT STICKS.

DARK BROWN WITH LIGHT STRIPES.

8-lbs. Brown Sugar.	3 Pints Water.
2-lbs. Glucose.	Peppermint Flavour.

PROCESS.—Bring the sugar, glucose, and water to the degree of crack in the usual way; pour the batch on an oiled slab and work in the flavour. Cut off a piece about $1\frac{1}{2}$-lb. and pull it over the hook until light and satiny, then roll out into a long stick, which then divide into 6 pieces of equal length, and lay them on the solid boil longways and at equal distances apart, then roll the boil into shape, bringing down one end to a point; pull out into convenient lengths, twisting them so that the stripes form a pretty spiral form round the stick. N.B.—For the stripes in this case, white sugar is often used and looks much better, but to do so two pans are necessary, one may be a small saucepan to boil two pounds. The white sugar is boiled separately in the ordinary way, otherwise process is exactly as described.

LEMON STICKS.

PULLED YELLOW CENTRE WITH YELLOW CASE.

8-lbs. White Sugar.	3 pts. Water.
2-lbs. Glucose.	Lemon Essence
Yellow Colour.	

PROCESS.—Boil the sugar, glucose and water to weak crack; pour the batch on oiled slab; work in the colour and flavour; cut off one third and pull over the hook until of a bright light yellow satiny appearance; remove it from the hook. Spread out the plain sugar and lay the pulled in the centre; case it nicely all round with solid, then commence to roll; bring one end down to required thickness; pull out into sticks as long as convenient; when cold, snip to lengths required.

ORANGE STICKS.

PULLED WHITE BODY WITH ONE BROAD RED AND TWO NARROW ORANGE
STRIPES.

8-lbs. White Sugar.	Red and Orange Colouring.
2-lbs. Glucose.	Oil of Orange.
3 pts. Water.	Tartaric Acid.

PROCESS.—Boil the sugar, glucose, and water to weak crack, 300°; pour batch on oiled slab; cut off about one third of the boil; divide this third into two pieces; colour one part to a deep red and the other to a deep orange; mix in the colours quickly and stand them aside on a piece of wood in a warm place till wanted. Now put the acid and flavouring into the larger portion of the boil and pull over the hook until white and spongy; remove it to the slab then take the piece of red sugar and draw it out about 12 inches long and $2\frac{1}{2}$ inches thick; lay it down the centre of the pulled sugar, then take the piece of orange sugar and pull that out about 2 feet, and half the thickness of the red, cut in two and place one piece on each side of the red. Roll, twist, and pull out the whole to the recognised thickness. When cold, snip in lengths required.

CINNAMON STICKS.

CLEAR PINK BODY, WITH FOUR NARROW WHITE STRIPS.

8-lbs. Sugar.	3 pts. Water.
2-lbs. Glucose.	Red Colour.
Cinnamon Flavour.	

PROCESS.—Bring the sugar, glucose, and water to the crack and pour out; cut off a small piece and pull it white; colour the body to a light pink, add the flavour, prepare the four stripes as before directed, lay them on the clear sugar, equal distances apart, roll out in lengths and snip off when cold.

CLOVE STICKS.

ALMOST TRANSPARENT, WITH A TINGE OF RED, STRIPED WITH WHITE
AND RED STRIPES ALTERNATELY.

8-lbs. Sugar.	3 pts. Water.
2-lbs. Glucose.	Cherry Paste.
Oil of Cloves.	

PROCESS.—Boil the sugar, glucose, and water to 300°; pour on oiled slab ; cut off small portion and divide it into two pieces ; colour the one deep red. Pull both the stripes and lay them alternately on the solid sugar ; form the boil into a roll, bring down one end (usually the left) to a point ; pull out in long lengths and twist ; when cold snip with scissors to size.

RASPBERRY STICKS.

PULLED WHITE CENTRE, CASED WITH RED AND STRIPED WITH NARROW WHITE STRIPES.

8-lbs. White Sugar.	3 pts. Water.
2-lbs. Glucose.	Red Colouring.
Raspberry Essence.	

PROCESS.—Boil the sugar, glucose and water to weak crack, **300°** ; pour the batch on plate ; cut in half and colour the one piece red, then flavour both halves with essence (raspberry and a little tartaric acid). Pull one half over the hook and cut off one third of it and lay it aside ; putting the other two thirds in centre of the red solid sugar and case it round ; now lay the remaining piece of pulled sugar in 6 lengths of equal thickness and distances apart on the top of cased boil. Roll out the boil to required thickness, twist and snip off into lengths when cold.

AMERICAN HONEY-COMB STICKS.

7-lbs. Sugar.	Colour.
2½-lbs. Glucose.	Flavour.

PROCESS.—Put in boiling pan the sugar and glucose with sufficient water to dissolve same and boil in the usual way to 285°, then pour on to an oiled pouring plate, flavouring with a little oil of lemon. Turn the boil up and commence to draw it out and refold till it gets a little stiff, now throw it over the hook and when well pulled replace it on the slab and flatten it out to about 15 inches long. Now take an iron tube about 18 inches long and two inches in diameter, oil the outside and lay it down the centre of the boil and roll the batch round it, pull it out a little and close up the left end. Now take a pair of small bellows and force as much air as you can down the pipe, and then commence to work the pipe slowly and when free from the sugar, again use the bellows and blow a little air gently into the hole left by the pipe ; pull out the batch smartly and close up the end. Bring the two ends together, pull out again and bring the ends once more together, repeat this process again. Break up in lengths when cold. To make a nice job of it a little practice is necessary.

AMERICAN CREAM STICK.

10-lbs. Sugar.	1-lb. Glucose.
Flavour.	Colour.

PROCESS.—Place sugar, glucose and proportion of water to dissolve, boil up to 260° by thermometer then add 1-qt. cream and boil up again till 270° and pour the batch on pouring plate; flavour with vanilla essence and knead np the whole till it gets stiff, now pull over the hook until flossy and spongy, replace on slab and draw out in bars about $2\frac{1}{2}$ inches wide. Wrap in wax paper. These goods will grain soft and be rich eating. Three colours are usually made : red, flavoured with rose, brown, flavoured with chocolate and the above white flavoured with vanilla.

TWISTED BARLEY SUGAR STICKS.

HAND-MADE.

8-lbs. White Sugar.	3 pts. Water.
2-lbs. Glucose.	Lemon Flavour.
Saffron Colour.	

PROCESS.—Put the sugar and water in a clean, bright pan and bring to a boil then add the glucose; put on the lid for 5 minutes; continue boiling in the usual way till it reaches the crack, 300°. Now add sufficient liquid saffron to tinge to a golden colour and pour the boil carefully over a smooth slab so that the sheet of sugar will not be thicker than one eighth of an inch. When the sheet has partly set, cut the whole length of it with scissors into strips one inch wide. Let an assistant take charge of the strips and twist them by taking hold of an end in each hand and turn them in opposite directions, forming a spiral column; when cold snip the sticks into required lengths and carefully weigh and bottle. To make these goods the operators must be very quick in their movements. The slab on which the sugar is poured must be warm as the thin sticks cool very fast and get brittle.

TWISTED BARLEY SUGAR STICKS.

MACHINE-MADE.

8-lbs. White Sugar. 3 Pints Water.
2-lbs. Glucose. Oil of Lemon.
Saffron Colour.

PROCESS.—Proceed with the boil exactly as for last recipe; when the sugar is on the pouring plate turn it up as if for drops and when set enough cut off pieces and pass them through barley sugar stick rollers. They come out three or four wide; be careful and separate the sticks and mark them into lengths by pressing the edge with a piece of sheet iron at equal distances while warm, so that when cold they will break up properly otherwise, being very fragile there is a lot of little pieces.

PEPPERMINT BULL'S EYES.

BULL'S EYES OR PENNET MACHINE.

FOUR CORNERED DROPS CUT AT ANGLES; BLACK WITH WHITE STRIPES.

8-lbs. Brown Sugar. 3 pts. Water.
2-lbs. Glucose. Peppermint Flavour.

PROCESS.—The process is exactly the same as for peppermint stick, viz:—Boil the sugar, water, and glucose to a weak crack, 300°; pour the boil on an oiled plate, flavour with peppermint and well work up. In a smaller pan have two pounds of white sugar with usual proportion of cream of tartar and water, boiled to the same degree; pull this over the hook until white and porous. Remove it to the plate and work it down into lengths about one inch thick; lay them long ways on the solid boil equal distances apart; make the whole boil into a thick roll bringing one end down to a point; draw off as for half-penny sticks but thicker, then with scissors snip them off in pieces about an inch long; hold the scissors in the right hand, the sugar in the left. Every time you make a clip turn the sugar half way round, so that the corners of each cushion will be at opposite angles.

N.B.—A machine for cutting Bull's Eyes, can be bought which does this work rapidly and satisfactorily. *See engraving.*

BULL'S EYES, VARIOUS.

THE formulæ given for the different kinds of sugar sticks will answer for the variety of bull's eyes. The process and ingredients are precisely the same. The sticks may or may not be drawn out a little thicker, according to the size of the drop required. Cream of tartar may be substituted for glucose in all recipes given for boiled goods. The sugar is not boiled quite so high for hand goods or pulled sugars as it is for machine drops, being of little lower temperature it works better, keeps pliable longer, and is less brittle when cold.

ROUND HAND-MADE BALLS.

8 lbs. Sugar.	3 pts. Water.
2-lbs. Glucose	Flavour.
Colour.	

PROCESS.—Boil the sugar, water, and glucose in the usual way to a weak crack, say 300°; pour the boil on the slab; colour and flavour to taste; work the batch up until stiffish, then roll the boil round, getting one end down to a point as directed for sticks. Pull off in lengths of about three feet and about one inch thick, then, with scissors, snip off in pieces about one inch long and roll round with the hand. An expert assistant is necessary for this operation, as the balls must be shaped while hot, and kept on the move till cold.

This general recipe will apply to all hand-made balls. For details of pulling, striping, casing, and variety the reader is referred to the various processes given for sticks and bull's eyes. They are all made and finished in this way. For smaller size, pull out the lengths thinner; for larger sizes thicker.

To make the various striped balls nicely, requires a good deal of practice. No amount of book learning will teach those who are quite ignorant of sugar boiling, but at the same time, if the reader has mastered the simpler process at the beginning of the book, he is quite capable of understanding this and working out his own ideas in his own way, but "hand-made balls" should not be attempted until the learner feels confident he can manage a boil easily and quickly, because there is no time to think after the sugar is on the slab. The manipulation must now have been acquired to an extent, so as to enable the operator to proceed as if by instinct.

BALL ROLLING MACHINE.

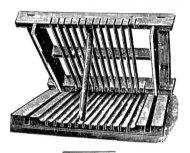

ROUND BALLS.

MACHINE HAND-MADE.

This contradiction of terms is only intelligible to a confectioner. I mean to distinguish goods made by this invention from those shaped through the ordinary rollers. This machine makes them perfectly round and more uniform than can be accomplished by hand, even by the most expert. While balls made through rollers are (I was going to say shapeless) however, they are anything but round, neither are they oval, oblong, or flat, still they are called balls for want of a better appellation.

The batch is prepared for the machine in the same way as for sticks; roll the sticks to the exact thickness; cut them off the same length as the gauge pin; put six or seven sticks at the bottom of the apparatus, then bring down the top and commence by lightly pressing and rolling the top part backwards and forwards; then bear a little heavier, giving a clear long sweep, and finish with a quick short motion ; empty the machine, and repeat the process until boil is finished.

CASED GOODS.

In giving directions for sticks and rocks, only a little has been said about cased goods and those who have read this work so far will understand what is meant. The process to simply case the sugar, is easy to a degree but art is necessary to make a nice job of it. The proportions of pulled to solid requires judgment. The colouring of the solid sugar is important for effect. The opaque boil in the centre shows up every speck and defect, therefore, thorough mixing of sufficient good colour, to give the case a deep tinge, is necessary for a bright appearance. Flavour and acids should be worked in to both solid and pulled sugar. A pinch of blue will improve the white pulled sugar, taking away the yellow shade. Beginners should look at their goods when finished ; the defects will suggest the cause. Nothing looks worse than sickly looking, half coloured, spotty cased drops. On the other hand, no goods are more brilliant and effective when well and carefully made.

ROSE BUDS.

| 8-lbs. White Sugar. | 3 pts. Water. |
| 2-lbs. Glucose. | Cherry Paste Colour. |

5 or 6 Drops Otto of Roses.

Process.—Boil the sugar, glucose, and water to the degree of crack, 300° ; pour on an oiled slab ; cut off about one third for pulling ; colour the larger piece a deep red and flavour both with the otto of roses ; pull the smaller piece over the hook till white ; spread out the larger piece ; lay the pulled sugar in the middle, casing it carefully round ; pass through small acid drop rollers. N.B.—Turn the boil on its edge every time you cut off a piece for machine, in order to keep the pulled sugar as near the centre as possible.

RIPE PEARS.

8-lbs. Sugar.	Red Colour.
2-lbs. Glucose.	Yellow Colour.
3 pts. Water.	$\frac{1}{4}$-oz. Essence Pear.

1 oz. Tartaric Acid.

Process.—Dissolve the sugar in the water, add the glucose, and boil to

305°; pour on oiled slab; cut the batch into three equal parts; flavour with essence of pear, together with a little acid; colour one part to a deep red and one to a deep yellow; pull the third portion over the hook, and lay it between the yellow and red pieces, so that one side would be yellow and the other a bright red; cut off into convenient sizes and pass through large pear drop rollers. These goods are sold either plain or crystallized.

MOTTO ROCK.

Had it not been for the many enquiries I have received from customers in reference to this class of goods, I would certainly have passed over "motto rock." I feel myself quite unable to give instructions clear enough to begin this, most laborious task a sugar boiler has to undertake. There is no doubt that hand-made goods look much prettier than any that can be done by machines; on the other hand, there is just this to be said, that it would be impossible to compete, as far as prices are concerned, with the machine made goods of the present day. By way of variety, it is very flattering to be able to decorate your shop and windows with some tasty stick or motto which will show the ability of a workman in such a striking degree. Nothing but practice, and a great deal of it, will ever make a proficient hand, but certainly patience and perseverance will overcome this as it will do almost everything else. Therefore, I will give the process as plainly as I can, in the hope that it will be found of practical assistance to those who aspire to be master of the branch. In the first place, see that your workshop is all in order, and everything is at hand. Have your pouring plate warmed by two or three previous boilings; boil your sugar a little below crack, say 300° by the thermometer. When the boil is on the slab, see that you keep it all in a heap; do not let the edges get hard, but keep turning them in. Pull the sugar directly it is cold enough to be handled. Colour the stripes, mixing the colour well in; keep them in a warm place while working the boil; turn them over occasionally, so that they may be kept moist all through. Should your stripes not stick when laying them on the boil, damp them slightly with a wet cloth. Suppose one wanted a boiling rock with the word LOVE running all through it: boil to just a little under the crack, 7-lbs. of good loaf sugar, with the usual quantity of cream of tartar. Pour it on a warm slab; cover one half of the boil to a red, and pull the other half over the hook; (if the slab be not very warm, lay both the red and the pulled sugar on a piece of hard wood, which will keep it moister than iron would,) then cut off a small piece of the red sugar, flatten in on the slab to cool, and harden. With this piece of sugar form the letter L, and work the white pulled sugar (which is stiffer) all round this letter, keeping it in shape. When this is done stand it on one side; take another piece of the pulled sugar and roll it round about $1\frac{1}{2}$ inch thick and case this all round with the red sugar, and case again with the white sugar over the red. This will give O; put this aside also, and take another piece of red sugar and form the V, working the white pulled sugar all between and round it. Form the E in the same way, and when done lay them in order—LOVE—and put whatever quantity of the white sugar you may have left round the word, and case the whole round with the remainder of the red sugar. The letters for this quantity of sugar should be about $1\frac{1}{2}$ inch high and in proportion. Roll the heap round, and bring one end down to a point and pull off the sticks to the required thickness; when chopped up in pieces the word will show all through the stick.

STAR ROCK OR ROCK VARIETIES.

THERE are many pretty assortments made in these rocks, and the perfection to which some workmen get them is something wonderful. It is nothing strange to notice the face of a watch, denoting some particular time of the day, staring from a bottle of these sweets, and even animals of all kinds, statues, and likenesses all follow in their turn, as well as stars of various colours and shapes. They are all made in the same way as the example in the preceding recipe. My remarks may practically assist, but the learner, if he has only them to rely on, must depend greatly on his own judgment and tact.

BOILED SUGAR TOYS.

IRON moulds are made by confectioners' machinists for casting boiled sugar in. They may be had to turn out all kinds of figures, such as dogs, cats, elephants, &c. They are very popular among the children, and sell well in certain districts, and show a handsome profit. The moulds are generally made in two parts; they must be well oiled; the sugar boiled as for drops, but not so high, fill the mould full and just before the whole mass sets, pour as much of the sugar out as will run; this will leave only a thin coating, which cling to the sides of the shapes, and will easily come out when the mould is parted, then you have the figure complete, but hollow. Boiled sugar whistles are made exactly the same way.

TO CRYSTALLIZE BOILED SUGAR GOODS.

SEVERAL descriptions of boiled sugars are sold crystallized, look very pretty and stand exposure to the atmosphere better. The process is very simple, and may be done with little trouble. When the drops have been made and set, break them up and sift them well in a coarse sieve; now shake them over a pan which is boiling, so that they get damped by the steam, and throw them in a heap of crystal sugar; mix them well up, so that the sugar adheres to the drops uniformly; now sift them out of the sugar again, and they will dry in a few minutes and be ready for packing. Another method, when the drops have been made and sifted, is to have a thin solution of gum or gelatine and shake it over them and rub them all together till damp all over; now throw over them sufficient crystal sugar to coat them and mix them up; when dry, sift again, weigh, and pack. N.B.—When being crystallized the goods should be nearly cold, or they will candy. Large French pears should be crystallized by the latter process, and be almost cold during the operation; being bulky, they retain the heat a long time, and therefore have a greater tendency to grain.

IMITATION INDIAN CORN.

8-lbs. White Sugar.	3 pts. Water.
2-lbs. Glucose.	Lemon Flavour

Yellow Colour.

PROCESS.—Boil the sugar, glucose, and water to weak crack, 305°; pour the boil on an oiled slab, flavour with oil of lemon and colour it to a yellow; cut this boil in two and pull one half over the hook; roll the pulled half out in lengths about the size of a corn pod; now put the plain yellow sugar through the Tom Thumb drop rollers, loosening the screws a little, and case the pulled sugars with sheets from the machine; if done carefully the result will be a good imitation of real Indian corn.

POP-CORN.

POP-CORN balls, bricks, cakes, &c., of various sizes are made from maize ; the species known as silver corn. The corn berries are shaken over a charcoal fire in a vessel known as a corn popper ; as they get hot, and the berries commence to burst, they must be kept continually in motion over the fire until the last grain has popped ; the popper is then emptied and the process repeated with fresh corn berries until the desired quantity is finished. They are then ready for packing.

POP-CORN BALLS.

ROAST the corn berries over a smokeless fire in a corn-popper ; keep shaking until every berry has burst ; boil sufficient sugar and water to the degree of feather, 245° ; add to each 7-lbs. of syrup, four ounces of dissolved gum arabic ; wet the popped corn in this syrup, and roll them in fine pulverized sugar until coated all over, then lay them aside ; when dry, repeat the coating process in the same manner until they have taken up the desired thickness of sugar. Weigh or measure sufficient coated berries, according to size of ball required ; moisten them with thin syrup ; partly form the ball by hand, then put it into a squeezer (something like a lemon squeezer), and press tightly into shape. N.B. —The corn berries may be coated in a comfit pan like other seeds or almonds, then form into balls in the usual way.

POP-CORN BRICKS.

PROCESS.—The corn berries are prepared as for balls ; boil brown sugar in the proportion of 8-lbs. sugar and 2-lbs molasses to ball, 250 ; pour the syrup over the corn and thoroughly mix them ; press them immediately into oiled tins. The process should be done quickly, and the seeds pressed as tightly as possible ; when cold, they are ready for sale, and may be cut to size with sharp knife.

POP-CORN CAKES.

PROCESS.—Prepare the corn as for balls, and pack them closely into strong square tins slightly oiled with olive oil of best quality ; boil to crack, sufficient brown sugar and glucose for quantity required, and pour the hot syrup over the pop-corns, just enough to make them adhere. When cold, cut them up with sharp knife to size.

IMPROVED COCOANUT & FRUIT GRATER.

THIS machine (by Brierley) is very strongly made and is especially useful for grating Cocoa-nuts for Jap and other kinds of Cocoa work. It can be regulated to grate finely or coarsely as required. Pine apples and other fruits can also be grated with it. It is constructed so that it will not bruise the Cocoanut or crush the material used.

JAP NUGGETS.

THESE goods seem to have come to stay, judging from the sale and display given them by retailers. They belong to a class of goods in which there is ample scope for variety. It is doubtful whether any two makers use the same formula. However, the process is practically the same in every case. I give the reader a choice of four recipes, which work well, but he may vary the ingredients a little, so as to identify himself with a particular make, which he may run as a speciality. The quantities given are for a small pan boiled over a furnace.

JAP NUGGETS, No. 1.

2-lbs. White Sugar.
4-lbs. Glucose.
4-lbs. Desiccated Cocoanut, unsweetened.
$1\frac{1}{2}$-lbs Farina.
2 pts. Water.
Yellow Colouring.

PROCESS.—Mix the ingredients in copper pan; boil on a slow fire to stiff ball, 250°, stirring all the time; add colouring to fancy. When ready, pour carefully on an oiled plate, making the sheet about half an inch thick; when cold, dust with pulverized sugar, and cut up with a sharp knife to size. N.B.—A few loose iron bars are useful to form a square on the pouring plate, in proportion to size of boil, that the exact thickness of the sheet may be determined.

JAP NUGGETS, No. 2.

2-lbs. White Sugar.
4-lbs. Good Brown Sugar.
5-lbs. Desiccated Cocoanut.
7-lbs. Glucose.
$2\frac{1}{2}$-lbs. Farina.
3 pts. Water.

PROCESS.—Put the sugar, glucose, and water in the pan; place it on a slow fire; stir in the cocoanut and farina, and boil to stiff ball, 255°, keeping well stirred. Pour on an oiled slab and cut up to size. Then set and dust with powdered sugar. In large factories, where this sweetmeat is made, machinery plays an important part; in fact the manipulation is practically all done by mechanism. There is the desiccator for preparing the cocoanuts; the steam pans which are fitted with beaters revolving inside, and fixed with chains and weights for lifting out, so that the pans may be emptied and cleaned without trouble; also breaks for rolling out the sheets to size; cutting machines which cut the nugget any size, the machines being so arranged that by simply altering a pawl on a ratchet wheel the size of the nugget is determined. Where this elaborate arrangement exists my formulæ will neither be desirable nor necessary nor do we pretend to suggest or advise. However, many tons are made in an ordinary boiling shop with only the usual appliances and the principle is to assist people thus situated.

JAP NUGGETS, No. 3.

4-lbs. Good Brown Sugar.   4-lbs. Desiccated Cocoanut, unsweetened.
3½-lbs. Glucose.   2-lbs. Farina.
3 Pints Water.

PROCESS.—As before, brown colouring should be used if required dark; it gives the goods richer appearance. When the boil is cut up the nuggets should be thrown into pulverized sugar.

JAP CUTTER

JAP NUGGETS (No. 4 American.)

5-lbs. Glucose.   10-lbs. Desiccated Cocoanut.
1-lb. Sugar.   1½-pts. Water.

PROCESS.—Put the sugar, glucose and water in the pan and boil to about 240°. Place the cocoanut in a wooden vessel which has been previously damped with water, pour over the nut a portion of the hot syrup stirring up the whole with a strong spatula. Let your assistant pour the remainder of the syrup slowly over the cocoanut while you mix it up with the spatula until the batch is thoroughly incorporated, if more cocoanut can be stirred in, do so, and make the mixture as stiff as possible. Now transfer the contents of the pan into a frame or between some wire bars on the slab, and flatten down the mass with a rolling pin. Let it stand for 2 hours and cut to size. Place the nuggets in granulated sugar.

BULGARIAN NOUGATS.

THIS sweetmeat, like Jap Nuggets, is made from a variety of formulæ. If well manufactured it commands a ready sale. Some very common stuff is vended on barrows, hawked on trays at seaside resorts and also sold in small shops chiefly owned by foreigners in poor neighbourhoods. This latter quality is in most cases, to say the least of it, a mysterious conglomeration of questionable ingredients. The recipes and instructions here given are for a good wholesome sweets.

It is almost necessary to have steam machinery for this purpose, because the process is long and tedious; small boilings hardly pay to make besides which there is a risk of burning.

BULGARIAN NOUGAT (No. 1. Best).

60-lbs. White Sugar.	14-lbs. Fondant Cream.
14-lbs. Glucose.	7-lbs. Gelatine.
14-lbs. Almonds, blanched.	Water.

1-oz. Essence Vanilla.

PROCESS.—Cover the gelatine with cold water and let it soak until soft, say about twelve hours. Dissolve the sugar and glucose in four quarts of water and boil in the usual way in a steam pan to a stiff ball. Turn off the steam, add the gelatine and stir until dissolved : now transfer the batch into the steam stirrer; melt the fondant cream and mix it in together with the almonds and essence of vanilla. Beat the whole well up for a couple of hours, then pour the mass into moulds or boxes, lined with wafer paper. When cold and set, it should be turned out and cut up into bars as required. By altering the colour and the essence, varieties may be made, such as raspberry, almond, &c.

BULGARIAN NOUGAT (No. 2. Cheap)

28-lbs. White Sugar.	12-lbs. Corn Flour.
14-lbs. Glucose.	2 qts. Water.
8-lbs. Almonds, blanched.	1-oz. Essence Vanilla.
7-lbs. Gelatine.	New Milk.

PROCESS.—Mix the corn flour with sufficient new milk to produce it the consistency of cream. Cover the gelatine with cold water and let it remain in soak for twelve hours or until quite soft. Let this begin the process: put the gelatine in a steam pan and melt it, then add the corn flour and stir well until the whole is thoroughly amalgamated; dissolve the sugar with 4 lbs. of the glucose in the water and boil in the usual way to the degree of crack. Remove the pan from the fire and add the remainder of the glucose. When the whole has partly cooled pour it gently into the steam pan, at the same time stirring in the almonds, and essence of vanilla. When the entire boil has been thoroughly mixed turn out the batch into deep moulds which have been thickly lined with wax or wafer paper. This nougat when cold and set is usually turned out in the block and cut up into bars as required. N.B.—The ingredients and method given in the above must be taken principally as a guide. There are so many different concoctions sold under this name that it would be impossible to give a definite formula.

NOUGATS, VARIOUS.

THE manufacture of French and other nougats is simply a question of mixing almonds, honey, sugar, egg-whites, and other good things in various proportions, giving the whole a delicate flavour and appropriate colour. Steam is always preferable as a means of cooking. When a furnace is used for this purpose, the fire must be very slow and the mass kept well stirred. The most popular flavours are raspberry, vanilla, orange, and almond. Best colours and essences only should be used.

VANILLA NOUGAT (Best).

14-lbs. Sweet Almonds, blanched.	24 Eggs—whites only.
4-lbs. Best White Sugar.	2-lbs. Glucose.
3-qts. Clear Honey.	1-oz. Essence of Vanilla.

PROCESS.—Beat the egg-whites in machine to thick froth; put the sugar, honey and glucose into a bright clean pan and place over a very slow fire, stirring continuously with a wooden spatula for about two hours, until the mass gets thick; then add the beaten egg-whites, and continue to stir until the mixing reaches the degree of stiff ball; then put in the almonds and the vanilla essence, stirring them also well in the boil. Now remove the pan and pour out the contents on wafer paper, spreading it out a full inch thick, cover the top also with wafer paper and smooth the entire sheet level; keep a flat board on top till cold and set. Remove the board and cut into bars, wrap in wax paper and pack.

This is an excellent sweetmeat when well made. For variety, change flavour, and colour suitably.

VANILLA NOUGAT (Cheap).

12-lbs. White Sugar.
3-lbs. Glucose.
4-lbs. Sweet Almonds, small.
3 pts. Water.
½-oz. Essence of Vanilla.

PROCESS.—Put the sugar, glucose, and water in a clean pan; place on a sharp fire and stir till dissolved then put on the cover and let boil for five or six minutes. Remove the lid and continue to boil to soft ball degree, then pour the contents on a damp slab (one over which cold water has been sprinkled). When cool, take a long flat spatula and work the sugar about until it becomes white and creamy, then add the almonds (which have been previously blanched and dryed), together with the vanilla essence. Keep working up the whole until of uniform consistency. Spread the mass on wafer paper in sheets one inch thick and also cover the sheets with wafer paper rolling the top smooth ; when set, cut into bars. Should the cream be a little thin, add some icing sugar when mixing ; if boiled properly this is not required. Most of the cheap nougats now in the market are made more or less according to this formula. For variety, change the flavour, and colour suitably.

AMERICAN NOUGAT.

THREE LAYERS.

6-lbs. Sugar.
4-lbs. Glucose.
16 Egg Whites.
1½ lbs. Almonds, blanched and dried.

PROCESS.—Dissolve the sugar and glucose in sufficient water up to a temperature of 252°. Stir the mixture one minute to let the heat out, have the egg-whites well beaten and add them with the vanilla flavour, well beating the whole together with spatula until quite stiff. Now take one third of the batch and place in the frame lined with wax paper and spread one-third of the almonds on top, then colour the remainder of the batch a light pink. Divide this lot into two portions and spread one portion on top of the one already in the frame, sprinkle more almonds over the top of this layer. Now colour the remaining portion of the pink a dark brown adding a small piece of pure chocolate and the remainder of the almonds mixing them all together and spread on top of the pink layer, smooth over and cover with wafer paper. Let it stand three or four hours and cut up.

N.B.—This same recipe will stand for Vanilla, Strawberry, and Chocolate Nougat made separately. Process the same only mix in the almonds with the egg white when beating up. A good chocolate colour is difficult to obtain in a whipped sugar. I have had better results from a dark brown added to a light pink bulk.

NOUGATINES.

4-lbs. Ground Almonds.   7-lbs. Castor Sugar.

PROCESS.—Place the sugar in a bright pan over a slow fire (without water); keep stirring until melted; see that the sugar is well scraped down from edges so that it gets all melted. When it becomes a rich brown colour, sprinkle in the ground almonds; now stir just sufficiently to keep the almonds off the bottom; when the latter are boiled in and thoroughly incorporated, remove the pan and pour contents on to an oiled slab. When cold enough to handle, turn the boil up as if for drops, and pass through a machine or snip off with scissors. Sift the nougatines and cover them with a thin solution of gum and throw them into a heap of icing sugar and mixing them up till well coated. Remove them to the drying room for twelve hours; they are then ready for packing.

CHOCOLATE NOUGATINES.

4-lbs. Ground Almonds.   7-lbs. Castor Sugar.

PROCESS.—Exactly as the previous formula. When shaped through rollers or by hand, the nougatines are dipped into melted chocolate (see chocolate for dipping); taken out with a fork and spread on trays until dry. N.B.—Nougatines must in all cases be coated or they become damp in a few hours. If coated with icing sugar, it is necessary to put them in a drying room for a day, otherwise the coating will peel off.

ICE CREAM CONFECTIONERY.

THIS form of boiled sugars has long been in vogue in America, and has lately appeared in the windows of several London sweet shops, principally in the West End, and sells very freely. It may be made as follows :—Boil 7-lbs. of loaf sugar with three pints of water ; add a small teaspoonful of cream of tartar ; allow to boil for ten minutes, then add one pound of fresh butter. It will then commence to froth up, and care must be taken that the pan is large enough, as the syrup will occupy twice the space than if no butter had been added ; boil this mixture to the degree of a very weak crack, (285° by the thermometer,) at which point it is done ; pour it on to the slab, which has been previously greased. As soon as the product begins to cool, turn it up and knead it until it gets stiff enough to pull over the hook. When on the hook pull it sharp until it gets as white as snow. The white is usually flavoured with vanilla or oil of lemon. It may be either pulled out in bars or left in the heap. It is easily broken in small pieces for retail purposes. During hot weather keep this toffee from the air, or it will be inclined to be sticky. This sweetmeat is very rich, and commands a good sale at the best price.

RASPBERRY AND STRAWBERRY ICE CREAM CONFECTIONERY.

This is made exactly as the last, with the addition of a little red colour before the boiling is poured out, or it may be coloured on the slab. Add a little essence of raspberry or strawberry and a pinch of tartaric acid just before pulling the boil. Colour the raspberry to a little deeper shade than the strawberry.

CHOCOLATE ICE CREAM.

To make chocolate ice cream, boil the same quantities as before, precisely in the same way in every particular. When the sugar has been poured out, work well into it $\frac{1}{2}$-lb. of powdered chocolate ; knead well up in order that the chocolate may be well mixed with the sugar. Sufficient chocolate should be used to give the boil a dark brown colour, otherwise the sweet would be too pale when pulled.

GLACES.

6-lbs. Sugar.	1½-lbs. Glucose.
Water to dissolve.	

Process.—Place ingredients in pan and boil in the ordinary way to 270°. Stand the pan in a frame or barrel top, and drop into the syrup.

one at a time such nuts or other fruit you wish to cover. Now take them out with a fork and place them on a clean oiled slab; when dry they are ready for packing which is usually done in wide mouth bottles. Brazil nuts, walnuts, Barcelonas, cherries and pineapple pieces are used for this process.

AMERICAN MARSHMALLOWS.

5-lbs. Pulverized Sugar.   5-ozs. Gelatine.
5-lbs. Glucose.   1-qt. Water.
Vanilla Flavour.

PROCESS.—Soak the gelatine in hot water until dissolved and put it aside Now put the glucose in boiling pan and place on the fire (without water) commence at once to stir until it melts and boil to 248°, remove the pan from the fire and stir in the 5lbs. pulverized sugar. Now pour into the batch the dissolved gelatine and well flavour with vanilla, then put the lot into a beater and beat well until stiff. Pour the batch back on the slab which has been well sprinkled with pulverized sugar, spreading it evenly and sprinkling more pulverized sugar on top. Let stand for three or four hours and cut up into squares.

This sweet is said to be a rare favourite in the United States.

CARAMELS.

CARAMEL CUTTER.

WHEN first brought over from America, these goods were certainly a treat. They were rather dear but they *were* good and the public appreciated them. Very soon the demand was universal, competition stepped in with the usual result viz.—the prices were lowered, the quality suffered, and anything cut to shape was called "caramels." However, several makers have kept up their standard of excellence, so that only those qualities which are identified by a particular brand or name find favour with the retail shopkeepers who study the interest of their customers. I recommend the making of an excellent article from good and fresh ingredients, using a distinctive name or brand, and, above all, keeping the quality up to the standard. It is better to please old customers with prime goods than try to deceive new ones with cheap and common confectionery! The following formulæ make really good caramels. For something very special, cream might be substituted for milk and the proportion of butter increased. Be careful to use best fresh butter and fresh milk or cream; condensed milk may be used when it is inconvenient to get new milk.

VANILLA CARAMELS.

8-lbs. White Sugar.	2 Tins Condensed Milk.
2-lbs. Glucose.	2 pts. Water.
1-lb. Fresh Butter.	Vanilla Flavouring.

PROCESS.—Boil the sugar, glucose and water to the degree of ball, 250°. Remove the pan a little off the fire; add the milk and butter, (the latter cut into little pieces) and stir well in with a wooden spatula until the whole is thoroughly mixed, then gently bring the mass through the boil and pour out on greased slab, making sheet about $\frac{1}{2}$ inch thick. When set, cut with caramel cutter, and when cold, separate the squares and wrap in wax paper.

COCOANUT CARAMELS.

8-lbs. Sugar.	1$\frac{1}{2}$-lbs. Desiccated Cocoanut, unsweetened.
2-lbs. Glucose.	2 Tins Condensed Milk.
1-lb. Fresh Butter.	2 pts. Water.

PROCESS.—Dissolve the sugar in the water, add the glucose, and boil up to ball, 250°. Remove the pan to side, then stir in the butter, milk, and cocoanut; bring through the boil. Pour on oiled slab or in frames about $\frac{1}{2}$-inch thick; when set, mark with caramel cutter; when cold, separate the squares and wrap in wax paper.

RASPBERRY CARAMELS.

8-lbs. Sugar.	1-lb. Raspberry Pulp or Jam.
2-lbs. Glucose.	2 Tins Condensed Milk.
1-lb. Fresh Butter.	2 pts. Water.
	Liquid Cochineal Colour.

PROCESS.—Boil the sugar, glucose, and water to degree of ball 250°; move pan to side of fire, add the milk, butter (cut small) and jam. stir the whole together, replacing the pan on the fire; add sufficient colouring; keep stirring the whole time until the whole comes through the boil; pour out; when set, mark with cutter, divide the squares, and wrap when cold.

WALNUT CARAMELS.

8-lbs. White Sugar.	1-lb. Shelled Walnuts, broken small.
2-lbs. Glucose.	2 Tins Condensed Milk.
1-lb. Fresh Butter.	2 pts. Water.

Saffron Colouring.

PROCESS.—As above. Caramels require careful watching and a lot of stirring, the boil being liable to catch and flow over. The fire must not be too fierce; when too hot, put an iron under one side of the pan to keep it up a little from the fire; keep constantly on the stir after the butter and the flavouring ingredients have been added.

CHOCOLATE CARAMELS.

8-lbs. Good Sugar.	$\frac{1}{2}$-lb. Pure Chocolate, unsweetened.
2-lbs. Glucose.	2 Tins Condensed Milk.
1-lb. Fresh Butter.	2 pts. Water.

Vanilla Flavouring.

PROCESS.—When the sugar, glucose and water have boiled to the degree of ball, 250°, and the milk, butter, and chocolate are all dissolved and incorporated, bring gently through the boil, then pour out on oiled slab or in frames. When set, mark deeply with caramel cutter; when cold, separate with sharp knife and wrap in wax paper.

AMERICAN CARAMELS.

THE following caramel recipes were sent to the writer from America by a brother confectioner, who was and is still employed in one of the best houses on the other side of the pond. They appeared in the fourth edition of the confectioners' hand-book, and were much appreciated at the time, but I am afraid in these degenerate days the luscious ingredients mentioned have been varied more or less according to the exigencies of price. However, here they are, and for those who can get a high price for a first-class article, they are well worth attention.

VANILLA CARAMELS, No. 1 Quality.

AMERICAN RECIPE.

6-lbs. Sugar.
2 qts. Sweet Cream.
Essence of Vanilla.
1½-lbs. Fresh Butter.
4-lbs. Glucose.

PROCESS.—Put the sugar, glucose, and cream in the pan; put on a slow fire and stir constantly; let boil to a stiff ball, then add the butter; keep stirring, and when it has well boiled through, remove the pan from the fire. Flavour with vanilla essence. Pour out on oiled plate; when set mark with caramel cutter; when cold, divide with sharp knife and wrap each caramel in wax paper.

VANILLA CARAMELS, No. 2 Quality.

AMERICAN RECIPE.

5-lbs. Sugar.
1-lb. Fresh Butter.
3 pts. New Milk.
½-oz. Cream of Tartar.
2 pts. Water.
Vanilla Flavouring.

PROCESS.—Boil the sugar, milk, and water with the cream of tartar on a slow fire; stir all the time till it reaches a stiff ball; add the essence of vanilla and stir it in gently. Remove the pan from the fire and pour contents on oiled slab; when set mark deep with caramel cutter; when cold, separate the squares with sharp knife. These caramels should be a cream colour.

RASPBERRY AND STRAWBERRY CARAMELS.

THESE flavours may be used in either of the last two recipes, best quality according to the first, second quality as the second. Walnut, cocoanut, &c., may be added for other flavours.

MAPLE CARAMELS.

BY using pure maple sugar, maple caramels may be made precisely as vanilla; the flavour of the maple sugar is sufficient and requires no additional essence. These caramels, will, of course, be dark.

CHOCOLATE CARAMELS, No. 1 Quality.

AMERICAN RECIPE.

6-lbs. Best Sugar.　　　　　　2 qts. Sweet Cream.
4-lbs. Glucose.　　　　　　　$1\frac{1}{2}$ lbs. Fresh Butter.
$1\frac{1}{2}$-lbs. Pure Chocolate, unsweetened.

PROCESS.—Put the sugar and cream in the pan; stir well together, then add the glucose; let boil to a stiff ball. Ease the pan off the fire a little and put in the butter cut into little pieces, then add the chocolate; constantly stir. Bring the mass through the boil, then add essence of vanilla. Remove the pan and pour contents on oiled slab, making the sheet about $\frac{1}{2}$-inch thick. Mark deep with caramel cutter when set; when cold, divide the squares with sharp knife and wrap in wax paper.

CHOCOLATE CARAMELS, No. 2 Quality.

AMERICAN RECIPE.

5-lbs. Sugar.　　　　　　　$\frac{3}{4}$-lb Pure Chocolate, unsweetened.
$\frac{3}{4}$-lb. Fresh Butter.　　　　$\frac{1}{2}$-oz. Cream of Tartar.
1 Quart New Milk.

PROCESS.—Dissolve the sugar in the milk; add the cream of tartar, and boil to the degree of ball. Ease the pan a little off the fire and stir in the butter and chocolate. Bring the whole to the boil and add extract of vanilla. Remove the pan and pour contents on the slab; mark and separate as directed in the last.

UNWRAPPED CARAMELS.

CARAMELS have usually been sold wrapped in wax paper. This is necessary when the goods are boiled very low and contain a large proportion of glucose. However, I have had large consignments from America of unwrapped caramels, which are having a good run. They are first prepared in the form of a paste which is kept in stock like fondant cream and used in different formulas to finish into unwrapped caramels of various qualities, flavours, and combinations. To have a good paste is essential to having a good caramel, it would not be worth while to give the details for making a caramel paste, as the ingredients obtainable on the other side are not always to be had here by small makers who cannot import, and this might lead to irregularities which it would be better to avoid. Caramel paste is now prepared by houses who make a speciality of it in very large quantities by the latest mechanical appliances for cooking, stirring, and mixing. Buying their ingredients in bulk they obtain just what is required both in substance and grade, and are consequently in a much better position to prepare an article of this kind than small makers on this side who have to buy what they can get. In the columns of the trade journals will be found advertisements of caramel paste importers, who will supply the article and give with it formulas for both wrapped and unwrapped caramels for which their paste is adapted. The process with the paste is simple and the recipes can always be improved upon so that no maker need be stereotyped as to exact result. I give the following instance from a paste branded " Excelsior."

UNWRAPPED CARAMELS.

3-lbs. Excelsior Paste.	8 lbs. Sugar
2 Gals. Cream or 5 Gals. Milk.	6-lbs. Glucose.
Caramel Flavour.	

Process.—Put all the ingredients together in a clean pan and place on a slow fire, keep well stirred until it reaches the soft crack, 270°; then remove the pan at once, stir in the flavour and pour the boil out, when set, cut up.

These caramels will keep in any climate, will not sugar or become rancied and will eat free. This paste may be also used for wrapped caramels as under.

No. 1.

12-lbs. Sugar.	4-lbs. Excelsior Caramel Paste.
12-lbs. Glucose.	1 Gal. Fresh Cream.
Caramel Flavour.	

Process.—As last, when set, cut up, and wrap in wax paper.

No. 2.

6-lbs. Sugar.	4-lbs. Excelsior Paste.
18-lbs. Glucose.	1 Gal. New Milk
Caramel Flavour.	

Process.—As for unwrapped caramels. Be careful to remove the pan quickly when batch has reached soft crack, flavour, stir and pour out at once and you will get a good colour.

OPERA CREAM CARAMELS.

10-lbs. Sugar.	½-lb. Almonds (chopped).
3-qts. Fresh Cream.	½-lb. Barcelona Nuts.
½ Teaspoonful Cream of Tartar.	¼-lb. Glacé Cherries.
½-lb. Walnuts (chopped).	

PROCESS.—Chop up the Nuts and Glacé Cherries separately and lay them aside. Now put the sugar, cream, and cream of tartar into a clean pan and boil to about 240° (not higher), and pour the syrup on a damp slab and let it get quite cold. Now use a spaddle and cream up by rubbing altogether against the slab; when all creamed cover with a damp cloth and let it remain for two hours. Now break off two pounds of this cream and knead into it the chopped walnuts, into another two pounds the almonds, colour another portion pink and knead into it the cherries. Colour a fourth portion of 2-lbs. brown, and work in the Barcelona nuts. You should now have three or four pounds of the cream left, divide this into two, colour one part to a red and flavour with raspberry, the other part flavour with vanilla, no colour. As you finish each portion press them into frames which have been lined with wax paper and roll them flat, at a thickness of a caramel; when set stiff cut with caramel cutter. This is a good line, especially for a retail shop.

BURNT ALMONDS

5-lbs. White Sugar.	2 Pints Water.
2½-lbs. Sicily Almonds.	Colours Various.
Flavours Various.	

PROCESS.—Boil the sugar and water in the pan; as soon as boiling, add the almonds, which must be kept off the bottom by stirring until the boil reaches the degree of ball, remove the pan from the fire, then with the spatula or palette knife grain the boil by rubbing part of the syrup against the side of the pan until it gets thin and creamy, then stir all together until it gets into a powder. Now turn into a coarse sieve, shake well up and separate those that adhere, then divide the batch into three or four lots. Put one lot with its fair share of siftings into the pan, cover over the stove with a sheet of thin iron to break the heat and put the pan on top of the iron; the siftings will gradually dissolve and adhere to the almonds which will become crisp when done (which you can tell by tasting); turn them out and serve the remainder in the same manner. They are often sold finished in this way, but in that case when the almonds have been put in the pan the second time each lot should be coloured and flavoured differently, then mixed. If required crinkly, boil in another pan to high crack, 315°, five pounds of white sugar; put the almonds back into the pan (which must have been cleaned); pour over them this syrup in two lots, stirring each time; in the latter case, colour the syrup for variety.

PRALINES SATINE

THESE beautiful sweets are very popular. When well made they are pleasing both to the eye and the palate but they must be kept air-tight or they soon lose all their attractiveness and become a sticky mass, the sweets having a great tendency to "sweat." In order to prevent this as much as possible use a little borax in each boil. The process is simple enough but it must be worked quickly, in fact, the beauty depends on the rapid manipulation of the sugar over the hook; keep the eye fixed on the colour; as soon as it becomes like a glossy satin with a close grain it is finished; lift it off the hook immediately and return it to the slab for casing; do not carry on the pulling operation till it becomes spongy, and be careful not to use too much colour; the tints should be light and delicate when the goods are finished. Machines are made for cutting pralines. Some are shaped and worked like a pennet machine, others consist of two frames, each fitted with knives, hinged at one end so that the top frame is lifted; then the length of praline stick is laid along the bottom one; the top one is then brought down until the knives touch the stick, then pressed gently until the stick is cut through, closing the ends and encasing the soft centre; the motion must not be sharp, or it will chop off the pralines, leaving the ends open.

VANILLA PRALINES

7-lbs. Best White Sugar.	1 Teaspoonful Cream of Tartar.
2-lbs. Fondant Paste.	1 Quart Water.
1-lb. Desiccated Cocoanut, fine.	Borax.
Green Colour.	

PROCESS.—Put the sugar, water and cream of tartar in the boiling pan and boil up to crack, 310°, in the ordinary way; while the pan is on the fire, take the fondant paste and work into it the desiccated cocoanut, with a little essence of vanilla and lay aside till required. When the boil has reached the required degree pour the sugar on to the slab; colour it a light green, and, when partly cool, pull over the hook until it becomes a delicate satin tint; return it to the slab, press the boil out, lay the fondant paste in the centre and case it all round with the pulled sugar; now carefully work the one end of the boil down to a point as for sticks and draw it out in lengths the required thickness; lay them on the machine and press gently until cut through; the pralines are then ready for packing. It is advisable to work small boils of these goods, as the casing being boiled high soon gets brittle. Turn the bulk round continually on the plate so as to keep the fondant paste exactly in the centre. Use chamois leather gloves to pull the sugar.

RASPBERRY COCOANUT PRALINES

7-lbs. Best White Sugar.	1 Teaspoonful Cream of Tartar.
2-lbs. Fondant Paste.	1 Quart Water.
1-lb. Desiccated Cocoanut.	Carmine Colour.
1-lb. Raspberry Jam, boiled stiff.	Borax.

PROCESS.—Work the jam and cocoanut into the fondant paste; boil the sugar, water and cream of tartar to crack; pour on to an oiled slab; colour to a light rose tint; when partly cool, pull and work off as in the preceding recipe.

BLACK CURRANT PRALINES

7-lbs. White Sugar.	1 Teaspoonful Cream of Tartar.
2-lbs Fondant Paste.	1 Quart Water.
1-lb. Black Currant Jam.	Borax.
$\frac{1}{2}$-oz. Tartaric Acid.	Purple Colour.

PROCESS.—Work the jam, acid, and colour into the fondant paste; boil the sugar, water, and cream of tartar to crack, and work off as already described.

COCOANUT PRALINES

7-lbs. Sugar.	1 Teaspoonful Cream of Tartar.
2-lbs. Fondant Paste.	1 Quart Water with Borax.
1-lb. Desiccated Cocoanut.	Lemon Flavour.
Yellow Colour.	

PROCESS.—As usual. Pralines of any sort or flavour may be made by following the directions given and substituting different essences, jams, chopped nuts, or almonds and colour to fancy.

CREAM BARS, &c.

THIS class of boiled sugars has become very popular. They are displayed in every variety in large as well as in small establishments. They very often consist of simply grained sugar "labelled" creams. This is a silly attempt at deception, alike dishonourable to the seller and detrimental to the trade. When the public ask for cream, they expect a soft, mellow, delicately flavoured article, which only requires bruising with the tongue in order to gain the full flavour with a substance which dissolves almost instantly. What a disappointment when the customer finds he has got a hard flavourless lump of almost dry sugar, or a chalky mixture as hard as a bullet. There is certainly a little more trouble to make creams than candies, but that is no reason why one should be sold for the other. The process for the different sorts is exactly the same, the colours, flavours, and arrangements alone differing, which observation will at once teach the learner what is necessary. I take it for granted that those who use the book require rather the key to the different kinds of goods, with instructions how to make the leading articles, than a list of repetitions, which a grain of sense and a moment's reflection would render unnecessary. Besides, something new is always wanted in the business. I have given methods for every class, and the reader will be dull indeed, if after a little practice he cannot suggest something which will be new to the trade. Some people are lucky enough to strike oil in this way. It may just be mentioned that large and expensive machines are made for creaming sugar, particulars of which will be gladly supplied by the trade machinists. They are used by large chocolate houses, as well as the leading confectioners but the details of those machines would be a little beyond the purposes of this book.

VANILLA CREAM BARS.

7 lbs. White Sugar.	3 Pints Water.
2 lbs. Glucose.	Vanilla Flavour.

PROCESS.—Dissolve the sugar with the water in a clean pan ; add the glucose and boil in the usual way to the degree of feather, 243° ; pour the contents on to a damp slab ; let remain till cold ; then, with a palette knife or wooden spatula, work up to a white cream, adding a tint of blue to bleach it. When the whole has become a smooth cream, return it to the pan and melt it just sufficiently that it may pour out smooth and level; stir in the flavour and run on pouring plate a sheet ½-inch thick; when set, cut into bars.

RASPBERRY OR ROSE CREAM BARS.

7-lbs. White Sugar.   3 Pints Water.
2-lbs. Glucose.   Raspberry or Rose Flavour.

PROCESS.—Dissolve the sugar in the water, add the glucose and boil to 243°; pour contents on slab, and when cold, divide the boil into three parts; colour one part red, add some pure chocolate to another, and to a third part add a pinch of blue; cream each part by rubbing on slab to a smooth paste. In rubbing in the pure chocolate, see that you have enough to make it a rich brown; for the red portion use just sufficient to give a light red rose pink. When all finished, melt each portion separately in the pan just sufficiently soft to run to a level surface; pour out first the red, then the chocolate on top of the red, then the white on top of chocolate; this will make a cream cake to cut up into bars. Some do not take the trouble to melt the cream, being satisfied to spread the paste out smoothing it on the top with palette knife; this answers the purpose but does not look so well.

COCOA NUT CREAM.

7-lbs. White Sugar.   3-lbs. Cocoanut, peeled and sliced.
2-lbs. Glucose.   3 Pints Water.
                    Red Colouring.

PROCESS.—Boil the sugar, glucose, and water in the usual way to the degree 245°; pour contents on slab; divide the boil into two lots; when cool, colour the one part to light pink and put a small touch of blue in the other; add the sliced cocoanut, half into each part, then commence to cream them by rubbing. When both parts have been mixed up into a smooth paste, it is ready for sale, being usually sold by cutting from the rough block. N.B.—Cut almonds, ground walnuts, &c., are used in the same way as directed for cocoanuts. The boils may or may not be flavoured, but a little flavouring improves them and makes them fragrant.

CRYSTALLIZED COCOANUT CHIPS.

Process.—Shave off the dark skin from a quantity of cocoanuts; cut them up in slices with a spokeshave or cocoanut machine. Bring to the boil a sufficient quantity of sugar, with the usual proportions of water; add the cocoanut slices and allow the whole to boil for say ten minutes, or until the sugar comes to a soft ball, keeping it stirred all the time; remove the pan from the fire and pour the contents into a coarse sieve which has been placed over a vessel to catch the syrup which will run off the chips. Immediately the chips are drained, turn them amongst a heap of fine crystal sugar and mix them up; in an hour's time, they will be ready to sift out. Prepare another quantity in the same manner, but have the crystallized sugar coloured red; when the second quantity of chips has been boiled and strained as last, turn them amongst the red sugar and mix them up directly; be careful the chips are not allowed to drain too long, or they will become too dry to take on the crystal; when sifted out of the crystal sugar, mix the white and red together. Cocoanut chips should be kept open to the air. Keeping them in covered boxes or in show glasses with the lids on they become sour in time. This method is a ready way, but is only suitable for retail purposes or quick wholesale trade. For best quality see next recipe.

COLOURED SUGAR FOR DRY CRYSTALLIZING.

PROCESS.—Place a large sheet of thick paper on a clean slab, in the centre of the paper put the quantity of sugar to be coloured in a heap, then in the middle of this heap pour liquid colouring of any shade required, now rub and mix up the whole with the hands until the colour is uniformly distributed. Now add a few drops of liquid ammonia and again mix up thoroughly, this will keep the colour fast and bright.

CRYSTALLIZED COCOANUT CHIPS.

BEST QUALITY.

PROCESS.—Prepare the cocoanuts by paring off the brown skin; cut them in thin slices and pack them in a crystallizing tin (see tools and materials used for making liqueurs, &c.); boil to the degree of smooth 217°, sufficient sugar in the ordinary way to make syrup enough to cover them. Pour this syrup over them while hot and stand aside for twelve hours, then drain off the superfluous syrup by removing the cork from the tin; spread the chips on trays and put them in the drying room for two or three days turning them over at intervals. When dry, put them again into the tin; boil a like quantity of syrup as before and let it stand till nearly cold; then pour it over the chips and let them remain undistributed for another twelve hours; then strain again and spread them on trays; when dry, they are ready for sale or packing. These, of course, will be white. To make the red chips, simply colour the syrup which is used for crystallizing.

SUGAR CANDY, PINK and WHITE.

SUGAR candy is made in a variety of colours. The foreign kinds which are imported in large quantities, varying in shades between very dark brown and pale yellow. The prices charged for these qualities being very little above the sugar value, are unprofitable to make, but the pink and white candy is not so common, and generally commands a remunerative figure, besides being attractive as a window decoration. The process is simple and interesting. Copper pans are sold by machinists for the purpose, but for small makers a rough copper or white metal pan will answer, so long as its sides are a little wider at the top than the bottom, in order that the crystallized sugar may fall out unbroken. Perforate the pan with small holes, about three inches apart, pass a thread through from one hole to another, so that the thread runs at equal distances through the centre of the pan, then stop up the holes from the outside with a thin coating of beeswax and resin to keep the syrup from running through.

When the pan has been got ready, boil to the degree of thread, or 230°, sufficient sugar to fill it, in the proportion of 7-lbs. sugar to 3 pints of water; then pour the contents into the pan and stand it in the drying room for three or four days. When the crystals are heavy enough, which you can tell by examining them, pour off the superfluous syrup; rinse the candy in lukewarm water and stand it in the drying room till dry. To make the pink, of course, colour the syrup, but be careful to tinge it very lightly. N.B.—When goods are undergoing the process of crystallizing, the vessel in which they are placed must not be disturbed.

CHRISTMAS PUDDING (Imitation).

7-lbs. White Sugar.	$\frac{1}{2}$-lb. Mixed Peel.
1-lb. Raisins.	$\frac{1}{2}$-lb. Sweet Almonds, blanched and chopped.
1-lb. Currants.	1-oz. Mixed Spice.
1-lb. Sultanas.	2 Pints Water

PROCESS.—Prepare the fruit by washing the currants in cold water, afterwards drying them; stone the raisins; blanch and chop the almonds; cut the peel in strips, then mix them together, adding the spice; boil the sugar and water to ball degree; remove the pan from the fire; grain the boil by rubbing the syrup against the side of the pan in the usual way. When it becomes creamy, add the mixed fruit, carefully stirring the whole till thoroughly incorporated; have some wet cloths ready, into which divide the boil; tie them very tight and hang them up until set hard. The blanched almonds are used to represent suet and should be chopped accordingly.

BROWN CREAM PUDDING.

7-lbs. Brown Sugar.	$\frac{1}{2}$-lb. Raisins.
2-lbs. Glucose.	$\frac{1}{2}$-lb. Mixed Peel.
1-lb. Currants.	$\frac{1}{2}$-oz. Mixed Spice.
$\frac{1}{2}$-lb. Sultanas.	2 Pints Water.

PROCESS.—Dissolve the sugar in the water, put the pan on the fire, and add the glucose; let the whole boil to a stiff ball, then pour the contents on to a damp pouring plate; when nearly cold commence to cream the boil by rubbing and working it about on the slab with palette knife or spatula until it becomes opaque, stiff and creamy. Have the fruits prepared and mixed as in previous recipe, then work them into the boil with spatula; now divide the boil into small basins holding about one pound each; press the cream well down and let remain till set. Take them out, brush over them a thin solution of gum, and dust them with powdered sugar to represent frosting, Before putting the cream into the basins sprinkle into them a little icing sugar to prevent sticking.

CANDIED NUTS.

TAKE any quantity of nut kernels, filberts, walnuts, Brazil nuts, or almonds, as preferred. Boil sufficient sugar with the usual proportions of cream of tartar and water, as for drops, to the degree of weak crack, say 300 by thermometer; remove the pan from the fire and drop n the kernels, a few at a time; lift them out with a long fork; lay them on tins or a cold iron pouring plate till set when they are ready for sale. Many prefer to roast the kernels before candying, but this is a matter of taste.

NOYEAU.

RASPBERRY noyeau is the kind usually made and kept in stock by confectioners. There are several ways of making it. I give two, which are perhaps the more recognised methods, but would suggest variety, such as pineapple, greengage, strawberry, black currant, &c. The only difference in the process would be the substitution of the different fruits and colours. The proportions would be the same and the process exactly as for raspberry noyeau. There is a wide field to choose from in this department, and no lack of good things, which can be easily incorporated to give novelty, both in appearance and flavour.

RASPBERRY NOYEAU.

OLD METHOD.

1-lb.	Gum Arabic.	1-lb. Blanched Almonds.
2 Pints Water.		Powdered Sugar.
2-lbs.	Raspberry Jam.	Liquid Carmine Colouring.

PROCESS.—Put the gum in a vessel; make the water hot and pour over it; let the gum remain in soak with an occasional stir until dissolved then strain; put the mucilage in the boiling pan; stand it over a slow fire; add the blanched almonds and jam and let simmer for 15 minutes. Have some powdered sugar on the slab; make a bay in the centre, into which pour the boil, then commence to work in sufficient of the sugar to form a stiff paste, adding colour enough to make the batch a deep red; roll the paste into a sheet about 1 inch thick; put wafer paper top and bottom, and cut it into bars with a sharp knife.

RASPBERRY NOYEAU, No. 2.

5-lbs. White Sugar.	1-lb. Almonds, blanched and dried.
1-lb. Glucose.	3 Pints Water.
2-lbs. Raspberry Jam.	Liquid Cochineal.

PROCESS.—Boil the sugar, glucose, and water to the ball degree, 250°; ease the pan off the fire; add the jam and almonds with sufficient colour to make the whole a bright red; let the batch boil through, keeping gently stirred until thoroughly mixed. Now remove the pan from the fire and see if the batch has turned opaque; if not, rub some of the syrup against the side of the pan, and stir in until the whole boil shows a little creamy, then pour out on wafer paper, keeping the sheet about three quarters of an inch thick; level the top down with palette knife and cover with wafer paper. When set, remove to a clean board and cut into bars with a sharp knife. In running sheets to thickness, arrange the loose bars on the pouring slate to form a square in proportion to the size of the boil.

WHAT TO DO WITH SCRAPS AND SIFTINGS.

IT is necessary to know how to use up the scraps, siftings, spoiled boils, candied and otherwise unsaleable goods. People who make jam or liquorice goods know, of course, what to do with them, but small makers, often accumulate a lot of waste, which seems always in the way. This should be avoided as much as possible, not only on the ground of economy, but for the good order and general appearance of the workshop.

Keep the acid scraps separate from the others; have two pans (earthenware will do), and make it a rule, when sweeping down the plates, to throw the acid scraps into one pan and the others into the second pan; keep them well covered with water, and, as the syrup gets too thick, put in more water, in order that the scraps may dissolve. When making dark goods, such as cough candy, cough drops, cocoanut candy, stick jaw, &c., &c., use a proportion of this syrup in each boil, dipping it out with a ladle. As a rule, a careful workman would use up his scraps every day. Some use the machine scraps by putting them in the next boil when the sugar is on the slab The writer's experience is that that method is objectionable, as it not only causes the boil to be cloudy, but very often grains it.

Dissolve the acid scraps in sufficient water to form a thin syrup; put in some whitening, powdered chalk, or lime; put the pan on the fire and stir until the whole boils. See that all the scraps are dissolved, remove the pan and let stand for an hour, then strain through flannel. Use this syrup in the same way as the other for making cheap goods.

LEMON SHERBET.

9-lbs. Powdered Sugar.   2-lbs. Powdered Tartaric Acid.
2½-lbs. Bi-carbonate of Soda.   ¼-oz. Essence of Lemon.

PROCESS.—If the tartaric acid is very dry, it is generally lumpy; crush it to a fine powder with a heavy rolling pin or thick glass bottle, then mix the sugar, acid and soda together; sprinkle the essence of lemon over the heap then work it up with the hands; afterwards pass it twice through a fine sieve; pack in bottles with well fitting corks. Take care that the ingredients and bottles are perfectly dry. One or two drops of otto of roses improves the fragrance and gives a bouquet.

PERSIAN SHERBET.

9-lbs.   Powdered Sugar.   2¼-lbs. Powdered Tartaric Acid.
2½-lbs. Bi-carbonate of Soda.   ¼-lb. Essence of Lemon.
¼-oz. French Cream.

PROCESS.—As for lemon sherbet, with the addition of the French cream or white of egg to make it frothy when mixed with water and carry the head. See that all the ingredients are thoroughly dry, any dampness will spoil the batch; be very careful the bottles or tins are dry, and when filled, are made air-tight.

RASPBERRY SHERBET.

9-lbs. Sherbet Sugar.	1-oz. Essence Raspberry.
2½-lbs. Acid, Tartaric.	Liquid Carmine.
2½-lbs. Bi-carbonate of Soda.	¼-oz. French Cream.

PROCESS.—Mix the colour, essence, and French cream, and thoroughly incorporate with the sugar, mixing with the hands till quite dry. Be careful not to use too much colour; (if too pale, more can be added), then add the acid and soda, working it well up together ; pass the heap three times through a fine copper wire sieve, bottle, and secure. These proportions give a good article—the last two cause a foamy head. A cheaper article can be made by increasing the proportion of sugar.

Many unprincipled people use a proportion of alum in lieu of so much acid, but this is despicable, as it has a baneful effect on the stomach and is prejudicial to health. Sherbet of all kinds is largely consumed by young people. Pineapple, rose, and other flavours are made, the ingredients being the same; the flavour and colour alone differing.

CHOCOLATE MAKING.

CHOCOLATE making, until recently, was considered a distinct business. Nevertheless, by reason of its very nature, it was impossible to dissociate it with the legitimate business of the confectioner. At all times the big guns had to rely mostly on the retail houses to distribute their goods. So select and independent was this special business, that market fluctuations seldom affected the prices.

The few, with what seemed like a tacit understanding, made the prices for wholesale and retail purposes, the dealers' profit being fixed, the bottom price being an open secret to the trade generally. This led to cutting amongst the wholesale houses, until the goods were handled intermediately at bare cost, the manufacturers and retailers dividing the profit.

This is altered to a great extent. Many smaller houses have had a look in with chocolates, and not a few of the large confectioners have a special department where the nibs are received and the cocoas and chocolates turned out in every variety, much to the general welfare and healthy development of the trade. We have also our small sugar boilers making their mark in this direction, turning out popular and profitable goods in many shapes. The fruit of Theobroma Cacao gives not.

only a pleasant flavour, but is nutritious in the highest degree, and adapts itself for mixing with sugar in various proportions with the best results.

In placing before the reader the following recipes and instructions for preparing chocolate and chocolate creams of various kinds, I have to acknowledge that I am indebted to the kindness of a personal friend of great experience in this line for whatever merit they may possess;

at the same time I have to offer him my apologies for the manner in which I have condensed his very carefully compiled manuscript. His minute and elaborate description of the process and machinery, which is employed in preparing the cocoa nibs for chocolate making, was not in accordance with my idea of a book of this description; my object all through this work being to teach the novice and assist those who have but imperfectly learned the business, or having learned one or two branches want a knowledge of the others. How far I may have succeeded in doing this I must leave those who use the book to judge. It is quite possible to say a great deal, and yet say nothing to the point. Long and intricate processess are generally confusing to the learner, and are passed over as being too difficult for him; at the same time, the diffi- culty may have been created simply by the manner in which the in- structions are written. I hope I shall not be found guilty of this. For these reasons, I have taken the responsibility of altering the chocolate recipes to their present shape. Where chocolate and cocoas are manu- factured on an extensive scale, and form the chief, if not the only, production of a particular firm, labour-saving machinery has from time to time been invented and introduced into the several departments with so much success, that the old-fashioned method is entirely super- seded. Formerly, the cocoa nibs were prepared for chocolate making by pounding them in a heated mortar with a heavy iron pestle, and after- wards ground smooth on heated granite slabs with a roller of the same material. This process was slow, dirty, and tedious. The employment of powerful and expensive mechanical contrivances now produce a much better chocolate paste at less than one-fifth the cost for manual labour. This paste may be bought pure from most of the large cocoa houses, and is admirably adapted for confectionery; it will answer the purpose for any of the following recipes. By adopting this course, it will be more convenient for the learner, and save an endless amount of un- profitable labour; besides, it would require experience in selecting cocoanuts suitable, and even if the learner should select sound, fresh nuts, there would be few country towns where he would have the opportunity of doing so.

SWEET CHOCOLATE.

10-lbs. Sugar. 1-lb. Fresh Butter.
2½-lbs. Glucose. 2-lbs. Pure Cocoa, unsweetened.
½-oz. Essence of Vanilla.

PROCESS.—Put the sugar, glucose and water in a clean pan, giving an occasional stir until boiling, put on the lid for five minutes. Remove the cover, see that the sides of the pan are free from sugar; if not, rub it round with damp cloth or sponge; put in the thermometer and boil to the degree of thread, 230°; add the cocoa paste (broken small) and the butter; keep stirring until the degree of a soft ball is reached; take the pan off the fire and pour in the vanilla flavour, and stir the lot till it gets quite stiff; pour out on greased tins; when cold, it eats soft and mellow. This is a delicious sweet and sells well.

CREAM FOR CHOCOLATE CREAM OR BARS.

10-lbs. White Sugar. 2½-lbs. Glucose.
3 Pints Water.

PROCESS.—Put the sugar, glucose, and water in a clean pan and boil in the usual way until the batch reaches the degree of feather, 240° (keep the sides of the pan free from sugar); pour out on a damp pouring plate and let remain till nearly cold; then, with a long palette knife or spatula, commence to rub the sugar against the plate and work it about until it changes from a clear syrup to a snow white creamy substance; then knead it with the hands until of uniform softness and no lumps left in the mass; it is now ready for use and may be kept covered in stoneware jars until required for the various purposes. In winter, the sugar need not be boiled so high; in hot weather, a little higher. When packing the cream away in jars, it is better to keep the top moist by laying on a damp cloth before putting in the cork. Seeing that cream keeps so well, of course, it is a saving to make much larger batches at a time. This can be easily arranged by multiplying the proportions according to size of pan and convenience. Those proportions are a guide, but the writer knows of no absolute *must be* this or that, and although he has made as many cream goods as most people, and with as much success, he has seen as fine a sample made in the same workshop when the boil was made up a little different. However, in submitting his own formula, it may be taken for granted that the writer is not a mile from the bull's eye.

CHOCOLATE CREAM ROLL, THICK.

10-lbs. Sugar. 3 Pints Water.
2½-lbs. Glucose. Pure Cocoa.
½-oz. Essence of Vanilla.

PROCESS.—Prepare the cream as in last recipe, but boil the syrup up to a strong thread, 250°, and add the flavour ; when creamed, break off portions and roll them to the desired thickness ; keep them on the move until they become firm enough to keep their shape ; have some melted chocolate, into which dip them once, twice, or three times, according to thickness of coating wanted.

CHOCOLATE CREAM BUNS AND CAKES.

10-lbs. Sugar. 3 Pints Water.
2½-lbs. Glucose. ½-oz. Vanilla Essence.

PROCESS.—Boil the sugar, glucose, and water in the ordinary way to the strong feather degree, 245°, then pour on to a damp slab ; let remain till nearly cold ; add the flavour and, with palette knife or spatula, work up the boil until white and creamy ; shape it with the hands or press it into tin moulds, then stand it in a warm place to harden a little on the outside. Melt some chocolate paste and cover the goods smoothly with it, using either knife or brush ; when dry, glaze them by brushing on a solution of shellac dissolved in alcohol. N.B.—In these last two recipes, the sugar is boiled higher than the "Cream for Chocolate Creams," because the goods are so large that the soft cream would not keep in shape. In melting pure chocolate, simply put it in a tin, together with a piece of lard or cocoa butter, stand it near the fire ; give it an occasional stir ; it will soon melt ; use no water, or it will run to powder and be spoiled. Sweeten if desired with ground sugar.

CHOCOLATE CREAM BARS, No. 1.

10-lbs. White Sugar. 3 Pints Water.
2½-lbs. Glucose. Vanilla Flavour.
Melted Chocolate.

PROCESS.—Prepare the cream as directed in "Cream for Chocolate Cream," or use some of that cream. Have some tins with edges one and a half inches deep ; use waxed paper and fit it neatly round the sides and bottom ; melt some of the cream on a slow fire ; flavour with vanilla as soon as the cream is sufficiently melted ; remove the pan and pour contents into the tins to make a sheet about one inch thick or less. When set, carefully empty, so as not to break the cake; have some melted chocolate and, with a soft brush coat the cream on both sides; lay them on wires till cold and set; cut up into bars the required size. N.B.—The knife for cutting bars of cream should be good, having a thin polished steel blade with a good edge. An old worn out thing breaks the cream and makes it irregular.

CHOCOLATE CREAM BARS, No. 2.

10-lbs. White Sugar.	3 Pints Water.
2½-lbs. Glucose.	½-oz. Essence of Vanilla.

Melted Chocolate.

PROCESS.—Prepare the tins by lining with waxed paper, fitting them smoothly; melt some sweet chocolate paste and pour it about a quarter of an inch thick on the bottom of the tins; when set, prepare some cream as directed for "Cream for Chocolate Creams," or use some of that cream melting it over a slow fire (not too hot); stir in the essence of vanilla and pour the batch into tins about one inch deep; when set, coat on top with melted sweet chocolate; when this lot is cold and quite set, cut up into bars with a sharp knife. N.B.—If bright metal or copper moulds are used waxed paper is unnecessary, while a better shape with pattern will be obtained.

COMBINATION CREAM BARS.

HAVE tins with sides two inches deep; line them smoothly with waxed paper; melt some cream as already directed; flavour with vanilla and pour it in the tin half an inch deep; when set, melt another lot of cream, colour it yellow, and flavour with essence of lemon; pour it on the top of the white cream; melt also a third portion of cream, colour it to a bright pink, flavour with raspberry and pour it over the yellow cream; when the whole lot gets cold and quite set, lift it out of the tin and spread some melted chocolate paste, top and bottom; when the batch is dry cut it up into bars. These goods look very pretty and sell well. N.B.—The object in lining the tins with waxed paper is to insure the cake turning out unbroken.

MOULDED CHOCOLATE CREAM BARS OR TABLETS BY HAND.

MOULDS for chocolate are either made in stout tin or copper of different devices, and generally to a size so that when filled the bars would weigh so much each, say $\frac{1}{4}$-lb. or $\frac{1}{2}$lb. nett.

First make bars of cream a little smaller than the mould, this is usually done from plaster of Paris moulds cut to size, printed in the starch trays like fondants, the imprints filled up with warm fondant cream flavoured with vanilla, when set take them out of the starch and brush clean. Now melt some sweet chocolate and pour it into the metal moulds, about one-eighth of an inch thick or less, turn the moulds about so that the chocolate may coat them all over, then take the cream bars and lay them in the moulds on top of the chocolate then with a brush, cover over the white cream with melted chocolate paste. in a few minutes the cakes may be turned out. If the chocolate paste be of good colour and evenly melted, it should carry a good gloss on its face. However, if too dull go over it with a camel's hair brush dipped in a solution of shellac dissolved in alcohol.

MOULDING CHOCOLATE BARS OR TABLETS BY MACHINERY.

THE above formula gives the process which is and has been practically the *modus operandi* till the time of writing but a new and elaborate machine has just been patented by Messrs. Bramigk & Co., whereby the cream tablet centres are moulded in chocolate without being touched by hand. Apart from the greater facility with which much larger quantities may be turned out, the finish of the goods is improved because the handling of chocolate makes it dull and lustreless.

The possessor of a machine of this description has his goods not only more uniform in shape and size and better in finish, but effects great economy in the use of chocolate, as the centres being made in exact proportion to the mould the amount of chocolate required is exactly determined. Although an explanation of machines of this magnitude are a little beyond the scope of an instructor of confectionery, it is as well to know that they exist and that the patentees will gladly show their advantages.

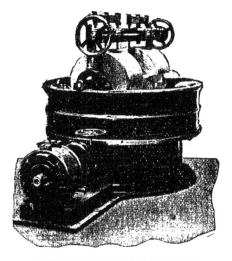

SWEET CHOCOLATES.

WHAT is known in the trade as Sweet Chocolates such as Medallion, Vanilla, shilling and plain cakes of this class can be made satisfactorily only by large houses. The quality of the goods depends a great deal upon the time they have been subjected to ponderous grinding, crushing and refining machines and the exactitude with which these perform the operation. The mixings are quite a secondary consideration, cocoa, sugar and vanilla being practically the only ingredients used.

Although it would be impossible for a small maker to compete with houses equipped with disintegrators, melangeurs and refining machines, nevertheless it may be useful to some and interesting to others to know how to make the different sorts on a small scale, hence the following recipes and instructions.

SWEET CHOCOLATE PASTE

5-lbs. Pure Cocoa.   3-lbs. White Sugar Powdered.

PROCESS.—Put the pure cocoa into a heated mortar, then with a warm pestle pound it until it is reduced to an oily consistency; then add the powdered loaf sugar, pounding away till it is thoroughly incorporated, now turn half of it into a tin and keep in a warm place; grind the other half on a warm slab with a heated roller until it is reduced to a smooth impalpable paste which will melt in the mouth like butter; serve the first half in the same way, then take the whole quantity and place on the stone again (this time the stone or slab must only be luke warm). Work it up and fill the moulds; giving them a shake to level the paste; when cold, it will turn out easily. Chocolate prepared in this way is ready for sale, or may be used for making chocolate drops or coating creams. Vanilla flavouring is an improvement.

CHOCOLATE DROPS (Plain).

WARM some sweet chocolate as described in last formula, adding a little lard, which will make it work free. When it is just sufficiently heated to be pliable, pinch off little pieces; roll them in the hand to the size of a small marble placing them in rows on sheets of white paper, each row about an inch apart; when the sheet is covered, take it by the corners and lift it up and down, letting it touch the slab each time; this will flatten the balls into drop shapes which on the bottom should be about the size of a sixpenny piece; when cold, they will slip off the paper without trouble.

CHOCOLATE DROPS (Nonpareil).

PROCEED exactly as for plain drops. When the drops have been flattened, cover the sheets of paper entirely over with white nonpareils (hundreds and thousands); when the drops are dry, shake off the surplus nonpariels.

CHOCOLATE CREAMS, By hand.

To make these, we must have starch trays and plaster of Paris moulds (see remarks on the Drying Room and Moulds for Creams). Smooth off the trays and mould with small cream moulds. Melt some cream (see Cream for Chocolate Creams); use the runner, and fill the starch trays; in an hour the creams will be set hard enough to be taken out of the starch; clean them off with a soft hair brush; they are then ready for coating. Warm some sweet chocolate paste until melted, then drop the creams into the melted chocolate, two or three at a time; lift them out with a long fork and place them on glazed paper or sheets of tin to dry; put them in a cool place to harden; pack carefully in paper lined boxes in such a manner that they hardly touch each other; if packed roughly, like most other sweets they become spotted and rough, spoiling the appearance altogether. N.B.—To thoroughly understand the formula, the novice is recommended to read all the instructions given in reference to starch work generally.

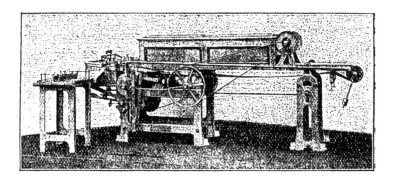

The "Climax" Patent Chocolate Coating and Cooling Machine.

CHOCOLATE CREAMS, by Machinery.

ALTHOUGH a great many chocolate creams are still moulded and covered by hand by good confectioners which command (as home made goods always do) a good price and make an attractive, if not an ornamental show in a window, still for the wholesale trade to be successful, it is absolutely necessary to provide not only machines but machines of the latest type, really the question of mixings and operations is more the business of the engineer than the workman. The manner of working and rapidity of turn out, as well as the size and shape of goods to be coated, governs to a large extent the density and heat of the chocolate used for covering, also the method and arrangements for the various mixings used. The above machine which is Messrs. Bakers' latest has been adopted by leading houses both at home and abroad. It is an improvement on their previous machines in so far as it covers a wider range of work, being specially constructed to make the Continental and most difficult grades of coated goods. When coating, it ensures a sound covering all over with the advantage of thick and heavy bottoms.

The output is very large, several rows being dipped and delivered at the same time.

The delivery is made from a continuous web, the goods being deposited on sheets of paper for convenience of lifting off. By a special contrivance the coating mixture is maintained at a fixed temperature and an even density which gives to the finished goods a uniform gloss and brilliancy.

The dipping tanks may be instantly changed from one kind of coating to another and is a great convenience to the practical working of a factory. A cooling apparatus is fitted to each machine. It will be apparent from this, perhaps rather meagre description, that the machine for this process is of the first importance, and that the details of working are reduced to simply feeding the mechanism.

MILK CHOCOLATE.

THIS sweetmeat has upset some of our stay-at-home confectioners. It would be difficult to name any single article in the trade for which there has been such a demand in so short a time, and from all appearances it has come to stay. How is it made? What's in it? have been often asked. Well, chocolate, sugar and condensed milk are the ingredients, to which is added a little flavour, but the preparation is another matter. In fact the whole secret of the fascination of this sweetmeat is practically the method of manipulation. The mixture is ground to the finest grade by being for a long time subjected to the crushing and grinding motion of two granite rolls which run at different speeds inside a huge revolving drum to which are adjusted scrapers that carry back the paste which has just passed through the rollers, to go through the process again. This operation continues, and during the process the granite rollers by a slow acting automatic gearing come into the closest contact with each other, the finest possible result being thus obtained.

The quality of milk chocolate depends practically on the fineness and minute disintegration to which the ingredients are reduced.

QUALITY OF CHOCOLATE.

GENUINE chocolate should eat with a cool sensation to the tongue, melt gently in the mouth like a piece of butter leaving no roughness or astringency, of a clear brown colour, the surface smooth and shining; when broken, it ought to be compact and close, not crummy. Adulterated chocolates may be detected by the gloss coming off when touched, being crummy when broken, and eating with a rough taste in the mouth. Chocolates should be warehoused in a cool place. Exposure to sun or gas turns it brown and specky, while a very moderate heat melts it.

CHOCOLATE FOR DIPPING.

This mixing is so often required by confectioners for so many purposes that a good general recipe will not be out of place. If the instructions are followed and a little discretion used with the colours, a light, glossy chocolate coating will result.

1-lb. Pure Chocolate.	Chocolate Brown Colour.
3-oz. White Wax.	Carmine.

Process.—Put the chocolate in a saucepan; stand on the furnace plate or near a fire; break up the wax into little pieces and stir it in until all is melted; then add the brown colour with a little liquid carmine, stirring the whole till thoroughly mixed; it is then ready for use. When mixing in the colouring, try a little on a piece of white paper until satisfied with the blend.

STARCH ROOM.

This is an important department in the works of a modern confectioner. In it are made gelatines, gums, liqueurs, fondants, fondant creams, and fancies of every description. There is perhaps no branch in this business giving greater facilities for the display of fertile brains, nimble fingers, and careful workmanship. The countless forms, shapes, and combinations which daily emanate from this branch by no means exhaust the possibilities. Every week sees fresh displays of new goods characteristic of the starch room; new designs, new ideas, and new colours, flavours, and ingredients are also introduced. Not only the confectioner, but the chemist and purveyors of good things are all contributing to the development of this branch. It would make many of the *old hands* turn in their coffins to look down the lists of some firms who cater for the trades' requirements and see the immense variety of fruits, flavours, colours, chemicals, spices, and other preparations they could put their hands on wherewithal to make goods to attract attention and tempt the palate of the public. Within the writer's recollection, a very small corner of a price list was sufficient to catalogue all the sundries which were supposed to be sufficient for the requirements of this industry, and, at best, the flavours were very indifferent in quality, while colours were few, common, and frequently unwholesome. The methods of working the whole range of these goods are practically alike, but the mixings differ, not only according to price, but also according to fancy, especially with regard to gelatine and gum goods. Perhaps no two workmen use exactly the same proportions, although they may obtain very nearly the same results. The quality and strength of the materials used

may account for this to some degree, but not altogether. Where prices are cut and competition is keen, one shilling per cwt. is an object, consequently the dearer ingredients are used so sparingly that the goods just hold together in an ordinary temperature, in hot weather they run, and in cold weather, if kept a long time they dry, shrink, and get hard. The instructions in this book give formulæ for first class of sweets, such as are ordinarily sold by high class confectioners, but there is room for variation. The expert reader may alter or arrange the qualities to suit his trade or prices but it is not advisable for a novice to do so until he has gained some knowledge by experience, and is able to judge what effect the lessening of this or the addition of that would have on the finished goods. To be original here, is to be great—a new mould, a new combination, or a new process that has merit, catches on at once. Experiments are easily made, and the material from which the moulds are made is inexpensive, *i.e.*, plaster of Paris.

Until very recently the engineer had not assisted us much in this department, and the workman had to rely upon himself for his variety and ideas. Now, not only the engineer but the artist has come to our aid, the former has given us the "Fondant Depositor"; starch tray filling and cleaning machines, etc., while the latter will supply us with rubber moulds which do away with the starch trays, or with artistic plaster moulds of all shapes and sizes for using with starch trays, Both machines and moulds are of great assistance, the former especially where quantity is wanted, while the latter which are inexpensive, make a much better shape and are more durable than moulds made by the hand.

TOOLS USED IN THE STARCH ROOM.

The tools and appliances needed for these goods are few, simple, and inexpensive, and may be enumerated as follows :—A confectioner's store, a copper boiling pan, a confectioner's thermometer, a wooden box to keep the starch powder in, which should be 4-ft. long. 26-in. wide, and about 2-ft. 4-in. high ; fix two pieces of narrow wood across this box, a foot from both ends, to take the bearing off the trays while being smoothed off and moulded. It will be observed that the mouth of this box is larger than the trays, that is for the purpose of catching all the starch that may run over the sides and ends of the trays while being smoothed off with a stick. The runner for filling the starch moulds is a very simple tool, being made by a tinsmith exactly similar to a tun dish or funnel used by publicans for putting into the necks of bottles and jars to empty the spirits or beer through ; have a hole in the bottom about half an inch in diameter: it has two little turnover handles at the top, opposite each other. The runner should be large enough to hold two or three pounds of syrup. When filling the moulds, hold the runner with both hands, by putting the little fingers through both handles; have also in the right hand, between the forefinger and thumb, a piece of stick long enough to reach the bottom of the runner, so that you may regulate the stream, or stop it altogether when required, by plugging the hole. A few trays will be necessary, and are mentioned in chapter on "drying room." The starch powder is in appearance like farina, and is used by all confectioners for moulding purposes. Glucose is a syrup, the best qualities of which are transparent; original casks generally weigh from 5 to 9 cwt. It may also be had in a solid form, and is packed in convenient bags containing 1 cwt. each. The syrup is generally preferred, but where the bulky packages would be objectionable, the solid may be used with success. Crystallizing tins should be of good strong tinned iron, 24-in. long, 14-in. wide, and 4-in. deep, with a hole at the bottom in one corner for drawing off the syrup when the goods have taken sufficient crystal. Crystallising tins made with two or three wire shelves are sold by confectioner's machine makers. A hand brush and a pair of bellows, are about the only tools required in the starch or moulding room. A handy man may make his own trays and starch box, or a carpenter would supply size mentioned, at about two shilings per tray.

THE DRYING ROOM.

This room is indispensable to make jubes, creams, pan goods, lozenges, &c.; in it goods are baked, dried, and crystallized.

The arrangements and constructions are simple, as the chief object is to generate heat; the next object is to utilize the space to the best advantage for the storage of the starch trays while the goods they contain are undergoing the finishing process. A moderate sized room, say from 14-ft. to 16-ft. square, if well racked, will hold a lot of stuff, and be large enough for a moderate trade; at any rate, it would be large enough to begin with. The racks are run up like shelves, but only support the trays at each end: they are usually made of timber, about 2-in. wide and 1-in. thick; the shelves are about 4-in. or 5-in. apart, with an upright between each row of trays. The room may be heated by an iron stove or by steam pipes; the position and construction of the stove would be determined by the flue, with due regard to the safety from fire and convenience for working; steam pipes, of course, run round the room under the trays; the degree of heat would be regulated according to the class of goods. A good rule, where a stove is used, is to keep the room a little above summer heat, putting the goods requiring most heat nearest the stove and *vice versa*. The starch trays should be made of good, hard, dry wood, about 36-in. long and 20-in wide, with sides a full inch deep; the ends should be quite 2-in. deep: so that, when the trays are packed on the top of each other, there is a space of one inch between the bottom of the one and the top of the other, the bearing, of course, would be on the raised ends. When the trays are not in use they should be kept in the drying room the starch powder soon contracts damp if exposed in a room where any boiling is going on and steam floating about; besides, warm starch powder gives better results, especially is this the case with liqueurs, creams and gums.

THE above engraving represents the three principal processes in moulding shapes. The figure with the stick in his hand over the smooth white tray is supposed to be smoothing off the starch ready for No. 2, who is making the indentations which No. 3 is filling. It is not quite as distinct as it might have been, it will however, give the reader a better idea of how the work is done than could have been conveyed in words, and, taken together with the instructions, will no doubt be sufficient to enable one to form plans for a beginning.

Manufacturers have, as a rule, an objection to allow strangers to look over their works. This block, may, therefore, be useful in illustrating a process it is so difficult to see worked out. Men are represented as smoothing and moulding, but this is generally done by boys or women and the trays are usually smoothed off in the starch bin, so that the starch powder which falls over the trays drop into the proper receptacle. I put the tray on the bench so that it might be seen.

TO MAKE MOULDS FOR PASTILLES, CREAMS, LIQUEURS, Etc.

ALTHOUGH there are rubber sheets with perfect impressions for all kinds and sizes of moulded goods which answer nearly every purpose for which we use trays, starch and moulds, yet many makers still keep to the old method while some adopt both.

Whether it is a question of cost, experience or practice, it would be difficult to say but a good deal of mould making is still done by the workman. This is how some are made. Dilute with water some good plaster of Paris to the consistency of paste and run it in a block about $1\frac{1}{4}$ inches thick; when it sets hard divide into pieces about one inch square, now take one of these cubes and with a pocket-knife carve it into the shape of a raspberry, another cube into a fondant, and so on for other shapes.

However there is another process for those who cannot use the knife dexterously. Buy from a pipe maker two or three pennyworth of clay, select a few moulds, sweets or other articles as patterns of which you require moulds taken, work the clay with the hand until it is soft and pliable then smooth the top and press the sweet or mould into the soft clay. See that it is nicely embedded and the clay close up to the edge, now pick it out gently with a pin to leave the impression as distinct as possible, now put some plaster of Paris in a small jug having a lip, add water sufficient to make a paste and run this into the indentations made in the clay and when set quite hard, take them out, trim them with a knife and cut the backs level, they are then ready for fixing to moulding stick. Another method is to soak a pound or two of gelatine until soft then melt it over the fire and pour it into a deep tin tray to set, try it now and again by dipping your finger into it, and when the impression does not close up quickly put in the moulds you wish to take the patterns from and let them remain in the gelatine until it is quite set, now pick the mould out carefully and fill the impressions with plaster-of-Paris as directed above, when the plaster sets firm pick them out of the gelatine. The advantage of running the plaster in gelatine instead of pipeclay is that the same impression will last for a number of castings if care is exercised in taking them out of the moulds, besides it is a much cleaner process. When you have your moulds made and trimmed with smooth backs, plane a piece of wood 26 inches long $2\frac{1}{2}$ inches wide and $\frac{1}{2}$ an inch thick, mark off 4 inches at each end to use for handles, then between the inside of the mark i.e. 18 inches, stick the mould firmly on with gum or glue in two rows a full inch apart. A separate moulding stick will be required for each pattern, unless for assorted shapes for mixtures when the variety is usually put on the same stick. Many use both sides of the stick putting a different pattern on each, when not in use always keep them hung up in a dry place.

Note.—Do not mix the plaster too thin for mould making or it will be porous when dry, which will cause the starch to adhere to them when moulding.

As it hardens quickly, mix only a little at a time rather thickly and use it at once. Perfect moulds may be bought cheaper than can be made by the workman whose time is of value.

GELATINE WORK.

This department has received special attention in every quarter, during the last few years. The great advance in the price of gum has almost put it beyond the reach of confectioners, except for very best goods. Therefore, gelatine, together with farinaceous and other substances, have been experimented with as a substitute for gum with more or less success. We have now an assortment of these goods, which, even to chronicle, would fill more space than we can spare for the entire subject, nor would it be profitable study for the learner, as I give the chief mixings for the principal selling lines, which, in themselves, make a fair variety, and would recommend the beginner to cogitate something new and get out of the beaten track.

In the formula, white sugar means Dutch crushed; granulated loaf or crystals; by gelatine we mean the sort generally used by confectioners, *i.e.* French, sold in cakes about one eighth of an inch thick, price from 70s to 100s per cwt. It is necessary to mention this, as there is a lot of these gelatines sold which, soaked according to instructions, would be quite dissolved and useless—the better the gelatine the more water it will hold. After gelatine goods have been crystallized in sugar, they ought to dry in an hour or two. Should they remain damp, there is too much water in their composition, either the gelatine has remained too long in soak, or the syrup has not been boiled high enough. Should they be too dry, the reverse is the case. It would be impossible to give positive instructions, on account of the different qualities of gelatine, but a mistake can be easily rectified, and the strength of the gelatine with which you are working can soon be found out by attention to these remarks.

CRYSTALLIZED ROSE AND LEMON JUBES.

14-lbs. White Sugar.
7-lbs. Glucose.
3-lbs. Gelatine, weighed when dry.
6-oz. Powdered Tartaric Acid.
4 Pints Water.
Saffron and Cochineal Colouring.
Rose and Lemon Flavouring.

PROCESS.—Put the gelatine in a vessel, cover it with cold water, and let it remain in soak for about twelve hours; then put the sugar, glucose, and water in the boiling pan; put on the furnace and boil in the usual way to a stiff ball, 255° (in summer to 285°); lift the pan off the fire and stir in the soaked gelatine, dropping it in a sheet at a time, and keep stirring till dissolved; let stand a short time till the scum rises, which then skim off; stir in the acid (which should be well ground); divide the boil in two; colour one part yellow and add a few drops of the essence of lemon; colour the other a light pink with liquid carmine and flavour with a drop or two of otto of roses; pour the mixture into oiled tins in sheets about $\frac{1}{2}$-in. thick; stand them in a cool place till stiff, then take them out; cut them first into slices, then into squares, either with scissors or jube machine; roll them in a heap of crystal sugar; sift them out; when dry (three or four hours), they are ready for sale or packing. N.B.—Under no circumstances colour gelatine goods with aniline dyes. Use liquid carmine for pink, saffron for yellow, and vegetable colours for the others. Always crush the acid finely before putting into the pan. Be careful in using the essence of pear, pine apple, and otto of roses, as too much imparts a disagreeable taste to the goods. Do not put the pan on the fire after the gelatine has been added, and add the gelatine, a sheet or two at a time, stirring till dissolved before adding more.

CLEAR PINK JUBE (Imitation Gum).

8-lbs. White Sugar.	1½-oz. Tartaric Acid.
8-lbs. Glucose.	3 Pints Water.
2-lbs. Best Gelatine.	Liquid Carmine.

Otto of Roses.

PROCESS.—Soak the Gelatine in cold water; boil the sugar, glucose, and water in the ordinary way to a stiff ball; remove the pan from the fire; add the gelatine and stir until dissolved; let the whole stand until the scum rises; skim this off and stir in the acid, flavour and colour; now pour into oiled tins; when firm, take out the sheets and cut up with scissors or machine, then rub them over with clean rag, with olive oil, and they will have a beautiful, bright appearance.

CLEAR RASPBERRIES.

8-lbs. White Sugar.	1½-oz. Tartaric Acid.
7-lbs. Glucose.	3 Pints Water.
2-lbs. Gelatine.	Liquid Carmine.

Essence Raspberry.

PROCESS.—Soak the gelatine by covering it with cold water for about twelve hours, then boil the sugar, water and glucose to a stiff ball;

remove the pan from the fire and gently add the gelatine; stir until dissolved; let it remain for a little time, then skim off the top; stir in the acid and colour a light red, adding the essence; have the trays smoothed off and moulded with raspberry shapes; run in the boil and let them remain in a cool place till set; sift out the goods; blow off any starch which may adhere and rub them up with a little olive oil to brighten. A pound or two of raspberry jam may be used instead of the essence.

CLEAR LIQUORICE JUBES.

8-lbs.	Brown Sugar.	2-oz.	Tartaric Acid.
6-lbs.	Glucose.	3 Pints	Water.
2-lbs.	Gelatine.		Aniseed Oil.
1-lb.	Block Juice.		Jetoline Black.

PROCESS.—Soak gelatine as directed. Bring the sugar, glucose and water to the degree of ball; remove the pan from the fire; stir in the gelatine and liquorice (previously melted); let it remain till a scum on top; skim this off, then put in a few drops of aniseed oil and sufficient colour to make it a black shade; pour in oiled tins making the sheet $\frac{1}{2}$-in. thick; stand in a cool place; when set, cut up in squares with scissors or machine and brighten with a drop of good olive oil. They are then ready for sale.

CLEAR PINEAPPLE JUBES.

8-lbs.	White Sugar.	1$\frac{1}{2}$-oz.	Tartaric Acid.
6-lbs.	Glucose.	3 Pints	Water.
2-lbs.	Gelatine.		Saffron Colour.
	Pineapple.		

PROCESS.—Have the gelatine soaked and proceed exactly as for clear pink jubes; when ready skim the boil carefully; colour with saffron and flavour carefully with essence of pineapple (only a few drops). These clear goods used always to be made of gum, and although we cannot give them the body and flavour of that famous mucilage, yet we give the appearance they were wont to be known by.

BLACK CURRANT JUBES.

8-lbs.	White Sugar.	1$\frac{1}{2}$-lbs.	Black Currant Paste or Jam.
6-lbs.	Glucose.	1$\frac{1}{2}$-oz.	Tartaric Acid.
2$\frac{1}{2}$-lbs.	Gelatine.	3 Pints	Water.
	Dark Purple Colouring.		

PROCESS.—Cover the gelatine with cold water and let soak twelve hours; boil the sugar, glucose and water in the usual way to the degree of ball; remove the pan from the fire and gently stir in the gelatine (a little at a time); add the black currant paste; stand aside till the scum forms; skim this off; stir in the acid and enough colour to make it a deep purple; pour the mixture into oiled tins in sheets $\frac{1}{2}$-in. thick; when set, take them out and cut up with scissors or machine. The black currant paste gives the best flavour.

CRYSTALLIZED APRICOTS.

8-lbs.	White Sugar.	1$\frac{1}{2}$-oz.	Tartaric Acid.
8-lbs.	Glucose.	3 Pints Water.	
2$\frac{1}{2}$-lbs.	Gelatine.		Apricot yellow colour.

Essence of Apricot or Apricot Pulp.

PROCESS.—Smooth off the starch trays and mould with large apricot moulds; have the gelatine ready soaked; boil the sugar, glucose and water to a stiff ball; remove the pan from the fire; stir in the gelatine until dissolved; stand the boil aside until the scum rises; skim this off; stir in the acid, colour and flavour with essence (or pulp); when thoroughly mixed, run into trays; let stand in a cold place till set, then sift them from the starch, blowing off any that may adhere. Turn them out and put them on a clean slab and sprinkle them over with cold water; mix them up so that they are equally damped; then cover over with dry crystal sugar; turn them over again and again with hands until they have taken a good coating, then they may be sifted and spread on trays to dry; before boxing, look them over; take out all the bad shapes and separate any that may be coupled together.

GELATINE COCOANUT BARS (Yellow).

8 lbs.	White Sugar.	1-oz. Acid, Tartaric.
6-lbs.	Glucose.	3 Pints	Water.
2$\frac{1}{2}$-lbs.	Gelatine.		Saffron Colour.
3-lbs.	Cocoanut Sliced.		Lemon Flavour.

PROCESS.—Soak the gelatine in cold water for twelve hours. Boil the sugar, glucose and water to a stiff ball, 255°; remove the pan from the fire; stir in the gelatine till dissolved; let stand for a few minutes and remove the scum from the top, then add the acid, flavour and cocoanut; gently stir the whole until well mixed; tinge to a bright yellow with saffron; pour into oiled tins making the sheets $\frac{1}{2}$-in. thick; when set, cut up into sticks to sell at four or eight a penny. N.B.—This boil may be divided into two lots, one half coloured red and flavoured raspberry, or a second boil may be made precisely as this one, altering the colour and flavour only.

WEDDING CAKE JUBES.

10-lbs. Sugar.	1-oz. Bi-carbonate of Soda.
8-lbs. Glucose.	2-oz. Icing Sugar.
2½-lbs. Gelatine.	Carmine.
1½-oz. Acid, Tartaric.	Saffron.
Essence of Lemon.	

Process.—Prepare the mixture as before ; when the gelatine has been added and the boil skimmed and flavoured, divide it into three lots ; colour one lot red, a second yellow, leaving the third lot clear ; pour the yellow mixture into oiled tins, making thin sheets ¼-inch thick ; mix the icing sugar, acid, and soda together in the powder ; drop it into the clear portion and stir until it swells up into a white foam, then run this on top of the yellow jube, about the same thickness ; allow this to set, then run the red colour on top of the white ; stand the tins aside till the jube sheet sets stiff ; remove them from the tins and cut them up with machine or scissors. When cut, roll them amongst fine crystal sugar until coated. This process makes a very pretty jube, showing the three colours in each jube ; the white centre shows up the yellow and pink. Let the pink jube be nearly cold before pouring it over the white layer.

CHEAP JELLY GOODS.

14-lbs. White Sugar.	2-oz. Tartaric Acid.
12-lbs. Glucose.	2 Pints Water.
3-lbs. Gelatine.	Colour.
Flavour.	

Process.—Soak the gelatine in cold water for twelve hours ; bring the sugar and water to the boil ; then add the glucose, and continue boiling till it reaches the degree of stiff ball ; remove the pan from the fire and stir in the gelatine and acid till dissolved ; colour and flavour to fancy ; remove the scum and run the batch into tins. Set the goods aside for twelve hours, then cut up into jubes and crystallize with fine powdered sugar. This is a cheap line; there is not much body in the jubes but they sell at a price and give satisfaction.

JELLY FANCIES.

12-lbs. Sugar.	3-lbs. Gelatine.
7-lbs. Glucose.	2-oz. Tartaric Acid.

3 Pints Water.

PROCESS.—Soak the gelatine in cold water for twelve hours. Smooth off the trays and mould them with fancy shapes. Boil the sugar, glucose, and water in the usual way to the degree of ball; remove the pan from the fire and stir in the gelatine gradually until dissolved; let stand for a few minutes. Take off the scum as it rises, then divide the boil, if required in more colours than one), colour and flavour each portion to fancy, then run the boil in the moulds; when set, sift the goods out of the starch, blow the dust off, and put them on a clean slab; sprinkle some cold water over them and roll them about until all are damped, then cover them with fine crystal sugar and mix them up till crystallized all over, and spread out on trays to dry.

The different recipes already mentioned will give the reader a general idea of how gelatine goods are made by using different colours, flavours, and shapes. An infinite variety can be produced. It could serve no good purpose to further multiply these formulæ for small goods.

ENGLISH DELIGHT.

ENGLISH delight, John Bull's pleasures, &c., &c., are made almost exactly as wedding cake jubes, the difference being that they are run into deeper tins and in thicker layers; cut up into blocks the whole length of the sheet and about $1\frac{1}{2}$ inches wide; and cut and sold from the blocks at per ounce.

JAM ROLEY POLEY.

10-lbs. White Sugar.	1-lb. Raspberry Jam.
5-lbs. Glucose.	1-lb. Desiccated Cocoanut.
2-lbs. Gelatine.	3 Pints Water.

Liquid Carmine.

PROCESS.—Soak the gelatine in cold water twelve hours; boil the sugar, glucose, and water sharply to a stiff ball; remove the pan from the fire; stir in the gelatine; stand aside till scum rises which skm off.

Divide the boil into two portions (mix together 1-oz. tartaric acid, 1oz. Bi-carbonate of soda, 2-oz. icing sugar); drop this powder and the desiccated cocoanut in to one half of the boil and stir briskly until the whole rises in a white foam, then run out into tins, in sheets about $\frac{1}{4}$-in. thick; now take the other half, colour it to a bright red, adding the raspberry jam; stir till thoroughly mixed and run this on top of the white sheet to about the same thickness; when cold and set, take out the sheets and make a roll of each. N.B.—Let the red portion be cool when run over the white, as the white being lighter will come to the top if disturbed by the mixture being too hot; or run the red layer first then the white on top.

RASPBERRY JELLIES.

9-lbs.	White Sugar.	3 Pints	Water.
6-lbs.	Glucose.	2-oz.	Tartaric Acid.
2-lbs.	Apple Jelly.	$\frac{1}{2}$-oz.	Essence Raspberry.
2$\frac{1}{4}$-lbs.	Gelatine.		Liquid Carmine.

Process.—Soak gelatine as usual; boil the sugar, glucose and water to a stiff ball; remove the pan from the fire; stir in the gelatine and let it remain till the scum rises; skim it off, then add the acid, jelly, flavour, and sufficient colour to make a bright red; now mould the batch into raspberry shapes and put them in a cold place. When set stiff, sift them out of the starch, blow off all dust, and put the goods in thin layers in a crystallizing tin and cover them with cold syrup. Let them remain undisturbed for twelve hours, then drain off all the surplus syrup, and turn out the raspberries on clean trays; when dry, pack. N.B.—When putting jelly goods in crystallizing tins, be careful that the layers are not thick, as they lay so close that the syrup cannot get in between them. A good plan is to have wire trays, and fix three or four loosely in each tin, taking their bearings on the ends of the crystallizing tin (machine makers sell them.) By this means, you will get more in a tin with a better result. Boil the syrup, in the proportion of 6-lbs. best white sugar to each quart of water, to the degree of smooth, 215°; it must be quite cold when used for gelatine work, or the goods will come out of the tins in a solid block.

BLACK CURRANT JELLIES.

9-lbs. White Sugar.	2-lbs. Black Currant Jelly.
6-lbs. Glucose.	2-oz. Tartaric Acid.
2¼-lbs. Celatine.	3 Pints Water.
Purple Colouring.	

PROCESS.—Soak the gelatine for twelve hours in cold water, smooth off, and mould fondant shapes in starch trays. Boil the sugar, glucose and water, as already directed, to a stiff ball; remove the pan from the fire; drop in the gelatine a few pieces at a time; stir till dissolved; let it remain a short time till the scum rises which skim off, then stir in the tartaric acid, jelly and sufficient colouring to make the mixture a bright colour, then mould the batch into starch trays. When the goods are firmly set sift them out, blowing off all the dust; place them in layers on wire frames (fitted for crystallizing tin); arrange the frames in the tins and cover with cold syrup; let them stand for twelve or fourteen hours undisturbed then drain off the surplus syrup; take them carefully out of the tins; pack them on clean trays; when dry they are ready for boxing. These goods require handling gently; they are very delicate and easily crushed.

PINEAPPLE JELLIES.

8-lbs. White Sugar.	3-oz. Tartaric Acid.
8-lbs. Glucose.	3 Pints Water.
2¼-lbs. Gelatine.	Saffron Colour.
Pineapple Flavour.	

PROCESS.—Soak the gelatine in sufficient cold water to cover it; mould the trays with pineapple shapes; boil the sugar, glucose and water as usual to a stiff ball and remove the pan from the fire; stir in the gelatine; wait till the scum rises and remove it, then add the acid flavour and sufficient colour to make a bright yellow; pour the mixing into the moulds; keep the trays in a cold place till set, then sift them from the starch and blow them clear of dust with a pair of bellows; pack them in layers on wire frames; put them in the crystallizing tins and cover with cold syrup; stand aside where they will not be shaken or disturbed for twelve or fourteen hours, then draw off the surplus syrup and put them on clean trays to dry. In flavouring these goods, use the pineapple gently,—only a few drops,—too much spoils the flavour.

CONCENTRATED TABLE JELLIES.

THE success of jellies in this form has made it a matter of importance, in order to encourage the already wide demand that the quality should not only be maintained but if possible improved. That the public has taken very kindly to them, is shown by the prominence given them in the best positions both in the windows and on the counters, not only of our confectioners but also the principal grocers and Italian Warehouse-men in the kingdom. There are several firms who make a speciality of these jellies and turn out really good goods ; at the same time there are others who sell on the merit of the former, whose rubbish is enough to stifle and kill the trade. " *'Twas ever thus.*"

The remedy must be with the retailers. This dishonourable and nefarious way of doing business does incalculable damage to the whole trade. It is therefore the duty of the shopkeeper to see that what he does sell is what he represents it to be and is the make of a responsible firm on whom he can rely in case of dispute or damage.

Seeing the quantity of foreign and even English conglomerations now in the market, at all sorts of prices, is the only excuse the writer has for making this interpolation. The materials used for concentrated jellies should be of the finest quality, great care in straining so that every speck is removed. The tins in which the jelly is run should be silvered and slightly rubbed with a clean rag dipped in the best salad oil. Strict cleanliness must be observed with everything used, as, when the jelly is inflated with the hot water for the table every impurity is magnified in a transparent mass. The gelatine used should be of a specially good quality. It is generally much thinner than that used for jubes, &c., consequently does not require to soak so long in cold water. As gelatine differs in thickness, it is impossible to say exactly how long it should be in soak ; however, say till soft enough that the blade of a knife can be forced through easily. The usual time required is from two to four hours.

CONCENTRATED RASPBERRY JELLY.

14-lbs. White sugar.	$\frac{1}{2}$-oz. Citric Acid.
8-lbs. Glucose.	2 quarts Water.
$3\frac{1}{2}$-lbs. Gelatine.	Carmine Colour.
12-ozs. Raspberry Fruit Extract.	

PROCESS.—Soak the gelatine by covering it with cold water for two or three hours. Boil the sugar with two thirds of the glucose and water to the degree of feather, 242° ; remove the pan from the fire ; stir in the remainder of the glucose with the gelatine and acid, colour to rather a deep red and add the flavour ; let it remain in the pan till the scum forms on top ; skim this off and run the mixture twice through a jelly bag ; pour it into tins, making a sheet a full inch thick ; stand in a cool place till set firm, then cut it up into bars 2¼-in. long and 1⅞-in. wide. This is the size for ½-pints, other sizes in proportion. The bars are then ready for packing. They may be either wrapped in wax paper or rubbed over with pulverized sugar and wrapped in plain paper, then, of course, in showy labels or card boxes.

CONCENTRATED STRAWBERRY JELLY.

14-lbs. White Sugar.	½-oz. Citric Acid, powered.
8-lbs. Glucose.	4 Pints Water.
3½-lbs. Gelatine.	12-ozs. Strawberry Fruit Extract.
	Cochineal Colour.

PROCESS.—Have the gelatine soaked in cold water. Boil sugar, water, and half the glucose to the degree of feather, about 242° ; remove the pan from the fire ; add the remainder of the glucose, gelatine and acid, stirring till all is dissolved ; let remain till the scum rises which skim off, then stir in colouring and flavour ; strain twice through jelly bag ; and run into tins making the sheet a full inch thick ; cut and pack as directed in the foregoing.

CONCENTRATED LEMON JELLY.

16-lbs. White Sugar.	2-quarts Water.
8 lbs. Glucose.	1½-oz. Citric Acid.
3½-lbs. Gelatine.	1-oz. Essence of Lemon.
Saffron Colouring.	

PROCESS.—Soak the gelatine as usual. Boil the sugar and water with half the glucose to the degree of feather ; remove the pan from the fire and gently stir in the remainder of the glucose with the gelatine and acid ; let the pan remain a short time then skim off the top ; strain twice through jelly bags, then tinge to a bright yellow and add the flavour (previously dissolved in 4-oz. spirits of wine); run the mixtures into tins ; cut to size when cold, and pack. If the essence of lemon makes the jelly cloudy, use 5 or 6 oz. of soluble essence of lemon.

N.B.—Oils and essences of lemon vary much in quality, here I recommend the best.

CONCENTRATED BLACK CURRANT.

8-lb. White Sugar.	3½-lbs. Gelatine.
7-lbs. Glucose.	½-oz. Citric Acid.
2-lbs. Black Currant Jelly.	4 Pints Water.
Purple Colouring.	

PROCESS.—Boil the sugar, glucose and water to feather; remove the pan from the fire; stir in the soaked gelatine, together with the jelly and acid; let the pan stand a little; remove the scum which rises to top; add sufficient colour to make a deep purple; then strain twice through jelly bags; run into tins; when set cut to size and pack. I use black currant jelly for the flavouring as no artificial article gives the true flavour of the fruit.

TURKISH DELIGHT (Lemon).

There are many many methods of making this. To do it properly requires a steam pan. However, small quantities may be managed on the fire. For steam batches, increase the size of boil according to size of pan and convenience.

4-lbs. Good Cooking Starch.	1-lb. Honey.
7-lbs. Ground Sugar.	½-oz. Soluble Essence of Lemon.
14-lbs. White Sugar.	1½-oz. Tartaric Acid.
3-lbs. Glucose.	4 quarts Water.

PROCESS.—Mix the starch with sufficient water to make a smooth paste, then add the ground sugar and stir well in; boil the remainder of the water and pour it boiling hot over this paste stirring till dissolved. Then boil the white sugar and glucose, with sufficient water, to a stiff ball; pour this syrup into the other ingredients and mix up the whole thoroughly, at the same time adding the honey, lemon and acid. Run the mixture into oiled tins making the sheet about 1-in. thick: when set, cut up into cakes; roll them amongst sherbet sugar; pack in boxes, using plenty of rough ground sugar between the layers.

N.B.—Great difficulty is often experienced to get the proper cooking starch; it is made from rice, comes from America and is sold in bulk by brokers.

TURKISH DELIGHT (Raspberry).

14-lbs. White Sugar.
7-lbs. Ground Sugar.
4-lbs. Ground Cooking Starch.
3-lbs. Glucose.
1-lb. Honey.
1½-oz. Tartaric Acid.
Carmine Colour.
Raspberry Flavour.
4 Quarts Water.

PROCESS.—Exactly same as last, with the exception of colour and flavour; use both sparingly, two or three drops of raspberry will be enough to flavour the whole boil.

GUM GOODS.

To manufacture gum goods on a small scale the process is a little tedious and tiresome and when one considers the present price of the raw material, and the time required to turn out a perfect jujube or pastile by fire heat, the writer is of opinion that it is neither an advisable nor profitable undertaking for the small confectioner. There are so many other branches to which the novice could turn his attention, in which the make is attended with less risk of failure while the goods are turned out and finished with despatch. In fact, the making of gum goods should not be attempted by a beginner as there are so many pitfalls in the process which can only be avoided by a trained and experienced workman. It would be impossible to coach a learner sufficiently by means of a book as to warrant the attempt. There are so many sorts and qualities of gums that it requires experience to select those suitable. Some gums are only partially soluble in water, others only in spirits of wine or essential oils and of no use for this business. The gums used by confectioners are gum arabic, mogador gum, and some sorts of East India gums.

These goods can only be made profitable where steam is used as a means of cooking, and, generally speaking, where this system is used, the workmen will have very little need of a book of this description. In a steam pan, batches of from one to two cwt. can be prepared in a quarter of the time twenty-eight pounds would take over the fire, so that it would be futile for a maker, by fire heat, to try to compete with those who have steam power; besides, the goods have a better appearance when cooked by the latter process.

The quantities are given for small boilings over the fire. For larger mixings or steam pans, it will be only necessary to increase the proportions.

CLEAR PINK JUJUBES (Gum).

16-lbs. Turkey Gum.	7 Pints Water.
6½-lbs. White Sugar.	Carmine Colour.
Otto of Roses.	

PROCESS.—It will be necessary to have two pans, one to fit in the other, leaving sufficient space between for a quantity of water. Put the gum (from which all the grit, &c., has been taken), together with the sugar and water into the inside pan; put both pans on the fire with water between them, and stir occasionally until all the gum is dissolved. See that the water between the pans does not get too low by evaporation (it will have to be renewed several times during the operation). It will take about seven hours to form a thick mucilage then strain through a very fine sieve or flannel, and let remain till the scum rises which skim off; flavour with a few drops of rose and tinge to a light pink. Run the mixture into tin trays which have been oiled; put them in the drying room until set stiff, then take them out and clear the dust off the top with an oily rag, and cut up with machine.

CLEAR PINK JUJUBES (Gum).

16-lbs. Turkey Gum.	7 Pints Water.
6½ lbs. White Sugar.	Pineapple Flavour.

PROCESS.—Same as for pink jubes, but pick all the dark pieces of gum out in order to get a clear jube and flavour with pineapple. Be careful in using the flavours, the slightest quantity is enough, too much and the jubes are spoiled.

LIQUORICE JUBES.

16-lbs. Turkey Gum.	1-lb. Block Juice.
5½-lbs. White Sugar.	7 Pints Water.

PROCESS.—The same as for clear jubes but the dark gum that has been sorted out for clear jubes may be used for the liquorice; the liquorice should be added when the gum and sugar is put on the fire; a little oil of aniseed is used by some, while others add a drop of capsicine to improve the flavour.

GUM PASTILLES (Lemon).

9-lbs. Turkey Gum.   5 Pints Water.
6-lbs. White Sugar.   Saffron Colouring.
Lemon Flavouring.

PROCESS.—The process given for the clear jubes was to have two pans, one fitting in the other with a space for water. This is adopted in order to keep the gum from sticking to the pan and burning, but with pastilles and other goods which are sold crystallized, a larger proportion of sugar is used therefore not so liable to catch, so that the outside pan is dispensed with and a slow fire used with great care and constant stirring.

Put the gum and water into the pan; place on a slow fire and stir with a wooden spatula till all the gum is dissolved, then strain the contents through a very fine sieve; return the strained gum to the pan and add the sugar; let the whole simmer over a slow fire for an hour, stirring all the time, when we should have a thick mucilage about the consistency of the white of a fresh egg. Remove the pan from the fire; let remain until the scum rises which remove; tinge with saffron and flavour with lemon. Have the starch trays smoothed and moulded with pastile shapes and run out the boil into them; stand the trays in the drying room until the goods are stiff enough to keep their shape, then sift them out of the starch, blow off the dust, and crystallise in syrup, luke warm.

GUM PASTILLES (Rose).

9-lbs. Turkey Gum.   5 Pints Water.
6-lbs. White Sugar.   Carmine Colour.
Rose Flavour.

PROCESS—Exactly as last, except in colour and flavour; tinge with liquid carmine and flavour with otto of roses. All kinds of crystallized gum goods may be made in this way, the shapes, colours and flavours alone differing. These can be easily copied or new ones invented.

CLEAR GUM DATES.

12-lbs. Turkey Gum.
6-lbs. White Sugar.
6 Pints Water.
Carmine Colour.

Lemon Flavour.
Rose Flavour.
Saffron Colour.

PROCESS—Make up the boil as usual. When the mucilage is ready, divide the boil into two; colour one half to a yellow and flavour with lemon; colour the other half to a light pink and flavour with rose. Mould into date shapes; when taken out of the starch, blow them off clean, then, with a rag dipped in olive oil, rub them up to make them look bright.

GLYCERINE PASTILLES.

36-lbs. Turkey Gum.
19-lbs. White Sugar.
3-lbs. Glycerine.
18 Quarts Water.

PROCESS—Put the gum and water into a pan and simmer for seven hours, then strain and add the sugar; continue to boil for another three hours, then mould in starch, and finish in the usual way. This is the genuine recipe of a celebrated chemist, who sells tons of these goods done up in small tin boxes at a big price.

Another method of making gum goods :—Some makers keep the gum soaked in cold water for days, giving an occasional stir two or three times a day until dissolved. They then use this mucilage, bring it to the boil, add the sugar and allow to simmer till finished; this saves time. Of course, the gum is dissolved in its proper proportion of water.

BEST WAY TO CRYSTALLIZE GUM GOODS.

13-lbs. Best White Sugar.
2 Quarts Water.

PROCESS.—Have the goods cleaned and put in crystallizing tins; bring the above quantity of sugar and water just through the boil, and stand aside until only milk warm, then pour it gently over the goods until covered, then slip the hands into the middle of the goods and, with the fingers, just ease this bulk so that the syrup will flow freely in between; withdraw the hands carefully and cover the tin; do not again disturb it for the next twelve hours, when the goods will be ready to drain and dry. To an inexperienced man, this method may seem a little dangerous and likely to spoil the crystal, but it will not do so if done carefully. Of course, it is understood the goods are not to be roughly stirred up, but simply loosened.

IMITATION GUM GOODS.

THERE is a quantity of goods sold as French, American, German, &c., gums, all more or less a mixture of the genuine article, with gelatine, farina, &c. Some are very good, others indifferent to taste, but most of them have a much prettier appearance than the original. We give the following couple of mixings which are perhaps the most general, and will give the reader an idea how the batch may be made up.

FRENCH GUM PASTILLES.

10-lbs. White Sugar.	5-lbs. Turkey Gum.
9-lbs. Glucose.	2-lbs. Gelatine.

3 Pints Water.

PROCESS.—Dissolve the gum in the water on a slow fire and strain it; then boil the glucose and sugar, with sufficient water, to a stiff ball degree; remove the pan from the fire; stir in the gelatine (which has been previously soaked) until dissolved, then add the gum mucilage, thoroughly incorporating the whole by stirring briskly with spatula; let the pan stand a little, then remove the scum and run the mixture into pastile moulds; when set firm, crystallize in syrup in the usual way. These goods are usually sold in three or four colours and flavours. The boil may be either divided and each portion coloured and flavoured separately, or more boils can be made and mixed when finished.

AMERICAN GUM PASTILLES.

10-lbs. White Sugar.	2-lbs. Glucose.
5-lbs. Gum Arabic.	2-oz. Tartaric Acid.
2-lbs. Gelatine.	4 Pints Water.

PROCESS.—Dissolve the gum in the water in the usual way; boil the sugar and glucose with sufficient water to the ball degree; then remove the pan from the fire; stir in the gelatine (which must have been previously soaked; mix in the dissolved gum and stir till thoroughly incorporated; colour and flavour as required, then run into starch trays; moulded with pastille shapes a little larger than ordinary; when set, crystallize with syrup almost cold. When gelatine is used the syrup must be nearly cold or the goods will melt in the crystallizing tin.

LIQUEURS.

THESE goods do not seem so popular as they were. One seldom sees them but in conjunction with other sweets which go to make up our best class of mixture. The plain brandy, rum, and gin almonds have left our windows, together with the decorated orange and lemon slices, wedding rings and a host of other goods, once the curiosity and delight of our youth.

Though these goods are simple and easy to make, still order and method must be practised to turn out nice goods of this class—the tons of common, coarse, miserable looking, empty rubbish, with which shops are filled in the shape of cheap mixture, is a disgrace to the trade, and is quite enough to account for the disappearance of the beautiful, full-flavoured juicy sweetmeats I call to mind. Still, in the best class of mixtures I have them still as sparkling and tempting as ever. No goods liven the colours and brighten the bulk more than well made liqueurs. There is no great skill in making; the process is simple enough, and, if the reader will but follow the instruction given with the few recipes there is no reason why he should fail. Good sugar should always be used, whether for white or coloured; the colours should be good and transparent and used sparingly; the flavours fresh and of the best quality; the starch should be thoroughly dry and warm; new starch must be spread on trays and left in the drying room for seven or eight days being turned over each day two or three times before being used; if it can be avoided the same starch should not be used for gelatine work; damping not only spoils the goods but is a great hindrance to the work; with good, dry, warm starch, the goods will be ready in a third of the time and look altogether brighter and better; when crystallizing, handle them tenderly, especially the large ones; do not put too many in a tin unless a wire sheet is between them to take the weight; method and discretion is all that is wanted to make the work run smoothly with a successful result.

BRANDY, RUM, OR GIN ALMONDS.

14-lbs. White Sugar.   4 Pints Water.

Process.—Have thoroughly dry and warm starch powder; smooth off the trays and print with the almond moulds; boil the sugar and water in the usual way to the degree of thread, 230°; lift the pan off the fire; let stand a little to cool, then pour in, say half a pint of spirit and immediately pull a cloth over the mouth of the pan to prevent evaporation as much as possible. After a few minutes, stir the boil gently and commence to run out into the printed impressions in the starch trays. When the moulds are all filled, sift a little starch powder over the goods, through a fine wire or hair sieve, and remove the trays to the drying room, racking them in a warm place. In six or seven hours they should be crisp enough. This can be easily tested by pressing one between the finger and the thumb; if ready, sift them out of the powder, blow them clean, then put them carefully in crystallizing tins and cover with syrup, lukewarm; let them remain all night. In the morning, drain off the superfluous syrup and spread them out on trays; when dry, weigh and pack. Gin almonds are white, brandy tinged with saffron, rum light red, flavoured with the spirit or essence. If the latter only a few drops are required to the boil.

ORANGE AND LEMON SLICES.

14-lbs. Sugar.	Orange Colouring.
4 pints Water.	Essence of Lemon.
Essence of Orange	Lemon Colouring.

PROCESS.—Exactly as the last; flavour when the sugar has been boiled: halve the lot; flavour and colour one part orange, the other part tinge with saffron and flavour with lemon. When the goods come out of the drying room, mix up some icing sugar with the white of an egg to a stiff paste, then, with an icing tube or paper cone, decorate the slices by running a thick thread round the edges and a little spot in the middle to represent the pip; afterwards, crystallize as usual.

WEDDING RINGS.

| 14-lbs. Sugar. | 4 Pints Water. |
| Colours and Flavours various. | |

PROCESS.—Exactly as for brandy almonds, but with a variety of colours and flavours; after the goods are sifted out of the starch powder if required dotted, prepare the icing as mentioned in the last formula, and put about six little dots on each ring; afterwards, crystallize.

LIQUEURS FOR MIXTURE.

| 28-lbs. Sugar. | 8 Pints Water. |
| Colours, flavours, and shapes various. | |

PROCESS.—Smooth off the trays and mould with mixed shapes in warm dry starch; boil the sugar with the water a little higher than the other, so that they will stand a little rough handling, say 235°; remove the pan from the fire and stir in the particular colour and flavour required then run into the moulds; when full, sift over them a little dry starch powder; put the trays in the drying room; in four hours these goods should be crisp enough for crystallizing which do in manner already described.

FONDANT CREAM WORK.

This department has developed more rapidly and more extensively than perhaps any other in the business, if we except chocolate, and even then the fondant cream has been a great assistance to the cocoa bean in providing the luscious centres for the variety in which this roasted berry has been used for coating. Fondant Cream is almost as useful to a confectioner as the stock pot is to the cook, we can work it into any conceivable size, shape, colour or flavour, we can use it alone or with any combination of nuts, fruits, berries or spices to make an endless variety of sweets both pretty and pleasant. Many pretty mixtures with all sorts of beautiful names are composed wholly or in greater part with the smaller variety of shapes made from these formulæ. Until quite recently the process of making was practically all done by hand, the syrup was creamed on the slab, the trays full of starch powder were smoothed, imprinted, filled, emptied and cleaned by the rather tedious process described on page (99). We have now machines for beating the syrup to a fine cream and an elaborate automatic arrangement which prints, deposits, and cleans the goods ready for sale or crystallizing in one continuous operation, saving an immense amount of physical labour and being much more economical in the way of space.

This machine has been in use for some years in America and has recently been adopted in this country with success. Readers to whom a description may be interesting would be much better repaid by visiting the sellers where they can see it, have the working explained, and also learn the advantages to be derived from its use.

For my purpose variety is a question of detail which I only mention to remind the reader that he or she must look for the greater part of it outside the covers of this guide. All the principal formulæ are given and the different processes noted; but when it comes to simply a matter of shapes, colours and flavours, I omit this, as a needless repetition. A fair study and a little practice with the recipes which follow, should enable anyone with average brain power to imitate anything he sees in this branch, and then with a pinch of genius to invent something new.

No. 1. FONDANT CREAM FOR CENTRES.

20-lbs. White Sugar.   7½-lbs. Glucose.

2½-quarts Water.

PROCESS.—Put the ingredients in a clean boiling pan and boil in the usual way to 240°, then remove the pan from the fire and pour contents on to a clean slab which has been previously dampened with cold water and let it remain until cold, then with a wooden spatula commence to rub this syrup to and fro against the slab until the batch turns white and creamy, when thoroughly done to a mass let it remain undisturbed for an hour, then put it away for future use in an earthenware pan covered with a damp cloth.

N.B.—This is but a small lot of fondant cream. It is usually made in much larger quantites even by a very small maker.

RASPBERRY AND VANILLA FONDANTS.

10-lbs. White Sugar.   3 Pints Water.

2½-lbs. Glucose.   Carmine Colour.

Raspberry and Vanilla Flavour.

PROCESS.—Boil the sugar, glucose, and water in the usual way to the degree of soft ball, 240° then remove the pan from the fire ; damp the pouring plate with cold water ; pour the boil on to it and let remain until cold. With a long palette knife or wooden spatula commence to work the syrup until it changes to a white glossy cream ; then divide the batch into two ; put one part in pan and remelt it, just enough to make it a consistency to mould ; add vanilla flavour and run it into the starch trays, which have already been impressed with fondant shapes ; now put the other portion in the pan and remelt ; colour it to a light pink ; flavour with the essence of raspberry and mould in same shapes ; when the goods are set and cold, sift them out of the starch and crystallize with cold syrup. N.B.—Have everything very clean when making fondants ; every speck will show ; a touch of blue will make the white a better colour.

CHOCOLATE AND VANILLA FONDANTS.

10-lbs. White Sugar.   3 Pints Water.
2½-lbs. Glucose.   ½-lb. Pure Chocolate.
Vanilla Flavour.

PROCESS.—Prepare the fondant creams as in last recipe ; when the boil has been creamed, divide into two, one part being twice the size of the other ; put the small portion in the pan to remelt adding the chocolate paste ; stir until the paste is dissolved and incorporated, but do not let the cream be too hot ; remove the pan from the fire ; have the starch trays moulded fondant shape ; run the chocolate cream in filling the impression only one third part full ; then remelt the white cream, flavour with vanilla and fill up the moulds ; when set, sift out the fondants and crystallize in cold syrup ; each fondant will be in two colours, white tipped with chocolate.

COCOANUT FONDANTS.

9-lbs. White Sugar.   3 Pints Water.
2½-lbs. Glucose.   Lemon Flavour.
1½-lbs. Fine Desiccated Cocoanut, unsweetened.   Carmine Colour.

PROCESS.—Proceed to make the cream as before directed and divide the batch into two equal parts ; remelt one part and stir in half the desiccated cocoanut with a few drops of lemon ; have the starch trays printed with fondant impressions and run them half full ; remelt the other portion of cream ; stir in the remainder of the cocoanut and colour to a pink adding a few drops of essence of lemon and fill up the impressions to the full ; crystallize in the usual way in cold syrup.

STRAWBERRY FONDANTS.

9-lbs. White Sugar.   2-lbs. Strawberry Jam.
2-lbs. Glucose.   3 Pints Water.
Carmine Colouring.

PROCESS.— Boil the sugar, glucose and water to a soft ball degree 240° ; pour the batch on a pouring plate which has been previously damped with cold water ; let the boil remain till nearly cold ; then with a wooden spatula or palette knife, work the syrup about till it becomes creamy, then mix in the jam ; return the whole to the pan and remelt ; add sufficient colour to make a bright pink then run into starch trays printed with suitable moulds ; when set, sift out the goods and crystallize in cold syrup.

CHERRY FONDANTS.

10-lbs. Sugar.
2½-lbs. Glucose.
Cherry Flavour.

3 Pints Water.
Carmine and Saffron Colour.

PROCESS.—Select some large preserved cherries: cut them in halves. Boil the sugar, glucose and water in the ordinary way to 245°; pour the batch on a damp pouring plate; when nearly cold, work up the whole with spatula till it becomes a white glossy cream, working in the flavour at the same time, then divide into three equal portions; colour one portion to a bright pink and another to a yellow, leaving a third white; knead each portion into a stiff paste, adding a little icing sugar to make it tough; pinch off small pieces and form them into balls about the size of a cherry making them a little flat on one side. On this flat part stick a half cherry squeezing into shape; place them in canvas trays and put in the drying room for a few hours to harden. Afterwards, crystallize with cold syrup. These goods are usually packed nicely in laced boxes. Other preserved fruits, etc., may be used in the same way. N.B.—If fondant cream is kept in stock it will be necessary only to melt portions instead of going through the *whole* process each time.

FONDANT MAKING BY MACHINERY.

The writer has seen this machine (The Mogul) in operation at a large factory in the East End of London and was surprised at its beautiful automatic action. At one end of the machine was a receptacle on which were placed six starch trays on top of each other. A movement of the mechanism, and the top five were raised while the bottom one was carried under a cover where it was emptied of its contents, refilled with starch powder, smoothed off and imprinted with fondant shapes, and then passing a little further on, the impressions were filled with cream. When the tray passed from each distinct process its place was immediately taken by the next in rotation which was treated similarly and so on, tray following tray with the greatest regularity and without a hitch, the finished fondants all of an exact size and perfect shape were dropping into a box very rapidly.

Practically any shape or size with or without pattern may be turned out by this automatic method at the rate of from 4 to 8 tray-fulls per

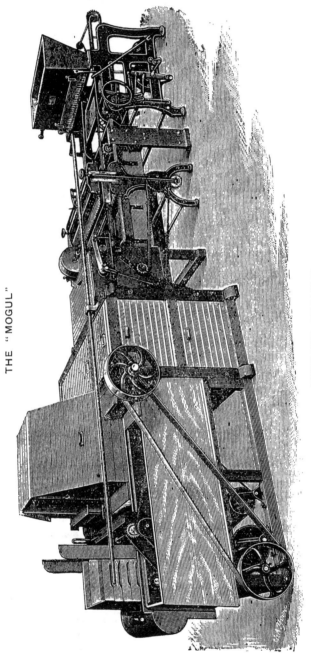

THE "MOGUL"

FONDANT MACHINE.

minute of finished goods, or ready for crystallizing or being covered with chocolate as may be wanted. The machine seems to require little attention except feeding. Bramigk & Co., 5 Aldgate, London, are the agents.

FONDANTS FOR MIXTURES.

10-lbs. White Sugar.	3 Pints Water.
2½-lbs. Glucose.	Colours Various.

Flavours Various.

PROCESS.—Boil the sugar, glucose and water as before directed to a stiff ball, and pour the sugar on a damp slab ; let stand till nearly cold then work it up with spatula till a glossy cream ; divide the boil into as many portions as you want colours, then remelt this cream ; colour and flavour to fancy ; run the batch into starch trays impressed with small fancy moulds of different shapes (leaves, fruits, flowers, etc., are taken as pattern for moulds); when the fondants are set, crystallize in cold syrup. Fondants for mixture are made a trifle harder, to prevent being crushed with the other sweets with which they are mixed.

DANDIES FOR MIXTURES (American).

9-lbs. Fondant Cream.	Colours.

Flavours.

PROCESS.—Divide the cream into three equal portions, flavour one portion vanilla, and work well up by kneading into it sufficient pulverised sugar to make it a good stiff consistence, then roll it out into a sheet less than one inch thick and put it aside. Take the second portion, colour it pink and flavour with raspberry essence, knead up to stiff paste by adding pulverised sugar then roll it into a sheet same size as last and spread this raspberry sheet on top of the white one. Now take the remaining portion, work into it some pure chocolate and a little brown colour, together with pulverised sugar to make stiff paste, then roll out in sheet like the others and place it on top. We have now three alternate colours in the one sheet which you must now take and roll up. Then for convenience, cut this thick roll into four pieces and roll each piece down into a long stick, a little thicker than a farthing sugar stick, and then cut them up into very short lengths placing them side by side on a tray ; let them remain for a few hours to harden and form a crust, when set enough to handle put them in a crystallizing tin, and cover with cold syrup which has been boiled to 215°, let remain for twelve hours then run off the syrup and spread on trays to dry. These goods go well with a mixture, they may be made in one or several colours, the paste may be mixed with chopped nuts or, a stiff fruit jelly may be used for a middle layer, or you can use lozenge cutters and cut the sheet up into different shapes and sizes, in fact any conceivable variety can be produced in this way.

BUTTERNUT CREAMS.

4-lbs. Fondant Cream.   1½-lbs. Walnuts.

PROCESS.—Chop the nuts fine. Warm the fondant paste and stir in the chopped nuts, when well mixed stand the pan off the fire then dip out half a teaspoonful at a time of this mixture and push each lot off the spoon in a little heap on the slab, when set, crystallize with syrup in the usual way.

CHOCOLATE BUTTERED CREAMS.

4-lbs. Fondant Paste.   1½-lbs. Walnuts.
Dipping Chocolate.

PROCESS.—Exactly as last but instead of crystallizing when set dip them in chocolate. These are first class lines for retail windows, for variety use Barcelona nuts, Brazil nuts and sweet almonds.

COCOANUT CREAM ROLLS.

4-lbs. Fondant Cream.   Grated Cocoanut fresh.
Vanilla.   Chocolate.

PROCESS.—Knead into the cream as much grated cocoanut as you can, then make it into a long roll about an inch thick and cut up in lengths of about 4 inches. Let them stand to set, then dip in chocolate and sprinkle them over with shredded cocoanut; when dry cut them in two at right angles.

A good line for the retail shop. For wholesale trade desiccated cocoanut should be used in lieu of fresh as the goods will keep longer but will not be so rich.

ROAST ALMOND CHOCOLATES.

4-lbs. Fondant Cream.   ½-lb. Sweet Almonds.

PROCESS.—Well roast the almonds then grind them. Now take the fondant cream and well knead in the ground almonds with sufficient pulverized sugar to make a stiff paste, roll out and cut up into balls, then dip in chocolate lifting them out singly with a fork and put on wire trays to dry.

PARISIAN CHOCOLATE BONBONS.

5-lbs. Fondant Cream.   ½-lb. Almonds.
Chocolate.   Vanilla.

PROCESS.—Warm the fondant cream, flavour with vanilla and run it in starch trays impressed with oblong shapes, when set take them out and brush off the starch. Well roast and chop up the almonds. Melt some sweet chocolate and stir them in till mixed. Now, well coat the fondant centres by dipping taking them out singly. When dry they are ready for sale.

BURNT ALMOND CHOCOLATE.

4-lbs. Almonds.   Chocolate.

ROAST and almost burn the almonds, then chop them not too fine. Now melt a small portion of chocolate and stir in the chopped almonds making a very thick paste, in fact stir in all the almonds you can, then with the fingers or a fork lift out a little at at a time and place it on wax paper in little heaps, when set they are ready for sale.

LEMON FRUIT BONBONS.

6 Lemons.   Castor Sugar.
Fondant Cream.

PROCESS.—Peel the lemons and squeeze out the juice into an earthen-ware pan then grate the outside of the peel and mix with the juice. Now add sufficient castor sugar to form a thick paste mixing it up with the hands until fairly stiff then nip off small pieces the size of a marble, shape them round and lay them separately on wax paper, let them stand in a warm place for an hour or so when a thin crust will form on the outside, they are then ready for dipping, see next formula.

ORANGE FRUIT BONBONS.

6 Juicy Oranges.   Castor Sugar.
Orange Colour.

PROCESS.—Exactly as last and tinge lightly with orange colour. Rasp berries, pineapples and almost every kind of acidulated fruits may be treated in this manner. When dry and ready for dipping warm some fondant cream, do not make it too hot but just so that it will work nicely, flavour and colour to suit. Then dip what goods are ready one at a time take them out and lay them neatly on wax paper. In about one hour they will be ready for packing. These goods may be dipped in chocolate. They are fine eating having all the natural flavour of the fruit juices.

PEPPERMINT CREAM PATTIES.

Fondant Cream. Peppermint Oil.

PROCESS.—Warm the fondant cream just sufficient to run through the funnel used for moulding fondants, &c., then stir in a few drops of good oil of peppermint and pour part of the cream into the funnel, then commence to let it drop in pieces the size of a half-penny (larger or smaller as wanted) on wax paper using the stick to regulate the quantity, with a little practice you will be able to make them regular and whatever size you wish. See illustration page (99).

LEMON CREAM PATTIES.

Fondant Cream. Lemon.
Colour.

PROCESS.—Exactly as last. Tinge with saffron, flavour with lemon.

CHOCOLATE PATTIES.

Fondant Cream. Pure Chocolate unsweetened.
Brown colour.

PROCESS.—Warm the cream and chocolate together, add a little brown colour if necessary, but if the chocolate is good and pure no colour is wanted. Drop on wax paper as directed.

ARTIFICIAL FIGURES.

FRUIT, eggs and any object may be taken from nature by this process to be transformed into sugar, afterwards glazed and coloured, to imitate nature so exactly as to deceive many persons. The moulds must be made in two, three or more pieces, so as to relieve freely without injuring the casting; each part must fit together exactly; for this purpose, make two or three marks or figures on the edges of the mould, to correspond with similar marks on the counterpart, so that the pieces to form each mould may be fitted with precision. Simple moulds in two pieces may be made by the workmen, such as eggs, apples, pears, &c., but where intricate objects are required, such as swans, baskets of fruit, &c., it is advisable to have them made by an experienced mould maker. Let the object from which you require the cast be partly embedded in soft pipe clay, or modelling wax, leaving so much of the mould exposed as you wish to form at a time (if in two pieces, say half), and oil it with sweet oil. Mix some plaster of Paris with water to the consistency of thick cream, and pour over the exposed half; when this has set, turn the object over and embed the half taken, now pour the plaster over the other half and the mould will be then complete; with a pen knife, scrape out a hole at one end into which the sugar may be poured. The moulds must be soaked an hour or so in cold water previously to being used, this is better than oiling as it keeps the sugar a delicate white. Boil the sugar as directed for candies or grained sugars; grain it and fill the moulds; in a few minutes run out as much sugar as will leave the mould; this will cause the casting to be hollow in the centre. Colour your articles to imitate the natural objects which they represent with liquid colours and camel's hair pencils; if a gloss is required the colours should be mixed with a strong solution of gum arabic or isinglass to the desired tint.

TO DECORATE FANCIES.

THIS is done with various colours, put on with a camel's hair pencil or brush the execution of which depends upon the ability of the artist; also, with what is called in the trade "piping"; this is made by mixing finely powdered sugar with the white of eggs to a stiffish paste which may also be coloured if required; it is put on by means of small pipes or tubes made purposely (by machine makers); or, a stiff paper bag may be used for this purpose. Fold some writing paper in the form of a cone, similar in appearance to what grocers usually do small parcels of sugar and tea in; the bag is filled with icing or piping; the mouth of the bag is turned down to prevent the escape of the piping; the point is then cut off with a pair of scissors or a sharp knife, to make a hole through which the icing passes to the goods. In using this bag squeeze the sides together when the icing will protrude from the small hole at the bottom. Some practice will be necessary before the learner can fully understand and work out this process satisfactorily. Some of the pipes which are used cannot be imitated by paper, the holes at the bottom having different devices, some fluted to form stars, while others are flat, which, when the icing is squeezed through forms a tape, others form various descriptions of fancy work. Where any quantity of this work requires to be done it is certainly cheaper and better to buy a set of tools, they are not very expensive and are always ready for use.

FIGURE PIPING.

A GOOD many fancies for the Christmas trade are made from an icing mixture. It would be impossible to give any idea of the process. The result entirely depends upon the dexterity of the workman. These beautiful imitations of men and women in gaudy dresses, as well as representations of animals, etc., all more or less true to nature, are really worked up almost in the same manner as an artist would a drawing, the only difference being that the artist uses his crayon while the confectioner employs his icing tubes. I can only assist the reader as far as giving the mixing for the icing used, and must leave the detail to the talent of the *would be*. These goods are mostly made by foreigners, the French being especially clever at it. Considering the prices at which they are sold wholesale, people must be wonderfully nimble with their fingers to make it pay. The ingredients are:—1-lb. icing sugar, the whites of two eggs and two teaspoonfuls of thick gum mucilage; beat up the egg whites with the gum, then mix the icing sugar gradually; continue beating with a flat spatula until the icing will stand up to a sharp point; a touch of blue will improve the white; colour other portions to fancy as required.

PAN ROOM.

IN this room is made all sorts of hard, round, oval, oblong and other shapes known in the trade as comfits. The method is one of the oldest known in the business. These goods have always held their own on the market as against everything new made by a different process, although we have had innumerable alterations and improvements in the tools, machines and appliances of the work, together with fresh ingredients for foundations and finish. Still, we adhere to the original process in all its essential details. In days gone by, these goods were made in a large copper pan suspended from the ceiling by means of two chains attached to a bar with a hook and swivel in the centre. It was constructed so as to hang on a level with the workman's breast over an open furnace or charcoal fire. By this means the pan was kept at a moderate heat while the length of the chain allowed the workmen to keep the pan on the swing giving it a motion that the contents should be kept rolling about. Syrup was prepared in small pans with which the goods were from time to time coated; the heat of the furnace and the friction caused by the motion of the pan grained the syrup, and covered the surface of the goods. As each coat dried another was added, and so on, making the comfits gradually larger and larger until the required size was attained, when the finishing touches were given. This is a very slow, sing song process compared to what can now be done by steam power and steam pans. Formerly, a good day's work by an experienced confectioner would not be more than about half a hundredweight of finished goods per day. At the present moment a man can superintend half-a-dozen or more pans, turning out two or three tons per week.

In face of these facts, it would be almost foolish for a small maker to try hand pans in the hope of being able to compete with others provided with requisite machinery, the cost of material and wages for labour would be more than the market price of the finished goods.

This pan is what is known as an oscillating pan and the first to supercede the hand pan. It is made of copper, with a strong inside lining which forms a steam chamber, into which the steam passes through a vulcanised rubber tube, right round the pan and exhausts itself by passing out through another tube (both tubes are shown), the pan is thus heated, the temperature being regulated by steam cocks. It is worked by machinery having a driving pulley attached to the main shaft which passes along the ceiling and connected to a steam engine. The quick regular motion of the pan causes greater friction and the steady regulated heat of the steam keeps the contents at a proper temperature. Goods made in these pans are more regular and may be finished in a better style than could be done by the hand process.

REVOLVING PAN.

THIS is another and newer shaped pan for the same purpose. This one simply revolves and does not oscillate like the one previously described. It is a question which pan does the best work, some workmen prefer one, some another; both have their merits and drawbacks but to judge from sales and preferences the revolver is the favourite; in fact, many newer houses have nothing else, while the older makers adding to their plant in most cases select this latter. Where large quantities are required no doubt the big revolver is on the job. The pan itself, like the other, is made of copper, and has a steam chamber but is supplied with steam through the shaft, the exhaust also passing out the same way therefore avoiding rubber tubes. In both cases these pans are delivered by the makers complete ready for the driving belt—price of the oscillating about £30, the revolver from £40 to £56, according to size. The sugar is generally melted in small steam pans to supply syrup for coating.

This syrup pan is made of copper having a jacket of the same material. Between the jacket and the pan, space is left for a supply of steam for melting and boiling purposes, the supply and exhaust being affected by means of taps fixed at the side of the pan for inlet and at the bottom for waste. The syrup pans are placed in the most convenient position, close to the comfit pans they are intended to supply. The formulæ in this branch will be of little interest to the majority of readers, because, as a rule, the firms who go in for pan work are either themselves or have in their employ experienced confectioners, at the same time it would be unwise to ignore altogether such an important department; besides, in my former editions much information which I thought was almost outside my purpose has been of great benefit, especially abroad.

NONPAREILS (Hundreds and Thousands).

THESE small comfits make the foundation for nearly all round work, such as rifle balls, rainbow balls and round marbles of any size. First sift some powdered sugar through a wire sieve (40 holes to the inch) ; then again sift what comes through in a lawn sieve, to separate all the fine dust ; use what is left in the lawn sieve ; put, say four or six pounds in the comfit pan ; set the pan in motion and turn on a little steam to heat the sugar ; let the pan revolve for a few minutes till the contents are warmed through, then add a little syrup, just enough to wet ; while the pan is turning round put your hand in and rub them about to keep the particles from sticking together while wet; when they get dry and free add a little more syrup; again rub them about and repeat the process, over and over again ; see that each coat of syrup is dry before adding another, also that the goods are separate and quite free. If they couple it is impossible to separate them ; being so small, careless work will show when they become larger, as they will be of very irregular shape and out of proportion in size ; when brought up to the size required, if wanted for nonpareils, take out three parts of them and stand them aside ; dissolve some best sugar to a thin syrup adding a pinch of blue ; give the goods left in the pan a coat or two of it, then gradually turn off the steam until the pan runs quite cold. While the pan is getting cold keep adding a little syrup, as the goods get dry (not too much) ; then let the pan run dead cold for some little time without adding any syrup ; in this way you will finish a nice white ; now stop the pan and pack the nonpareils on trays. Put in another portion of the unfinished goods ; start the pan and turn on the steam ; when they get warm, colour a portion of the syrup yellow ; give them a few coats at intervals until they show a decided colour, then turn off the steam ; letting them get gradually cold, still adding a little yellow syrup ; when quite cold let the pan run for a little time until the sweets are dry and comparatively hard, then stop the pan and take them out. Put in another portion ; colour the syrup red and finish in the same way and still another, and finish a light blue, and so on, according to the number of colours required; when all is finished, mix together and they are then ready for sale. Should the nonpareils be wanted for bottoms for larger balls, of course, no colouring will be required until they have reached the size you want; in that case as the goods increase in bulk the pan will get too full, a portion must be taken out from time to time and put aside for stock bottoms.

GREEN PEAS AND CORAL BEADS.

THESE goods are raised from the nonpareils as described in the foregoing formula. Put any quantity of bottoms in the pan, start it to run and turn on the steam; put on coat after coat of syrup until the nonpareils have come up to the size of a pea, then use best syrup, colour it green; make the shade to represent nature as near as possible; give the goods several wettings with the coloured syrup; when you see them come to colour, shut off the steam: add a few more coatings a little thinner: as they become cold stop the supply of syrup and let the pan run until they are dry, when they are finished. Coral beads and red currants are made in exactly the same way. The art lies in the colour and finish, striking the shades and finishing clear. This is done by regulating heat, lowering it gradually, thinning off the syrup, and putting in just the quantity at proper intervals, running the pan until the goods are cold and dry enough to prevent spotting and specking.

RIFLE BALLS.

PROCESS—They are raised in the same way as green peas; the syrup may be used thicker, but not too thick or the balls will go out of shape; the pan is kept pretty hot until they are nearing the size wanted. Then commence to thin off the syrup and look to the finishing; when brought fairly nice and smooth take them out of the pan and divide them into as many portions as you want colours; put those for white in the pan first and finish off with syrup made from best sugar, then work the yellow, then the orange, then the red; working them this way the pan does not require so much cleaning, as the light colours used first will not harm the darker ones; the mauve and blue shades are used last. Rifle balls are made in all sizes; the process is the same, only that the very large ones are taken out of the pan once or twice and put in the drying room to harden during the operation.

CHING CHANGS.

PROCESS—They are made and finished in exactly the same way as rifle balls; when finished take them out of the pan; have a changing board which is usually a roughly constructed tool, consisting of a square frame in which strips of wood are fixed edgeways, a quarter to half-inch apart (according to the size of the marble); the edges of the wood are coloured and the balls are run down them, making two coloured rings round each. These goods were at one time very popular and now sell fairly well.

ANISEED BALLS.

PROCESS—Same as for rifle balls, but the syrup is made from common sugar and flavoured with a little oil of aniseed. The shades of colour vary with different makers but are all of a reddish brown.

BIRDS' EGGS.

PROCESS.—Sift four pounds of mogador or other good caraways, free from dust; put them in the pan; turn on a little steam and set the pan in motion; when the seed warms put on a little thin solution of gum, just enough to wet them, then throw them about with the hands to separate them, adding a dust of dry flour; when dry, wet them with a little thin syrup; keep moving them about with the hands; see they are parted; when the first coating of sugar is dry, add another, and so on; when they begin to get large, the sugar may be used thicker and more steam turned on the pan until they get nearly the required size, when the steam should be slackened and the syrup thinned; when they look fairly well and dry take them out of the pan; divide them into lots for colouring. Now wash the pan out; prepare some finishing syrup; replace the portion for whites first in the pan; start it and turn on a little steam; use the syrup sparingly; let each coat dry before adding another; gradually reduce the supply of steam till the pan is quite cold and finish an opaque white; a pinch of blue in the syrup will improve it. Now use another portion and colour the syrup to fancy, finishing in a like manner, and so on, until they are all coloured. These goods are usually sold spotted; to do this, spread them on trays and take a short, coarse haired paint brush in the right hand, dip it in some liquid colouring and strike it lightly against a stick, held in the left hand, over the goods, the spots will fly off on the comfits ; when different colours are used and carefully put on, the result is very pretty.

CARAWAY COMFITS.

PROCESS.—Follow the last formula by sifting the seeds, then putting them in the pan ; wet with thin gum ; dust with flour and syrup to size. *Scotch Carvie* is made very small (all white), English Caraway much larger (pink and white, sometimes pink, white, and yellow).

CORIANDER COMFITS.

PROCESS.—Put 4-lbs. of sifted coriander seeds in the comfit pan ; start the pan in motion ; turn on a little steam. When the seeds are warm, put on a thin coating of gum mucilage, then a dust of flour ; use the hands to keep them free, then coat with syrup until they reach the required size ; finish as already directed. These goods are usually made all white and are used largely for mixtures, plain and purled. Some raise the rifle balls from these seeds. In the latter case they are of course, coloured. Corianders are also purled by the same process as for cinnamon comfits, when used for Scotch mixtures.

CINNAMON COMFITS.

PROCESS.—Take 4-pounds of cinnamon or *cassia lignea*, which is a cheaper sort ; soak in water for a few hours to soften, then cut up in pieces, about one inch long and very narrow, with a pair of scissors or machine which is made for this purpose ; put them in the drying room till hard, then remove them to the comfit pan ; start it in motion and turn on the steam. When the sticks are warm, give them a coating of thin liquid gum and a dust of flour ; use the hands to feel they are free ; give them a few coatings of syrup, then put on the remainder and finish through the purling pot *i.e.* a small vessel like the top of a funnel used to fill bottles, having a small hole at the bottom, in the centre. An iron rod runs down the middle of the funnel, having its point to fit in the hole. This rod is moveable, being fixed with a screw, so as to regulate the supply of syrup through the funnel. This arrangment is suspended over the centre of the pan and is kept full of syrup, which is allowed to run over the goods as the pan revolves, the thickness of the stream being regulated by the iron rod. Keep the pot well supplied with very hot syrup during the operation and the pan revolving slowly at a good heat so that the sugar which is dripping on to the cinnamon sticks will dry instantly, and give that nice white, rough appearance.

COMFITS WITH BOILED CENTRES.

A great variety of pan goods are made from boiled centres. Rollers are made by machinists to produce shapes for this purpose. Some of them are very pretty. In this way bulk is produced much quicker and cheaper. The boilings intended for pan bottoms are made in the same way as directed for boiled sugars. The sugar should be boiled very high and no more glucose or cream of tartar used than is necessary to cut the grain, otherwise the finished goods may become damp and soft. The sugar bottoms are worked up, coloured, and finished in the same manner as seeds.

COCOANUT PERFECTIONS.

Process.—Take any quantity of desiccated cocoanut, unsweetened ; mix with it a thin solution of gum and work it into a firm, stiff paste, well binding the cocoanut. Cut off pieces and roll into lengths a little thinner than a lead pencil ; dust well with icing sugar and stand close together on a slab, then saw them into pieces about $\frac{1}{2}$-in. long with a thin, sharp knife. Pack them on canvas trays and put in the drying room till hard and dry, then put into a cold pan. Work round them carefully a coating of thin gum and flour ; sift them out of the pan and put them again on trays to harden in the drying room ; when dry, replace in the comfit pan ; give them three or four coatings of cold syrup ; between each coating throw in a handful or two of dry sherbet sugar, then let them revolve till dry (all this time with a cold pan) ; now turn on a little steam and, when the goods have warmed, give them two or three more coatings of syrup, but no more dry sugar. Now shut off the steam and give them a further wetting or two and finish in a cold pan ; take out on clean trays and put in the drying room till hard and firm. If wanted coloured, the last wetting or two would be with coloured syrup.

The goods are a little difficult and troublesome to make, but look very pretty if well done ; they are comparatively new, and of Yankee origin.

SUGARED ALMONDS.

PROCESS.—Pick and clean 20 or 30 pounds of well-shaped almonds, Jordan, Valencia, or sweet Barbary, and put them in the pan. Start revolving and turn on the steam till they get warm, then give them a wetting of liquid gum ; rub them about with the hands till they are all damp ; throw in a handful or two of flour amongst them and keep them moving till they are dry. When dry, take them out and spread on trays ; put them in the drying room for, at least, twelve hours ; see that the gum and flour have covered them all over, especially at the points, or they will finish with broken tips, or what is known as pointed. When taken from the drying room, put them again in the comfit pan ; start the pan running and turn on the steam ; when the almonds get warm, put on a little syrup ; when that dries, renew the quantity with a dust of flour ; examine the almonds from time to time, by lifting a handful out of the pan, and see that they are taking the syrup all round, if not, pick out the faulty ones (to be gummed again with the next batch) ; bring up the others by repeated coatings of syrup and finish off with best thin syrup and a cool pan. N.B.—Always have the goods and pan cool when colouring. Never leave the finished goods in the pan when dry, or they might sweat and show white marks when separated. The colouring process should not take too long. From half-an-hour to forty minutes is about the time.

PAN GOODS WITH LOZENGE BOTTOMS.

A GOOD many bottoms are made from lozenge paste, such as Victorias, &c. They should be perfectly dry and hard before putting in the pan, or they will run out of shape and couple when they get warm. Use the flour freely with first coatings of syrup ; do not have the pan very hot until they are well in shape and the first coating dry on them. Work off in the usual way.

GLAZING PAN GOODS.

PROCESS.—The goods to undergo the process of glazing must have been finished as if for sale. Have the pan clean ; put in the goods ; set it in motion and turn on steam enough just to warm them, then drop in a cake or two of hard white wax ; let them run round until they have taken a finely polished surface, then shut off the steam and let the pan revolve till the goods are nearly cold. At no time must they be hot, or they will not take the gloss. In pan work, as in other departments, too deep colours should be avoided ; the lightest shades and tints are prettiest and, when mixed, look delicate and tempting.

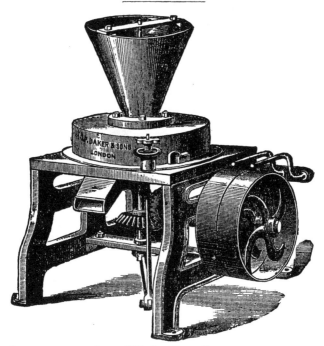

Sugar Mill, for Steam Power.

LOZENGE MAKING.

The process of making dry goods is very simple, at the same time, it requires experience and a good deal of practice to enable one to tell just when this and that is right or to add a little more sugar or a little more liquid in order to make the batch just the consistency needed. I can assist the learner only by telling him how I should do this in order to make that, but many little unforeseen and unprovided for events occur, especially to beginners, to mar their progress which does not always occur to one at the moment of writing. It is impossible for me to infuse into the brain and muscle that dexterity and acuteness which experience and practice alone will impart, however clearly I may write the directions.

THE "CLIMAX" LOZENGE MACHINE.

141

I see no obstacle which may not be overcome by anyone determined to succeed, even if he has no more to guide him in this branch than my book, in addition to his own reason and common sense.

This branch (with the exception of the cream lozenge) would only be important to small makers who have a wish to make up their own recipes for special lozenges, such as cough, medicated, or something out of the ordinary run, unless they were prepared to lay down plant in order to compete with big makers. The making of lozenges by hand, as far as the common sorts go, is a dead letter. Thirty years ago the lozenges were mixed, rolled, stamped and cut by hand, journeymen confectioners assisted by boys or women being employed for this purpose. Generally speaking, more men were employed in this department than in any other. It is not so now. As in the comfit room, machinery has been introduced and abolished the need for assistants. The latest arrangements in this way mix, roll, print and cut automatically. At first, they worked a little roughly, but at the moment of writing the engineers have so perfected their appliances that everything works smoothly, turning out goods almost perfect at a fraction of the cost for manual labour.

The latest machine of this kind I have seen is called the Climax. I think it embraces almost every improvement, being fitted with pinning, printing and embossing gear. To this machine is attached a patent friction pawl for working the pinning motion. By this, the skip can be altered without stopping the machine and can be adjusted to an exact skip, which cannot be done with ratchet wheels. I believe this is the only machine so fitted. The embossers can be made to emboss any design. The scrap delivery plate is adjustable and can be altered to prevent drag. The machine also cuts rings which formerly had always to be cut by hand. The printing block is fixed so near the cutters that the lozenges do not get out of truth, consequently the printing is exact and in the proper place. The goods are delivered direct on to the trays. This apparatus turns out two or three tons of lozenges per day, but is also made in smaller sizes. I should have liked to have shown a better drawing of this magnificent piece of engineering skill, but it is too large and complicated to give anything like an intelligent view of it on these small pages.

Dough Mixing Machine.

The luxury of making lozenges by machinery does not end with the machine principal—mixers and brakes must be used to provide sufficient paste to keep it employed. The above shows a mixer. The inside is covered with brass, the arms or beaters of gun metal. Studs are fixed at the bottom. The arms are double and set at angles—this prevents the paste from getting into a lump and ensures a thorough mixing in about eight minutes. The machines are made in different sizes.

The Brake.

This shows a brake or kneading machine, made of solid brass. The plates on which the paste works is also made of the same material. It is fitted with reversing gear, so can be worked from either side. The scraper which is attached, scrapes the rollers clean. A small machine of this kind will thoroughly knead 20 cwt. per day. attended to by one girl.

These machines are useful where a moderate quantity is required even where the larger lozenge machine is not used. I have perhaps said enough to show how a small maker would be handicapped by his bigger brethren with the apparatus at command. However, as I already mentioned where special mixings are required for which a special price can be got, the old-fashioned method would come in and the following instructions prove useful.

However simple the process is, one must have some tools. We cannot do without a sugar mill to grind the sugar, the old method of pestle and mortar being out of the question. These sugar mills are made in various sizes, at prices from £10 to £50. A small one would do for a decent trade. They are simple in construction, easily taken to pieces, and are regulated by screws, so that the sugar may be ground coarse or fine as required. There are several other purposes besides lozenge making for which ground sugar is required, such as sherbet, icing, drop dusting, &c., making the sugar mill a useful tool to both confectioners and pastry cooks. The larger sizes are fitted with fast and loose pulleys to be worked by steam power. The other tools necessary are two marble slabs, one to mix on, the other on which the paste may be rolled out in a sheet the thickness required and for cutting, the size of slab, say 4-ft. by 2-ft. 3-in. or larger with polished surface; a brass rolling pin about 2-ft. long, fitted with moveable gauge to regulate the thickness of the sheet; a palette knife about 18-in. long; a soft hand brush; a box containing starch powder; cutters of various sizes and shapes; stamp and dyes for motto lozenges, &c. These are the special tools but we shall also require trays and other odds and ends in a general way. The trays should be made of good dry pine, say about 3-ft. long, 2-ft. wide, and an inch deep. The timber should be a full half-inch thick when planed.

GENERAL DIRECTIONS.

A FIRST-CLASS lozenge is composed of best ground sugar mixed with a mucilage made from gum arabic or tragacanth. The finer the sugar is ground the more opaque and smooth the lozenge will be when finished. If a rough or transparent lozenge is required, such as fruit or cocoanut, the sugar should be ground coarse. This is known in the trade as grip or wire sugar. Dissolve the gum in hot water, in the proportions of one pound of gum and two pounds of water; if the gum be broken up small about twelve hours would be sufficient to reduce the whole to a liquid, then strain through a fine cloth. Put the sugar in a heap on the marble slab; make a bay in the centre into which pour in the gum mucilage, then commence with the palette knife to gradually work in the sugar from the edge just as if you were mixing up flour and water for bread for the oven; if for white lozenges add a pinch of blue to bleach the colour. During the process, if it kneads too dry and crummy, add a little more gum, or if too sticky a little more sugar. For coloured goods such as ginger, rose, musk, &c., add the colour and flavour with the gum, so as to be thoroughly incorporated during the process of mixing. When the paste gets very stiff, cut a portion off and roll it out into a sheet; put the gauges on the rolling pin, that it may come to the proper thickness, lift the sheet up two or three times and dust a little starch powder under it to keep it from sticking to the slab; during the operation turn it over three or four times with the knife and roller; dust over the face of the sheet a powder composed of half starch powder and half ground sugar; rub the sheet well with the ball of the hand to give it a smooth surface; use the brush freely to face it up; handle it as little as possible; commence to cut by taking a straight line over the left near the edge and however slowly continue to work in parallel lines; keep the cutter clean and empty it often into trays which have been dusted with starch powder. A cheap mucilage is made up of glucose and gelatine with gum which we shall mention in turn.

Should any readers attempt to make lozenges from these instructions, begin with cough, as the usual colour of them will not show the defects; at any rate, do not attempt white goods, or the result will surprise you— instead of a white you will, ten to one, get a dull sort of a dusty drab, which is the result of too much handling in preparation.

PEPPERMINT LOZENGES.

14-lbs. Powdered Sugar.   ½-oz. Oil of Peppermint.
1 quart Gum Mucilage.

PROCESS.—Put the powdered sugar in the middle of a marble slab; make a bay in the middle of the heap; pour in the gum mucilage and flavour; add a pinch of blue; work the whole up to a stiff paste; roll out portions into sheets to required thickness with gauged rolling pin; rub the ball of the hand lightly over the face of the sheet to smooth it ; now brush over the surface with hand brush and cut into lozenges with round cutter. Peppermint lozenges are made in many sizes and thickness ; put the goods on trays and stand in drying room till crisp and hard.

EXTRA STRONG PEPPERMINT LOZENGES.

7-lbs. Icing Sugar.   1-oz. Oil of Peppermint.
1Pint Gum Mucilage.

PROCESS.—Work together the sugar, gum and flavour with a pinch of blue into a stiff paste ; roll out into sheets and cut with round cutter ; pack into trays and stand in drying room till hard. The time required in drying room depends on the thickness of the goods. N. B.—Extra strongs are usually so stamped, which is done after the lozenges are cut and spread on trays. They differ in quality according to the quantity of mint added. For very best, Mitcham peppermint oil is used ; for cheaper kinds the American oil of peppermint is employed.

MUSK LOZENGES.

1 Drachm Best Musk.   28 lbs. Lozenge Paste.
6-oz.   Lime Water.   Carmine Colouring.

PROCESS.—Bruise the musk and mix it with the lime water ; put it in a vessel and let it stand in hot water for twenty-four hours ; mix with the above quantity of lozenge paste (prepared as already directed) ; colour with carmine and cut with small round cutters ; stamp each lozenge, musk. If an essence of musk be used, the lime water must be omitted

MUSK LOZENGES.

1 Drachm Pure Musk in Powder.   28-lbs. Lozenge Paste.
½-oz.   Tartaric Acid.   Carmine Colouring.

PROCESS.—When preparing the paste, work in the powdered musk and acid together with sufficient colour to give the batch the usual tint ; roll out in thin sheets and cut with oval or round cutter. A better quality is made by using more flavour and are stamped musk.

MUSK LOZENGES (Cheap).

28-lbs. Icing Sugar.   Essence of Musk.
Gum Mucilage.   Carmine Colour.

PROCESS.—Prepare the paste as usual ; roll out thin and cut with round cutter. It is hardly possible to give exact quantities of flavouring for the cheap musk lozenge now sold. Essence of musk, natural or artificial is used, and that so sparingly, that it would be difficult to tell what they were flavoured with.

ROSE LOZENGES.

| 14-lbs. | Lozenge Paste. | $\frac{1}{2}$-oz. Tartaric Acid. |
| 1 Drachm Virgin Otto of Roses. | | Carmine Colour. |

PROCESS.—Prepare paste in usual way ; add sufficient colour to make batch a light pink, roll out the sheets thin ; cut with small cutters and stamp rose.

ROSE LOZENGES (Cheap).

28-lbs. Lozenge Paste. $\frac{1}{2}$-oz. Artificial Otto of Roses.
Carmine Colouring.

PROCESS.—Like most lozenges, these goods are flavoured and coloured according to price, the process of course is the same.

GINGER LOZENGES.

14-lbs. Lozenge Paste. $\frac{1}{4}$-oz. Essence of Lemon.
$\frac{1}{2}$-oz. Jamacia Ginger, powdered. Yellow Colouring.

PROCESS.—As usual ; mix ingredients thoroughly together. Better or cheaper qualities by adding more or less ginger

CAYENNE LOZENGES.

14-lbs. Lozenge Paste. Otto of Roses.
$\frac{1}{2}$-oz. Best Extract of Cayenne. Carmine Colouring.

PROCESS.—As usual ; cut out with round, oval, or octagonal cutter.

COUGH LOZENGES, No. 1.

14-lbs. Lozenge Paste. $\frac{1}{2}$-oz. Oil of Aniseed.
1-lb. Block Juice. 1-oz. Tolu.
1 Drachm Morphia.

PROCESS.—As usual ; cut with small round, oval, or octagonal cutter, 40 to the oz.

℞ N.B.—Lozenges containing morphia or other scheduled poisons, should only be sold by chemists.

COUGH LOZENGES, No. 2.

14-lbs. Lozenge Paste. 1-oz. Ipecacuanha Powder.
1-lb. Block Liquorice. $\frac{1}{4}$-oz. Oil of Aniseed.
1 Drachm Morphia.

PROCESS.—As usual ; cut with small oval cutter.

COUGH LOZENGES, No. 3.

14-lbs. Lozenge Paste.　　　1-lb. Block Liquorice.
1-oz. Essence of Cough Drop.

PROCESS.—As usual ; cut with oval cutter, and stamp.　This is a very good lozenge.

N.B.—If the colour is not deep enough to fancy work in a little brown colouring.

CINNAMON LOZENGES.

14-lbs. Lozenge Paste.　　$\frac{1}{4}$-oz. Oil of Cinnamon.

PROCESS.—As usual ; mix thoroughly ; some houses colour to a pale brown, others to a shade of red.

MAGNESIA LOZENGES.

14-lbs. Lozenge Paste.　　$1\frac{1}{2}$-lbs. Magnesia.
Oil of Cassia Flavour.

PROCESS.—Before adding the gum to the paste, mix the sugar and magnesia together and sift them, then add the gum and oil of cassia ; cut with round cutter.

TOLU LOZENGES.

14-lbs. Lozenge Paste.　　2-oz. Tolu, dissolved in spirits of wine.

PROCESS.—As usual ; cut with oval cutter.

LAVENDER LOZENGES.

11 lbs.　Icing Sugar　　$\frac{1}{2}$-oz. Oil of Lavender.
1 Quart Gum Mucilage.　　Lavender Colouring.

PROCESS.—Mix ingredients thoroughly together ; roll out in thin sheets ; cut with fluted cutter.

ANISEED LOZENGES.

14-lbs. Lozenge Paste.　　$\frac{1}{4}$-oz. Oil of Aniseed.
Extract of Liquorice.

PROCESS.—As usual ; use as much liquorice as will make the batch brown.

IPECACUANHA LOZENGES.

14-lbs. Lozenge Paste.　　$\frac{1}{2}$-oz. Ipecacuanha Powder.
1-oz. Tartaric Acid.　　10 Drops Otto of Roses.

PROCESS.—As usual ; cut with small octagonal cutter.

CHALK LOZENGES.

7-lbs. Icing Sugar.   ¼-oz. Powdered Nutmeg.
¾-lb Prepared Chalk, Powdered. 1 Pint Gum Mucilage.

PROCESS.—Sift the sugar, chalk, and nutmeg together, then add the gum and make a paste in the usual way : cut with small cutter.

LETTUCE LOZENGES.

7-lbs. Lozenge Paste.   4-oz. Extract of Lettuce.

PROCESS.—As before directed.

PAREGORIC LOZENGES.

14-lbs. Lozenge Paste.   1-oz. Tartaric Acid.
1-oz. Tincture Paregoric   Carmine Colour.

PROCESS.—As usual.

ANTI-ACID OR HEARTBURN LOZENGES.

10-lbs. Icing Sugar.   4-oz. Magnesia.
½-lb. Prepared Chalk.   20   Drops Oil of Cinnamon.
Gum Mucilage.

PROCESS.—Mix by sifting the icing sugar, chalk and magnesia together dry, then add the gum and cinnamon to make a stiff paste ; roll out in thin sheets ; cut with small cutter.

NITRE LOZENGES.

14-lbs. Lozenge Paste.   4-oz. Powdered Nitre.
Lemon flavour.

PROCESS.—Work in the flavours, making a stiff paste ; roll out thin ; cut into lozenges with oval cutter.

QUININE LOZENGES.

7-lbs. Lozenge Paste.   ¼-oz. Sulphate of Quinine.

PROCESS.—As usual ; oval cutters.

ANTI-BILIOUS LOZENGES.

8-lbs.   Lozenge Paste.   6-oz. Magnesia.
6 Drachms Turkey Rhubarb.   1½-oz. Carbonate of Soda.
20 Drops Oil of Cinnamon.

PROCESS.—Thoroughly mix in the ingredients as usual ; cut with small cutter.

149

LONG LIFE LOZENGES.

8-lbs. Lozenge Paste.   ½-oz.Turkey Rhubarb.
4-oz. Jamacia Ginger, Powdered.

PROCESS.—As usual.

OFFICIAL RECEIPES of the BRITISH PHARMACOPŒIA.

LOZENGES.

Preparation with Fruit Basis.

Take five hundred times the quantity of the drug ordered for one lozenge ; mix it intimately with fifteen and a half ounces (or four hundred and thirty-nine and a half grammes) of Refined Sugar, in fine powder, and three hundred grains (or nineteen and a half grammes) of Gum Acacia, in powder.   Make the mixture into a paste with one fluid ounce and a quarter (or thirty-five and a half cubic centimetres) of Mucilage of Gum Acacia and two ounces (or fifty-six and three quarter grammes) of the black-currant paste of commerce previously softened with boiling distilled water, adding any additional Distilled Water that may be necessary.   Divide the mass into five hundred equal lozenges. Dry them in a hot-air chamber at a moderate temperature.

Preparation with Rose Basis.

Take five hundred times the quantity of the drug ordered for one lozenge ; mix it intimately with seventeen and a half ounces (or four hundred and ninety-six grammes) of Refined Sugar, in fine powder, and three hundred grains (or nineteen and a half grammes) of Gum Acacia, in powder.   Make the mixture into a paste with five fluid drachms (or seventeen and a half cubic centimetres) of Mucilage of Gum Acacia and a sufficient quantity of the official Rose Water.   Divide the mass into five hundred equal lozenges.   Dry them in a hot-air chamber at a moderate temperature.

Preparation with Simple Basis.

Take five hundred times the quantity of the drug ordered for one lozenge ; mix it intimately with seventeen and a half ounces (or four hundred and ninety-six grammes) of Refined Sugar, in fine powder, and three hundred grains (or nineteen and a half grammes) of Gum Acacia, in powder. Make the mixture into a paste with one fluid ounce and a quarter (or thirty-five and a half cubic centimetres) of Mucilage of Gum Acacia and a sufficient quantity of Distilled Water. Divide the mass into five hundred equal lozenges. Dry them in a hot-air chamber at a moderate temperature.

Preparation with Tolu Basis.

Take five hundred times the quantity of the drug ordered for one lozenge ; dissolve what salts of alkaloids may be ordered in three fluid drachms (or ten and a half cubic centimetres) of Distilled Water ; mix the solution intimately with seventeen ounces (or four hundred and eighty-two grammes) of Refined Sugar, in fine powder, and three hundred grains (or nineteen and a half grammes) of Gum Acacia in powder. Thoroughly incorporate with the mixture any other drugs ordered for the lozenges, and three fluid drachms (or ten and a half cubic centimetres) of Tincture of Balsam of Tolu. Make into a paste with one fluid ounce and a quarter (or thirty-five and a half cubic centimetres) of Mucilage of Gum Acacia and any additional Distilled Water that may be necessary. Divide the mass into five hundred equal lozenges. Dry them in a hot-air chamber at a moderate temperature.

TROCHISCUS ACIDI BENZOICI.

Benzoic Acid Lozenge.

	IMPERIAL.	METRIC.
Benzoic Acid	½ grain. ...	... 0·0324 gramme.

Mix with the Fruit Basis to form a Lozenge.

TROCHISCUS ACIDI CARBOLICI.

Phenol Lozenge.

	IMPERIAL.	METRIC.
Phenol	... I grain. ...	... 0·648 gramme.

Mix with the Tolu Basis to form a Lozenge.

TROCHISCUS ACIDI TANNICI.

Tannic Acid Lozenge.

	IMPERIAL.	METRIC.
Tannic Acid	½ grain. ...	... 0·0324 gramme.

Mix with the Fruit Basis to form a Lozenge.

151

TROCHISCUS BISMUTHI COMPOSITUS.

Compound Bismuth Lozenge.

	IMPERIAL.	METRIC.
Bismouth Oxycarbonate	2 grains. ...	0·1296 gramme.
Heavy Magnesium Carbonate	2 grains. ...	0·1296 gramme.
Precipitated Calcium Carbonate · ...	4 grains. ...	0·2592 gramme.

Mix with the Rose Basis to form a Lozenge.

TROCHISCUS CATECHU.

Catechu Lozenge.

	IMPERIAL.	METRIC.
Catechu	1 grain. ...	... 0·0648 gramme.

Mix with Simple Basis to form a Lozenge.

TROCHISCUS EUCALYPTI GUMMI.

Eucalyptus Gum Lozenge.

	IMPERIAL.	METRIC.
Eucalyptus Gum	1 grain. ...	... 0·0648 gramme.

Mix with the Fruit Basis to form a Lozenge.

TROCHISCUS FERRI REDACTI.

Reduced Iron Lozenge.

	IMPERIAL.	METRIC.
Reduced Iron	1 grain. ...	... 0·0648 gramme.

Mix with the Simple Basis to form a Lozenge.

TROCHISCUS GUAIACI RESINÆ.

Guaiacum Resin Lozenge.

	IMPERIAL.	METRIC.
Guaiacum Resin	3 grains. ...	... 0·1944 gramme.

Mix with the Fruit Basis to form a Lozenge.

TROCHISCUS IPECACUANHÆ.

Ipecacuanha Lozenge.

	IMPERIAL.	METRIC.
Ipecacuanha Root, in powder ...	¼ grain. ...	... 0·0162 gramme.

Mix with the Fruit Basis to form a Lozenge.

TROCHISCUS KRAMERIÆ.

Krameria Lozenge
Synonym—Rhatany Lozenge.

	IMPERIAL.	METRIC.
Extract of Krameria	1 grain. ...	... 0·0648 gramme.

Mix with the Fruit Basis to form a Lozenge.

T.ROCHISCUS KRAMERIÆ ET COCAINÆ

Krameria and Cocaine Lozenge.

Synonym—Rhatany and Cocaine Lozenge.

	IMPERIAL.	METRIC.
Extract of Krameria... ...	1 grain. ...	0·0648 gramme.
Cocaine Hydrochloride	1-20th grain.	0·00324 gramme.

Mix with the Fruit Basis to form a Lozenge

TROCHISCUS MORPHIN.E.

Morphine Lozenge.

	IMPERIAL.	METRIC.
Morphine Hydrochloride ...	1-36th grain. ...	0·0018 gramme.

Mix with the Tolu Basis to form a Lozenge.

TROCHISCUS MORPHINÆ ET IPECACUANHÆ

Morphine and Ipecacuanha Lozenge.

	IMPERIAL.	METRIC.
Morphine Hydrochloride ...	1-36th grain. ...	0·0018 gramme.
Ipecacuanha Root, in powder	1-12th grain. ...	0·0054 gramme.

Mix with the Tolu Basis to form a Lozenge.

TROCHISCUS POTASSII CHLORATIS.

Potassium Chlorate Lozenge.

	IMPERIAL.	METRIC.
Potassium Chlorate...	3 grains. ...	0·1944 gramme.

Mix with the Rose Basis to form a Lozenge.

TROCHISCUS SANTONINI.

Santonin Lozenge.

	IMPERIAL.	METRIC.
Santonin	1 grain. ...	0·0648 gramme.

Mix with the Simple Basis to form a Lozenge.

TROCHISCUS SODII BICARBONATIS.

Sodium Bicarbonate Lozenge.

	IMPERIAL.	METRIC.
Sodium Bicarbonate...	3 grains. ...	0·1944 gramme.

Mix with the Rose Basis to form a Lozenge.

153

TROCHISCUS SULPHURIS,
Sulphur Lozenge.

	IMPERIAL.	METRIC.
Precipitated Sulphur	2500 grains.	162 grammes.
Acid Potassium Tartrate, in powder ...	500 grains.	32·4 grammes.
Refined Sugar, in powder	4000 grains.	259·2 grammes.
Gum Acacia, in powder	500 grains.	32·4 grammes.
Tincture of Orange	500 minims.	29·5 cubic centimetres.
Mucilage of Gum Acacia	500 minims.	29·5 cubic centimetres.

Mix the Tincture of Orange with the powders; add the Mucilage of Gum Acacia to form a suitable mass. Divide into 500 lozenges. Dry them in a hot-air chamber at a moderate temperature. Each lozenge contains 5 grains (0·324 gramme) of Precipitated Sulphur.

MIXINGS FOR CHEAP LOZENGES.

THE high price of gum, no doubt, accounts to a great extent for substitutes used in making a lozenge paste for cheap goods. The formulæ differ with different makers. The writer knows lozenge hands who at present are making a paste by simply melting glucose and working as much ground sugar into it as possible. Others use glucose and gelatine, and some use a mixture of gum, gelatine and glucose. Readers who are called upon to make lozenges, where price is the only consideration, will find the following workable and answering this purpose. However, if this is still too expensive, the gum may be left out, then the gelatine, but I hardly think anything cheaper than glucose can be found, and this will do at a pinch by itself, but the quantity must be increased.

CHEAP COMMON PEPPERMINTS.

28-lbs. Icing Sugar.	1-lb. Gum.
2-lbs. Glucose.	1 Quart Water.
1-lb. Gelatine.	Oil of Peppermint.

PROCESS.—Soak the gelatine until it will take no more water; dissolve the gum in the water; warm the glucose and dissolve the gelatine in it, then mix the dissolved gum, glucose and gelatine together; put the sugar in a heap on the slab; make a bay in the centre and pour in the mixture; add the oil of peppermint, working up the whole into a stiff paste, adding more ground sugar if required, then roll the batch out in sheets; cut into lozenges; place them on trays; put them in the drying room till hard. Musk, rose, and any other sort may be knocked up in a similar manner.

CREAM LOZENGES.

THE following is a capital mixing for cream lozenges of every description. This class of goods can be made on a small scale at a profit—no drying room is required, and the quality of the goods depends entirely on the manipulation. The operator must use great care and discretion when handling the colours. Bright, but deep tints are required, at the same time heavy, solid colouring is to be avoided. Nearly all fruit flavourings require a little acid to throw them up, which must be ground to a fine powder and mixed with some dry sugar, then sifted together. This will make it permeate the batch better and easier. In making white dissolve a touch of blue in the water (always work your white first on the slab). Keep the other colours on different parts, so that one does not smear the other. Goods are often spoiled through carelessness in this respect. This paste can be made into a thousand and one different shapes, colours, blends, and varieties, such as blocks, rolls bars, nuggets, cocoanut quarters, lozenges, pic-nics, cubes, plain and parti-coloured forms of every kind.

As stated under various headings through this work, no good purpose could be served by a wearisome repetition of mixings on the same lines. I give the principal articles made in each class and surely new departures will suggest themselves to the readers. These goods are always changing. Should the inventive faculty not be fully developed in any particuiar case, I should recommend the subject to study the windows of confectioners and buy a sample of anything he would like to make, as I find those who cannot conceive for themselves are wonderfully good imitators.

CREAM LOZENGE PASTE.

28-lbs. Ground Sugar.	$\frac{1}{2}$-lb. Gelatine
3-lbs. Glucose.	$\frac{1}{2}$-Pint Water.

PROCESS.—Soak the gelatine in water till quite soft; put one pound of the icing sugar with the half pint of water in a clean pan and bring it to the boil; remove the pan from the fire and stir in the glucose; replace the pan on the fire until just hot enough that you could easily bear your hand in the syrup, then take it off and stir in the gelatine till quite dissolved and thoroughly mixed; put the bulk of the icing sugar in a heap on the slab, making a bay in the centre, into which pour the mixture together with any colour or flavour required, then commence to work in the sugar from round the edge first and so on, till the whole is worked up into a stiffish paste; it is then ready for the various purposes. Goods made from this paste will be ready for sale in a few hours; they will soon get hard enough in a dry workshop, a hot room is not necessary.

RASPBERRY CREAM LOZENGES.

PROCESS.—Make the paste as above directed; work in sufficient carnation paste to give the batch a bright red tint (be sure the colour itself is good and brilliant); mix in $1\frac{1}{2}$-oz. of tartaric acid and two ounces of best raspberry essence to each $\frac{1}{2}$-cwt.; roll out into sheets the thickness required and cut with oval cutter; pack on trays and stand them in a dry place for a few hours, when they may be weighed and boxed. Use the dust very sparingly during the process; cut firmly; keep the cutter clean and dry, emptying it every few strokes.

VANILLA CREAM LOZENGES.

PROCESS.—Prepare the paste as described adding a little dissolved blue to bleach the colour white; use two ounces of extract or essence of vanilla to every $\frac{1}{2}$-cwt. batch with one ounce of acid; sift the acid amongst the dry sugar before putting in the mucilage; roll out into sheets and cut with oval cutter.

CHOCOLATE CREAM LOZENGES.

PROCESS.—Work into the cream paste, already described, three pounds of pure cocoa (melted) to every batch of $\frac{1}{2}$-cwt., colour to shade with chocolate brown colouring; add the colouring when the batch has been partly mixed, not too much at a time, as some of these colours are very powerful; see that the cocoa is all melted before putting it with the sugar. In melting cocoa do not add water or it will be spoiled, simply put it in a saucepan and stand it on the stove plate ; it will soon run to a syrup.

MIXED CREAM LOZENGES.

PROCESS.—From the same paste. See that your colours are the very best and the flavours concentrated ; use powdered acid with raspberry, lemon, orange and rose ; the other flavours usually made of almond, chocolate and vanilla ; in the first two no acid, the latter optional. The names will suggest the colours to be used. For all practical purposes, four colours are enough, lemon, vanilla, raspberry, and chocolate. In mixing colours, always have the largest portion white, they show up the others. Use as little dust as possible during any operation with this paste, it takes the gloss off.

COCOANUT CREAM LOZENGES.

28-lbs. Ground Sugar.　　　　5-lbs. Cocoanut, grated fine.
Carnation Paste Colouring.

PROCESS.—See that the cocoanuts are fresh and milky ; break them ; throw the milk away and pare off all the brown skin, then grate them finely ; put the sugar in a heap on the slab ; make a hole in the middle ; put in the nut and commence to work the whole into a paste of medium stiffness ; the size of the nuts will determine the exact quantity of sugar —you may want a little more or have too much—knead in just sufficient to make a paste pliable, though stiff. The nuts should be fresh and used as soon as they are opened. No liquid is necessary, except that which exudes from the grated kernel. Lozenges made according to these instructions will keep soft, moist, sweet, and of good flavour for a long time. Divide the batch into two portions, one portion double the size of the other ; colour the smaller portion with carnation paste, a deep tint ; leave the larger portion white, then roll out part of the white into a sheet the required thickness ; put it aside, then roll out part of the red into a sheet ; the red should only be half the thickness of the white sheet ; lay the red sheet evenly on the top of the white and press them together, then run the rolling pin over the two until the exact thickness is obtained ; dust very sparingly and cut with oval cutter ; put them on trays in a dry place and they will be ready for sale in a few hours.

COCOANUT CREAM ROLLS.

PROCESS.—The same mixing for paste as for cocoanut cream lozenges; colour a small portion a deep tint with carnation paste; work in a little more sugar into the red to absorb the moisture of the colour so as to make the red the same consistency as the white; roll out both the red and white proportions into sheets, considerably thicker than for lozenges; place the white in this case on top of the red; press the two together, then roll them round carefully to thickness required.

IMITATION COCOANUT QUARTERS.

PROCESS.—Use the same mixing as for cocoanut cream lozenges; colour a small portion with chocolate brown to imitate the skin of the cocoanut; roll out the white paste to the thickness of the white portion of the natural cocoanut kernel; roll out the brown paste very thin to imitate the skin of the cocoanut; lay the white paste on top of the brown; run the rolling pin over the sheet, then cut off small pieces, triangular shape, and press them in a cocoanut shell to take the shape. The cocoanut shells for moulding should be carefully sawn into quarters; the paste should be sufficiently stiff to keep the shape; let the paste stand in the moulds a little time to harden. In the wholesale, where the demand is great, iron moulds, of course, are preferable.

BLACK CURRANT LOZENGES.

14-lbs. Powdered Sugar. 1-oz. Tartaric Acid.
6-lbs. Black Currant Paste. Gum Mucilage.
Black Currant Colouring.

PROCESS.—Put the sugar on the slab; make a bay in the centre; pour in the gum; add the acid and black currant paste; mix the whole thoroughly into a stiff paste adding more sugar if required; dust the slab with a mixture of half sugar and half starch powder; roll the sheets out one-eighth of an inch thick; cut with round cutters; pack on trays and stand the goods in a drying room till hard.

Coltsfoot Rock Machine.

COLTSFOOT ROCK.

16-lbs. Ground Sugar.	1 Quart Gum Mucilage.
½-lb. Block Liquorice.	¼ oz. Oil of Aniseed
3-oz. Gum Dragon.	¼ oz. Essence of Lemon.

1-oz. Essence of Coltsfoot.

PROCESS.—Soak the gum dragon in water for twenty-four hours and press it through a sieve ; put the sugar in a heap on the slab ; make a hole in the centre ; pour in the gum, liquorice (which has been previously dissolved), aniseed and lemon ; make up the whole and knead to a very stiff paste, working in more sugar if required, then pass through machine on trays ; stand in the drying room till hard enough for packing.

BATH PIPE.

PROCESS.—Prepare the same paste as for coltsfoot rock leaving out the essence of lemon ; break off a small piece ; roll it out with the hands until nearly the thickness wanted then use a long, flat board to finish rolling ; press very lightly on the board and the pipe will be equal in thickness the whole length with a smooth surface ; spread the goods on trays ; put them in the drying room till hard. The paste must be kneaded as stiff as possible, or the pipes will get flat while in the drying room, as they lie in one position till hard.

ROSE, LEMON, AND PEPPERMINT PIPES.

THESE pipes are made from lozenge paste worked up very stiff ; flavour and colour as name indicates ; colour the rose with carmine, flavour with otto of roses ; lemon, colour with saffron paste, flavour with essence of lemon ; for peppermint, work in a little blue to make a perfect white ; flavour with oil of peppermint ; proceed in exactly the same way as for bath pipes ; finish with flat stick.

REGENT PIPE.

THIS pipe is striped with different colours. The body and stripes are made with lozenge paste, prepared in the same manner as bath pipe ; cut off little pieces and colour red, blue or yellow ; spread out the white body and lay the stripes on alternately, practically the same as directed for boiled sugars ; squeeze them out in lengths with the hands ; roll them round, twisting the stripes spiral shape, and finish with flat stick.

ON LIQUORICE GOODS.

To manufacture this class of goods successfully requires distinct and heavy plant, including steam melting and mixing pans, sifting and mixing machines as well as powerful presses.

The process of making, drying and preparing for the market is long and tedious, the best brands such as "Solazzi" and "Corigliano" occupying several weeks if not months from the pressing of the root till the delivery of the liquorice stick. The commoner sorts made from the block juice are prepared more quickly but still require some time in the drying room.

Makers of repute are comparatively few and confine themselves almost solely to producing variety from the root in question, their mixings and manipulations are their own and in most cases the result of years of experiment. No useful purpose would be served by giving details of processes which mean a large outlay, as those interested to this extent would be better guided by a practical man having the latest experience in this particular branch.

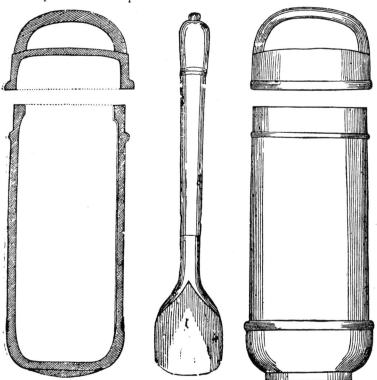

Pewter Ice Cream Freezer and Spatula.

ON ICE CREAM MAKING.

ICES of various descriptions are now almost considered a branch of our modern retail confectioners, in fact, during the summer months, many of our best shops look to this for the greater part of the takings. Since the introduction of the frozen custard into this country it has been the favourite refresher with a great portion of the public but especially the young. At one time the trade was almost exclusively in the hands of foreigners, but at the present moment they only go to swell the great army of purveyors in this branch. The vast amount of money spent weekly on ice cream, not only in hot weather, but all the year round would seem incredible were it tabulated.

Many gigantic places in London and other large towns have been reared on the profits made in making and vending this commodity, while moderate fortunes are made every season, even now, by wide-a-wake jacks who send out numbers of barrows attended to by their own countrymen. Competition is now perhaps greater than at any former period and although fancy prices cannot be got for common stuff, yet there is a good profit to be obtained on good and well made cream. It is most important for a good trade to have the quality A1. Youngsters will walk a long way to get what they want to their liking, and are generally good judges of what is best and *who* sells it. That is a fact, most people with my experience will admit, and to this fact I attribute the success of the strangers. They generally make ice superior to Englishmen because they have more patience to work it better with the spatula and are more particular in the preparation. There are many machines in the market for the rapid freezing and beating of the custard which shopkeepers employ to save labour, and, to a large extent, spoil the product. I have yet to see the mechanical contrivance equal to the old fashioned method in producing smooth, soft, still, firm, mellow creams, which are served up in the restaurants and cafés owned by foreigners. Few, if any of them, use a machine. One can see the pewter freezer with the long handled spatula sticking out at the top, standing at one end of, or underneath the counter, while in a good many establishments owned by Englishmen we find the cheap American machine, which grinds and freezes the contents by its rapid motion to a hard, frosty, congealed mass.

Still, confectioners want to know why Italian and Swiss jacks get most of the trade. With ice cream, as with everything else, the writer is of opinion the best sells best and pays best. During the summer months the sweet trade is quiet. If we want to add an adjunct to our business, let us do it well and cater with a good article, at least as good as our neighbours. It is the duty of your humble servant to give a selection of all the mixings and processes, the better processes and qualities of course I recommend, but where circumstances and conditions make it imperative to be both economical and quick, the reader will have the opportunity of finding the mixing and process in its place.

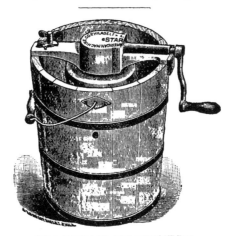

ICE CREAM MACHINERY.

AMERICAN ICE CREAM FREEZERS.

We have in the market at present a large selection of freezing machines at moderate prices. The contrivances are both ingenious and capable of producing a frozen mixture in a short time of fair quality. America is at the front as far as prices are concerned, and, although perfect in construction and calculated to do all that is said for them, the specimens I have seen from that country are of rather a gingerbread type. The freezing pots are made of strong sheet tin, some of them of copper tinned inside. The iron work is galvanized and the tubs are made of white cedar wood. My objections to these machines are that the pots are too thin, thereby freezing the mixtures too quickly, notwithstanding the rapid motion of the beater which works inside the freezer, the cream when frozen is roughish. It would not be possible to make a first-class ice cream in these machines, but they are cheap, effective, and quick, and will do for a third rate trade.

11

CROWN FREEZING MACHINES.

SINGLE.

DOUBLE.

THESE English machines are much stronger and are altogether better adapted for the purpose. The freezers are made of best pewter. The mechanical parts are simple, strong, and effective, while the tubs are well made of oak—they are much dearer than the foreign make. If we consider durability, they would come out in the end much cheaper, besides pewter is much preferable as a metal for freezing. In it the custard gets well mixed and beat up before it begins to congeal, as the pewter pots are so much thicker than the Yankee tin ones. Still the ices made by machine, at least any I have yet seen, are not equal to those made in an ordinary pewter freezing pot. In this case the process is slower, but the result can be made to far excel that by the quicker method. Zinc freezers are also largely used and are very cheap, they are not so durable, at the same time, they do very well for common or custard ice cream. When making ices from the fruit or when acid is used, it is imperative that pewter freezers be used, as the acids act upon zinc, destroying the delicate flavour and colour of the cream. When using a freezer a tub and spatula are also necessary.

It is more economical to buy the tub with the freezer—then it is the proper size; if too large, there is a waste of ice; if too small, the cream gets soft very quickly. A pewter spatula is also necessary—a flat stick sharpened at the point is not strong enough to scrape the frozen mixture from the sides and bottom of the freezer, and a knife scratches the pewter and is dangerous.

The Schafer Patent.

THE above machine is not only ornamental but useful, and fills a gap in shops where females are the only assistants. Cream and water ices may be frozen by this process equal in quality to that made by many machines requiring a deal of manual labour in preparing and turning, and this process has the advantage of keeping the contents in prime condition for a long time in the hottest weather.

The process is quick and clean, also economical in the use of both ice and salt; where the sale is moderate and intermittant with a lack of physical energy the qualities of "The Schafer" will be appreciated as it requires little preparation and no turning.

Directions are supplied with every machine. They are sold by Messrs Clarke, Nicholls & Coombes, and machine makers generally.

HOW TO MAKE ICE CREAM.

PREPARE a custard or water mixture from any of the following recipes as directed; pour the mixing into the freezer and place it in a tub; now fill up the space between the freezer and the tub with ice broken in pieces, about one inch and a half in diameter, mixed with coarse salt; fill up the tub till within $2\frac{1}{2}$ inches from the top of the freezer; put on the cover and proceed to turn the freezer round; it will be rather stiff at first, but will soon get freer, when the cover may be removed and the frozen mixture, which adheres to the sides and bottom be scraped off with spatula.

The action of the freezer will now be so easy that it may be turned very fast with little exertion; keep the sides and bottom free from frozen mixture, well mixing the hard scrapings in the body of the custard as it begins to stiffen; use the spatula to beat it up smooth; keep turning and beating until the spatula will stand upright in the cream when the process is finished. If the cream is to be served out in glasses during the day, drain off part of the water from the tub which the action of the salt upon the ice causes, by means of the tap fixed in the bottom; also scrape the sides down from time to time, this will keep it from getting hard and lumpy. N.B.—When freezing by machine, simply put the custard or other mixing in the freezing pot; place it in position; fill tub with ice and coarse freezing salt, and turn the handle till frozen.

CUSTARD ICE CREAM, No. 1.

2 quarts New Milk.	6 or 8 Fresh Eggs.
1-lb. White Sugar.	2-oz. Fresh Butter.
$\frac{1}{4}$ to $\frac{1}{2}$ oz. Vanilla Essence.	

PROCESS.—Well whisk the eggs with a fork or whisk then stir them into the new milk adding the butter and sugar; put the whole into a

165

clean pan and place on a slow clear fire; keep stirring all the time well rubbing the bottom of the pan until the mixture comes to the boiling point when it will get thickish; be careful that it does not quite boil or it will curdle; remove the pan from the fire and strain through a fine hair sieve; stand it aside until cold; when quite cold put the custard in the freezer adding the vanilla and freeze either by hand or machine as directed; a tinge of saffron would make the cream look richer.

CUSTARD ICE CREAM, No. 2.

1 quart New Milk.	$\frac{1}{2}$-lb. White Sugar.
2 Fresh Eggs.	$\frac{1}{2}$-oz. Fine Gelatine.
$\frac{1}{4}$-oz. Vanilla Flavour.	

PROCESS.—Whisk the eggs and mix them well with the new milk and sugar; put the whole in a clean pan on a slow fire and stir until it comes nearly to the boil then remove the pan from the fire and stir in the gelatine until it dissolves; stand aside until quite cold; add vanilla just before freezing.

This cream is usually preferred being smoother and having a better body, though only in appearance.

CUSTARD ICE CREAM, No. 3.

1 quart New Milk.	$\frac{1}{2}$-lb. Sugar.
1 pint Water.	$\frac{1}{2}$-oz. Gelatine.
$\frac{1}{4}$-oz. Vanilla.	

PROCESS.—Mix the milk, water and sugar together in a clean pan; put the whole on a slow fire; stir occasionally until nearly the boiling point then remove the pan from the fire and stir in the gelatine till dissolved; strain and freeze as directed when cold.

This is a fairly good cream though not rich; in freezing, be careful it does not get lumpy; do not freeze too rapidly and keep the sides of the freezer well scraped stirring the hard edges well into the body; the poorer the custard the more likely it is to get icey.

CHEAP ICE CREAM.

| 3 quarts New Milk. | 2-lbs. White Sugar. |
| $\frac{1}{4}$-lb. Farina or Corn Starch. | |

PROCESS.—Dissolve the farina in part of the milk then mix the whole together and simmer on a slow fire (not boil) until it thickens; remove the pan from the fire, stand aside till cold, and then freeze.

N.B.—In practice, the custard is usually made at night and frozen first thing in the morning. However, that depends upon circumstances and run of business. It is almost superfluous to add that these formulæ may be altered a little; the addition of eggs and other good things will always improve the quality, and when eggs are cheap one or two in the common creams would be much appreciated no doubt.

RASPBERRY ICE CREAM.

2 quarts New Milk.	2-oz. Fresh Butter.
1 lb. White Sugar.	Raspberry Flavour.
6 Fresh Eggs.	Carmine Colour.

PROCESS.—Whisk the eggs and stir them into the milk adding the sugar and butter, then heat the whole in a clean pan almost to the boiling point keeping the contents well stirred; remove the pan from the fire strain through a hair sieve; when cold, add the flavour and colour to a rose pink not too heavy. Freeze as already directed.

RASPBERRY ICE CREAM, No. 2.

1 quart New Milk.	2-oz. Thin Gelatine.
½-lb. White Sugar.	Raspberry Flavour.
Carmine Colour.	

PROCESS.—Mix the milk with the sugar and bring it to the boiling point; remove the pan from the fire; add the gelatine and stir till dissolved; stand aside till cold then colour flavour and freeze in the usual way.

LEMON CREAM ICE.

2 quarts New Milk.	1-oz. Thin Gelatine.
1-lb. White Sugar.	Juice of 2 Lemons.
3 Fresh Eggs.	Saffron Colour.

PROCESS.—Whisk the eggs and stir them into the new milk together with the sugar in a clean pan; bring the whole to the boiling point; strain and stand aside till cold then add the lemon juice; colour to a soft yellow and freeze as directed.

AMERICAN ICE CREAM.

3 quarts Best Cream. ¾-lb. White Sugar.
¼ to ½-oz. Extract of Vanilla.

PROCESS.—The above is a real Yankee recipe. Dissolve the sugar in the cream; add the vanilla; as soon as the sugar is dissolved freeze as directed; it is unnecessary to apply heat at all to the custard. This mixture increases in bulk to almost double during the process of freezing.

DESSERT ICES.

THIS is the better class or after-dinner ices. The variety is so numerous that to chronicle the names would fill a small volume. Let it suffice to enumerate the more popular kinds which will almost be sufficient for any purpose the reader may require, because, with a little variation in the ingredients and flavours the variety may be worked out to any extent. Wines, fruits, pulp, extracts and essences used in this class may be altered, increased, or reduced to suit any particular palate. The excellence of any dish is judged by the taste and palate to whom it is served. Let it be noted that fruit, pulp and other preserved goods that are heavier than the cream should be mixed in when the custard is partly frozen or, naturally, they would fall to the bottom, the set cream will hold them in position and the process of mixing, whether with beater or spatula, will distribute them throughout the body, Wines and spirits must be added when the custard is cold; when adding acid or lemon juice be careful not to curdle.

DESSERT ICE CREAM.

GENERAL RECIPE.

1 quart Fresh Cream.   4 or 5 Fresh Eggs, according to size.
8-oz. Powdered Sugar.

PROCESS.—Whisk the eggs then stir them in the cream adding the sugar; put the whole in a clean copper pan; place it on a slow but clear fire stir it until it nearly boils when it will get thick then strain through a fine hair sieve; stand aside until cold; add the flavouring ingredients and freeze according to instructions already given.

N.B.—This cream will be understood to form the body for the following flavours.

RASPBERRY ICE CREAM.

RUB fresh raspberries through a fine sieve; add a pint of this pulp to every quart of the above custard; pour it into the freezer; when the custard has been partly frozen colour with a little cochineal and finish the process.

STRAWBERRY ICE CREAM.

THIS fruit is prepared exactly the same as raspberries—scarlet strawberries are the best for the purpose—a small pinch of citric acid or the juice of a lemon will improve either of them; add, when partly frozen, colour lighter than for raspberry.

PINEAPPLE ICE CREAM.

An ordinary sized pineapple to every two quarts of cream should be prepared by peeling and bruising through a fine sieve; add to the custard when partly frozen the juice of a lemon; colour with saffron water and finish freezing.

COCOANUT ICE CREAM.

PEEL and grate a small fresh cocoanut for every quart of custard to be frozen; when the custard is taken from the fire, stir in the cocoanut, then strain; freeze when cold.

PARISIAN COFFEE ICE CREAM.

MAKE a strong infusion of Mocha coffee and add half-a-pint, in which is dissolved 3-oz. sugar to every quart of custard to be frozen.

N.B.—When infusions of any kind are added to the custard, it is necessary to sweeten them with a little extra sugar, so as not to reduce the standard sweetness of the custard.

TEA ICE CREAM.

ADD to every quart of cream half-a-pint of a strong infusion of good black tea.

CHOCOLATE ICE CREAM.

MELT near the fire 4-oz. of pure cocoa paste with a little butter; add this quantity to every quart of custard when partly frozen.

NOYEAU ICE CREAM.

To every quart of custard add one glass of noyeau and one glass of sherry just before freezing.

ALMOND ICE CREAM.

BLANCHE and grate 4-oz. Jordan and 1-oz. of bitter almonds; add this to each quart of custard, prepared as directed, and freeze.

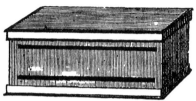

Neapolitan Ice Box.

MIX with one pint of water the yolks of fourteen eggs and two glasses of maraschino wine; add sugar to taste; place the whole in a clean pan: put it on a slow fire and stir all the time until near the boil; remove the pan from the fire and well whisk the mixture until it foams, then pour it into a Neapolitan ice box; place the box in a tub surrounded with small pieces of ice, well mixed with freezing salt, for four or five hours, or till required; when wanted, take out the box and dip it in tepid water for a second; remove the cover and the block will drop out. Part of this ice may be scooped out and the space filled up with cream custard ice, if preferred.

NEAPOLITAN ICE PARTI-COLOURED.

PREPARE custard or water ices two or three different colours and flavours; freeze them, but not too hard, then take the Neapolitan box and spread a layer of red (raspberry), then a layer of white (vanilla), and on top a layer of yellow (lemon), filling up the box; place the box in the ice tub surrounded with broken ice and salt for a couple of hours; it will then be hard, when it may be removed from the box; cut into slices and serve.

LEMON WATER ICES.

2	Fresh Eggs, whites only.	¼-oz.	Tartaric Acid.
¾-lb.	Powdered Sugar.	1	Quart Water.
	Essence of Lemon.		

PROCESS.—Whisk the whole together and freeze as already directed.

N.B.—When making the mixture for water ices the palate will be a good guide ; make the preparation stronger than if required for drinking as freezing considerably reduces the flavour.

LEMON WATER ICE (Best).

THIS is made precisely the same as last but instead of using essence of lemon, squeeze the juice of eight and the peel of three pared very thin, to every quart of water with the whites of three eggs and powdered sugar to taste ; strain and freeze.

RASPBERRY WATER ICE.

PROCESS.—Squeeze the raspberries through a fine sieve ; use half a pound of this pulp to every quart of water with a pinch of citric acid and the whites of two eggs, sugar to palate.

STRAWBERRY WATER ICE.

PROCESS.—Prepare in exactly the same way ; the strawberries should be in good condition. NOTF.—Any kind of fruit pulp may be used for flavouring ices the process is the same. Apples, pears and other hard fruits require boiling before being strained.

CHERRY WATER ICE.

PROCESS.—Bruise in a mortar a pound of Kentish cherries with the stones ; add the juice of two lemons, half a pint of water, one pint of clarified sugar, one glass of noyeau and a little colour ; strain and freeze.

ICES FROM JAMS.

When fresh fruit is not to be had jams may be used ; although not so good as fresh fruit they are to be preferred to artificial flavours. Dissolve the jams in boiling water, strain through a sieve and use in the same proportiou as fruit pulp.

NESSELRODE OR ICE PUDDING.

PREPARE a custard of one pint of cream, half a pint of milk, the yolks of six eggs and half a pound of sugar ; flavour with a stick of vanilla and one ounce of sweet almonds powdered ; stew over a slow clear fire and stir until it gets thick being careful not to let it boil ; stand aside till cold then add a wine glassful of brandy ; partially freeze then add two ounces of raisins and four ounces of preserved fruits cut small ; mix well and mould. (Basket shape generally used).

Ice Moulds.

THE above shows a small group of moulds used for ices. They are made in a great variety of designs and sizes, usually of bright pewter some copper, the former is preferable being easily cleaned and does not corrode. A well-made mould is necessary to give a finish to a well prepared cream.

Ices served from some moulds are, for general style and natural appearance simply perfection.

TO MOULD ICES.

THE recipes for any of the mixings, either cream, custard or water, will answer for the moulds. The process of moulding is very simple and easily explained. Prepare a mixing from any of the formulæ and pour it into the mould, put on the cover, wrap the mould in paper, put it in a tub and surround it with broken ice and freezing salt for at least two hours or let it remain embedded until required, then take it out of the ice, clean off the paper, &c., dip it into luke warm water and lift it out again directly, take off the cover and turn it on a dish in the usual way. These ices are decorated in various ways when sent to table according to the nature of the mould—for instance, a few leaves are used when it represents fruit.

FRUIT PRESERVING, Etc.

No work which professes to treat on the confectionery business could be considered complete without more than a passing reference to fruit preserving. This business to-day can hardly be considered apart from sweet making. Most of the leading firms who make and supply the wholesale trade with hard and soft confections are, more or less interested in jams, jellies, peel, &c., while many of the retail people look to this branch for their summer trade. This is as it should be. Those who know anything of the trade are aware that during the summer months the ordinary sweets are almost a dead letter. Fruits, with all their tempting freshness are in season and the contest between our every-day luxury and the annual visitors is unequal; consequently we must either take a back seat and wait our turn, or pay attention to the opponents and turn them to account. The jam trade has perhaps been a little overdone of late—prices are low and competition keen. There may be many reasons for this state of things but the principal one in the writer's opinion is that a number of people possessing more or less capital were so influenced by some remarks made by a prominent politician some years ago as to the profits to be derived by growing fruit and making jam, that they rushed into the speculation without investigation, hence the erection of large and small jam factories all over the country both private and joint stock. What was and is the result! The shareholders and creditors in most cases could better answer this question, but most of us connected with the trade could reckon a good many who have come to grief. As a rule, jams and preserves are not sufficient in themselves to build up a successful trade. In the busy season a lot of space and labour is required. When the rush is over it is practically found impossible to reduce the staff and expenses in the same ratio as the trade may have fallen off, consequently, what is gained in season is more than absorbed with expenses during the quiet time. All these circumstances go to make this business fitted in every way to fill up the sweet-maker's slack times and find employment both for his hands and machinery, thereby making a prosperous and profitable consolidated concern.

This is my experience, and one who has been closely connected with the trade for more than thirty years, has filled the post of principal jam boiler in more than one large factory and has the satisfaction of stating that he has received many tangible proofs of his employers' esteem during that time.

JAMS, JELLIES, and MARMALADE.

PERHAPS the result of my long experience will be useful. The following hints and wrinkles must not be taken as if written in a dogmatic strain. The experience of one man may help another. None of us know everything. It is only a *bigot* who refuses to learn. I give them as a practical man and for what they are worth to the beginner.

Jams, jellies, or marmalades, if properly boiled with their proportion of good sugar, will keep good for years in either, glass, china, or earthenware vessels without the aid of vinegar, whisky or spirit of any kind. The old style of covering the preserves with paper soaked in spirit is a needless expense. If the surface is slightly oiled with a drop of the best olive oil it will prevent any incrustation forming on top. It is not essential to make the covering of the vessel air-tight, but so long as it will keep the dust from the contents that is the chief object. It is a fallacy to suppose that jam made from wet fruit will not keep, but dry fruit is preferable, especially with raspberries and strawberries, as they keep their colour better in boiling. Most preserve makers use a preservative of some kind, such as Bush's preservative, salicylic acid, &c. Perhaps to avoid running the risk of the jams becoming mouldy, (the result of a faulty boil or two,) it may be wise always to employ a small portion of some reliable preservative. As regards the quality of sugar used for preserving it should be good, strong, grainy and white, *i.e.* Dutch crushed, crystal or granulated ;—cheap, soft pieces or raw sugars will not do, as they lose weight in boiling, deaden the colour and reduce the quality to a syrupy, sticky mass.

Dry fresh fruit, good white sugar, a good fire or plenty of steam are the conditions for getting a clear, sparkling, free, full flavoured preserve of a nice jelly consistency. If we cannot always get dry fresh fruit, we should always be able to get good sugar, a clear fire or plenty of steam. These are two out of three conditions for the very best jam. If we cannot get perfection let us get as near to it as we can. The proportions of sugar to fruit given in the formulæ are not, and cannot be, stereotyped. If the fruit is green, use a little more sugar ; if soft and wet, a little less. Too ripe or wet fruit should always have green gooseberry or apple juice added to give it body and congealing properties. When filling whole fruit or currant jam let it stand a little to congeal, then stir before pouring out or the fruit will float on top. See that the edges of the pots are wiped with a damp cloth before tying down, or the smears will show through. Use vegetable parchment paper to cover with instead of gut skin or bladder. If the latter get damp from any cause such as the jam touching, they give off an offensive smell; besides which the parchment looks cleaner. Glass vases, butter coolers, cream jugs, sugar basins are very expensive to fill, the breakages are more than are dreamt of by the proprietors in most places. A pretty label on a clean jar, with a neat white parchment covering is the best finish to a well made jam.

GLUCOSE IN JAMS.

MANY manufacturers use large quantities of glucose in making jams. Some think it cheapens the bulk and causes it to congeal. Opinions differ. I should myself use but very little of it had I a jam factory of my own—too much causes the preserve to be heavy, syrupy, and stringy. However, a little may keep the jam from getting dry or sugary on top.

APPLE and GOOSEBERRY JUICE in JAMS.

THIS is tender ground on the question of adulteration. That which improves can hardly be called an adulterant in the true sense. Experience teaches that in many fruits and conditions of fruit the addition of a little juice adds to the flavour, brilliancy and consistency of the jam, especially is this the case with raspberries, strawberries, and other fine fruits, unless freshly gathered.

After a few days, raspberries and blackcurrants have a tendency to acidity. In this case, a little juice is very useful, and, even where the fruit is quite fresh the addition will improve the result but it must not be overdone. In the formulæ given I recommend apple juice in place of water when the fruit is in ordinary condition. In the event of having fruit out of condition from any cause, I recommend a much larger proportion of apple or gooseberry juice, allowing one pound of sugar to every extra quart of juice, having seen many difficulties got over in this way. If the apples or gooseberries are good, the congealing properties are very great, consequently a rich, free jam is the result. On the other hand, if they had been boiled without, it would have been dry and thick. The juice is easily made. Simply cut up into slices a quantity of cooking apples, put them in a clean pan, cover them with water and boil till they are soft and pulpy; as they become thick add more water; when done strain through coarse jelly bags or fine sieve. Gooseberry juice is prepared in the same way. Juice for steam pans is prepared by another method in a steam tub, details of which will be found in their proper place. In order to be better understood, I have separated the preserves boiled over the furnace from those prepared by steam power.

JAMS, JELLIES, &c.

FIRE HEAT.

RASPBERRY JAM, No. 1.

14-lbs. Fresh Raspberries.   12-lbs. White Sugar.
1 Quart Water or Gooseberry Juice.

PROCESS.—Put the above proportions in a clean pan (copper or brass); place on a clear open fire or confectioners' furnace; stir constantly until the sugar dissolves then occasionally till it begins to thicken when it must be closely watched and kept on the move by stirring well, rubbing the bottom of the pan with spaddle. If the boiler is a beginner, directly the boil feels a little thick ease the pan off the furnace by standing a piece of iron under one side between the furnace and the pan. Now commence to try it by lifting out the spaddle, hold it over the pan—at first the jam will run off thin, then a little thicker, then drop off in webs; it is now done and should be lifted off at once and contents potted. Considerable practice is required to test jams by this method, but when acquired much time is saved and the consistency determined more accurately. When looking at the jam falling from the spaddle, hold it opposite a window if possible. The old method of taking a little out on a cold plate to see if it congeals may be practised in addition to the other test at first, although with quick fires, while the sample is cooling the bulk may be burning. Jam should be potted as soon as boiled; give the bulk a stir round with the ladle every time you fill the jug. If the jam is allowed to stand in bulk after boiling for even a quarter of an hour, the delicate flavour is destroyed, for that reason it is advisable to fill into pots or jars as soon as possible.

RASPBERRY JAM, No. 2.

14-lbs. Raspberries.   12-lbs. White Sugar.
2 quarts Gooseberry Juice.   2-lbs. Glucose.

PROCESS.—As for No. 1. A little colour may be required to brighten the bulk. An excellent jam.

RASPBERRY JELLY.

Fresh Raspberries.   White Sugar.

PROCESS.—Press the raspberries through a cane sieve, then squeeze the pulp through jelly bags; boil the juice in the proportion of 9-lbs. of white sugar to each gallon; try the boil as directed in No. 1. When the jelly is potted, skim the top almost directly with a wooden spoon. The pulp left in the jelly bag may be used for cheap jams.

STRAWBERRY JAM, No. 1.

14-lbs. Strawberries.   2 quarts Gooseberry Juice, or Water.
12-lbs. White Sugar.

PROCESS.—The same as for raspberry jam, No. 1. Unless the strawberries are freshly gathered it is almost necessary, in order to get a good jam, that gooseberry juice be added instead of water. Strawberries do not congeal readily, a tinge of red colouring is often necessary.

STRAWBERRY JAM, No. 2.

14-lbs Strawberries.   7-lbs Gooseberry Pulp.
18-lbs. White Sugar.

PROCESS.—Use the gooseberry pulp after it has been put through the cane sieve; proceed as for No. 1 raspberry. A little colour is necessary. This is a good jam. N.B.—Cheaper qualities may be made by adding more pulp. Glucose is too heavy for this jam—it makes it tough.

WHOLE FRUIT STRAWBERRY JAM, No. 1.

14-lbs. Freshly Gathered Strawberries.   12-lbs. White Sugar.
3 Pints Water.

PROCESS.—Pick the strawberries free from stems; put the sugar and water in the pan and bring it to the boil; allow to boil for seven or eight minutes, or, say 240 by thermometer, then add the strawberries (put them in carefully not to break them), boil sharply for twelve minutes or until the syrup thickens; the spaddle does not show the web with this fruit; keep stirring all the time after the fruit is added;

if it is likely to flow over add a few drops of best salad oil or a piece of fresh butter the size of a Barcelona nut; when the jam is ready, pour the bulk into a shallow vessel and stir till it cools a little so as to mix the fruit with the syrup and every time the jug is filled give another stir.

WHOLE FRUIT STRAWBERRY JAM, No. 2.

14-lbs. Freshly Gathered Strawberries.   ½ Gallon Gooseberry Juice.
16-lbs. White Sugar.

PROCESS.—Dissolve the sugar in the juice and boil for a few minutes adding the strawberries, and continue to boil keeping stirred all the time until ready which may be told by the spaddle test ; the time on a sharp fire would be about twelve to fifteen minutes after the strawberries have been added.   This, in the opinion of most people, is a much superior jam to even the pure article, No. 1, the consistency is better and the flavour more pungent.   Use the oil or fresh butter mentioned in last formula if required.

N.B.—I question if this could be labelled " pure strawberry jam."

BLACK CURRANT JAM, (Whole Fruit).

14-lbs. Black Currants.   12-lbs. White Sugar.
3 Pints Water.

PROCESS.—Pick the currants free from stems ; put them together with sugar and water in a clean pan and boil in the ordinary way keeping the mixture well stirred all the time till ready, which may be tried in the usual way with spaddle. This method is much preferred to rubbing the fruit through sieves. Take it as an axiom that the less the fruit is handled, bruised or boiled the better the preserve in every respect.   It is a mistake to suppose that any kind of sugar will do for black currants. To make good jam good sugar must be used.

BLACK CURRANT JAM (Whole Fruit), No. 2.

14-lbs. Black Currants.   ½ gallon Gooseberry Juice.
16-lbs. White Sugar.

PROCESS.—Same as above. Most people prefer it with the addition of gooseberry juice—which makes a rich jelly and mellows the flavour.

BLACK CURRANT JAM, No. 3.

14-lbs.   Black Currants.   16-lbs.   White Sugar.
½ gallon Gooseberry Pulp.   3 quarts Water.

PROCESS.—Put the currants and water into the boiling pan and boil in the ordinary way stirring all the time until .they get soft which will be about fifteen minutes after they commence boiling, then remove the pan from the fire and pass the hot pulp through a small sieve (ten holes to the inch), then return the pulp, add the sugar and the gooseberry pulp and boil off in the usual way. This makes a really good jam and saves the time of picking over the currants. A little glucose may be used with this fruit, in the proportion of 14-lbs. equal to 10-lbs. sugar for sweetening and preserving properties.

BLACK CURRANT JELLY.

14-lbs. Black Currants. 1 gallon Water.
7-lbs. Gooseberries. White Sugar.

PROCESS.—Put the currants, gooseberries and water in the pan and boil till quite soft and pulpy then strain through jelly bag, measure the juice in the pan and allow 7-lbs. sugar to every gallon and boil off on a good fire. The jelly is easily tried with a spaddle. Directly it flakes, lift off the pan and pour into selected vessels quickly as this congeals very fast. Almost as soon as it is filled out the scum should be skimmed off the top. N.B.—Should a pure black currant jelly be wanted, keep out the gooseberries—the process is the same. The above formula is considered better than when made from black currants alone.

RED CURRANT JAM (Whole Fruit), No. 1.

14-lbs. Red Currants. 11-lbs. White Sugar.
3 Pints Water.

PROCESS.—-Pick the currants free from stems and proceed exactly as for black currant jam. Gooseberry juice instead of water will much improve the result.

RED CURRANT JAM, No. 2.

14-lbs. Red Currants. 11-lbs. White Sugar.
6 Pints Water.

PROCESS.—Boil the currants and water together until soft, then press through a small sieve to keep back the stems ; put the hot pulp back in the pan ; add the sugar and boil off.

PLUM JAM.

14-lbs. Plums. 11-lbs. Sugar.
3 Pints Water.

PROCESS.—Put the ingredients in the pan and boil in the usual way until the mixture drops in flakes,

179

DAMSON JAM.

14-lbs. Damsons.   13-lbs. White Sugar.
3 Pints Water.

PROCESS.—As usual. Glucose may be used in the last two recipes, say 10-lbs. sugar and 4-lbs. glucose, instead of 13-lbs. sugar.

GOOSEBERRY JAM.

14-lbs. Gooseberries, red or green.   12-lbs Sugar.
3 Pints Water.

PROCESS.—As usual.

APPLE JELLY.

CUT up a quantity of cooking apples into slices; put them in a pan and cover them with water and boil till quite soft; if they get too thick, add more water; they must be stirred nearly all the time while boiling; when ready strain through jelly bags. Measure out the juice back into the pan and add from 4-oz. to 6-oz. of sugar to each pint, according to thickness and quality of apples, then boil off as already directed.

ORANGE MARMALADE.

PUT a quantity of Seville oranges into a vessel and cover them with boiling water; when soaked for ten minutes commence cutting with a knife the rind of each orange into four equal parts; open and separate the pulp from the rind, putting each in different places; when finished take the chips (rind) and cut up into very thin strips with a sharp knife or machine; put into a pan, cover with cold water and boil till quite tender; if the water is changed once or twice during this process the result will be better. When ready, strain through a cane sieve just fine enough to keep back the pips; now mix the pulp and chips together; weigh them and for every pound add one pound of best white sugar; put the whole in the pan and boil off on a brisk fire; stir all the time and try with spaddle same way as directed for jam. If clear marmalade is wanted, keep out the greater part of the chips. To make marmalade on a big scale, see instructions under steam power.

JAMS, VARIOUS.

BLACKBERRY, cranberry, raspberry and currant, &c., jams are made in exactly the same way as similar fruits for which I have given instructions. I think it would be a waste of time to enumerate them.

Steam Pan.

PRESERVES BY STEAM POWER.

STEAM is now almost universally used as a means of boiling, especially for the wholesale trade. Compared with furnace work, the saving in labour is no less remarkable than the facility with which it can be made. Jam cooked on a fire or furnace requires constant attention and continual stirring so that one man has all his work cut out to look after one pan and may turn out from five to eight cwts. per day of ten hours, according to the size of pan and class of fruit, while, with less fatiguing labour, he could, with the help of a lad, attend to six steam pans, each making 1¼ cwt. per boil. That would be on the average, 9-cwt. every forty minutes, besides, the operation would be conducted in less smoky and altogether cleaner surroundings.

The construction of the necessary mechanical contrivances is neither very costly nor requires a lot of space. Any machine maker would be able to advise as to the best position for the pans, &c., after seeing the proposed factory or department, but it is well to know that a good supply of steam is absolutely necessary, in order to make good preserves, so that in buying a boiler be careful to buy it large enough. Allow 4-horse power for every pan to be erected. It is also necessary to have what is known as a "steam tub." This is generally a glucose barrel, fitted with a perforated copper coil. This coil goes down the centre of the cask and takes two or three circles round the bottom. The tub is used for pulping apples, boiling orange chips, &c. The steam passing through the small holes soon reduces the raw fruit to a pulp and is of great service in keeping a supply of juice for jelly or pulp for jam. The pressure of steam for boiling purposes should not be less than 35-lbs., while from 40 to 50 would not be too high. The quicker the boiling the better the colour and less loss by evaporation. Tables, benches, &c., must be erected according to the size, shape, and convenience of the workshop.—N. B.—See also instructions for boiling by fire heat.

FRUIT PULPING, STRAINING, AND SEPARATING MACHINE.

This machine is very useful to large makers for extracting pips, stalks, stones, &c., from raspberries, strawberries, currants, plums, apples, dates, &c. The best are made with copper cylinders, copper lined feeding head, and the shaft cased with gun metal. This prevents the iron from touching and discolouring the fruit. Several tons per day may be pulped through a good machine.

GOOSEBERRIES.

ABOUT the first fruit of the season of service to a jam maker are gooseberries.

As soon as they are full grown (but not ripe) they make good jam and excellent jelly, while the juice and pulp are useful as a body for many fruit jams and jellies, such as black currant and red currant jam, strawberries, &c., in fact, gooseberries are second only to apples as a universal and reliable ingredient for improving, giving body and brightening the more expensive fruits when perhaps a little off colour.

GOOSEBERRY JAM, BY STEAM, NO. I.

112-lbs. Gooseberries.   96-lbs. White Sugar.
Water.

PROCESS.—Put the berries first in the pan, then the sugar, add a pailful of water, turn on the steam and commence to stir with a long stick until the sugar dissolves ; then only occasionally. When it commences to boil the bulk will rise in the pan and throw off a lot of steam ; as it goes on boiling the cloud of steam will gradually get less ; as the boil gets thicker it gets darker ; now commence to try it with a flat stick having a sharp edge; dip the stick into the boiling pan; lift it out again immediately and hold it before your eyes; at first the liquid will run off thin ; keep repeating the process and you will notice every succeeding time you look at the falling syrup from the stick it will get thicker until it will drop off in webs or flakes, then the jam is done. Shut off the steam at once, turn the contents into a cooler and fill into packages.

Of course to try the jam in this way requires practice. However, the knack is soon acquired. From the time it commences to boil until finished with a supply of steam at 40 pressure, would be about twenty minutes. N.B.—The above was the writer's proportions when the fruit was in fair condition. If the fruit is very green use a little more sugar; if ripe a little less. A steam pan of the ordinary type will boil this quantity.

GOOSEBERRY JAM, No 2.

| 112-lbs. Gooseberries | 35-lbs. Glucose. |
| 70-lbs. White Sugar | Water. |

Process.—Put the berries, sugar and water in the pan; turn on the steam and stir until dissolved, then add the glucose and boil off as for No 1.

RASPBERRY JAM, No. I.

| 60-lbs. Raspberries. | 60-lbs. White Sugar. |
| 1 Pailful Gooseberry Juice or Water. | |

Process.—Where jam is made in quantities fruit generally arrives picked from stems. Raspberries should be used as quickly as possible. They soon lose colour and turn sour if kept any length of time. Put the above quantities into the pan, turn on the steam and stir till the sugar is dissolved; then only occasionally till ready. The process is the same as for gooseberry jam, No. 1. If water is used instead of juice, 56-lbs. sugar will be sufficient.

RASPBERRY JAM, No. 2

| 60-lbs. Raspberries. | 14-lbs. Glucose. |
| 45-lbs. Sugar. | Water or Gooseberry Juice. |

Process.—Same as for No. 1, gooseberry. Glucose is no improvement and very little saving on cost.

STRAWBERRY JAM.

| 60-lbs. Strawberries. | 60-lbs White Sugar. |
| Gooseberry Juice or Water. | |

Process.—Same as for No. 1, gooseberry jam. A pailful of gooseberry juice is a great improvement; if water is used, 54-lbs. sugar will be sufficient.

WHOLE FRUIT STRAWBERRY JAM, by Steam.

| 60-lbs. Strawberries, freshly picked. | 60-lbs. White Sugar. |
| Gooseberry Juice or Water. | |

Process.—Put the sugar in the pan with a pailful of juice or half a pailful of water, turn on the steam and let the contents boil until the syrup is pretty thick ; now drop in the fruit gently without crushing it ; continue the boiling until done, which may be tried in the usual way. If the strawberries have a tendency to flow over the pan, add a few drops of salad oil or a small portion of fresh butter about half the size of a walnut. When the jam has been turned into the cooler stir the batch well up so that the syrup and fruit will be evenly distributed. The gooseberry juice will cause it to congeal better ; if water is used, 54-lbs. sugar will be sufficient.

BLACK CURRANT JAM, by Steam.

60-lbs. Black Currants.   60-lbs White Sugar.
Gooseberry Juice or Water.

Process.—The same as for gooseberry jam, No. 1. The currants in this case should be picked by hand free from stems.

BLACK CURRANT JAM, by Steam, No. 2.

60-lbs. Black Currants   60-lbs. White Sugar.
Gooseberry Juice or Water.

Process.—Put the currants in the boiling pan with a pailful of water, turn on the steam and stir the contents until they boil for about ten minutes when the fruit will be soft ; then pass through a small sieve or pulping machine and replace in the pan ; add the juice and sugar and boil off as usual.

RED CURRANT JAM.

60-lbs. Red Currants.   56-lbs. White Sugar.
Gooseberry Juice or Water.

Process.—As for black currants.

PLUM JAM.

112-lbs. Plums.   96-lbs. White Sugar.
Apple Juice or Water.

Process.—Exactly as for gooseberry jam. Apples are generally in season when plums are ready for jam making. The juice from apples is to be preferred to water.

DAMSON JAM, No. 1.

112-lbs. Damsons.   100-lbs. White Sugar.
Apple Juice or Water.

Process.—Same as for gooseberry jam.

185

DAMSON JAM, No. 2.

112-lbs. Damsons.   80-lbs. White Sugar.
28-lbs. Glucose.

Process.—As for gooseberry jam. Glucose may be used for either plum or damson ; it may cheapen the bulk but will not improve the jam. Jam, in which glucose has been added is denser, consequently, in small packages where the preserve is practically sold by measure there is not much gain by the addition.

APPLE JELLY.

Fill the steam tub three parts full of clean cooking apples ; put on the cover and turn on the steam ; let them steam for about twenty minutes, then shut off the steam ; remove the cover and see if they are all smashed and pulpy ; if not give them a little more steaming, then, with a long spaddle bruise any that may not be broken against the side of the tub ; fill up the tub to the top with cold water and again turn on the steam till the mixture boils then strain through jelly bags. Put into the jam pan three pailfuls of this juice, straining through muslin or a fine hair seive, together with 21-lbs of best white sugar and boil with a pressure of not less than 40. Stir till the sugar dissolves and boil until the jelly hangs in webs upon the stick then shut off steam ; remove the scum and pot ; while the filler-out is at work, an assistant, with a spoon, should follow to crack any bubbles and remove any further scum.

N.B.—No glucose should be used in jelly making. The boil if slightly tinged with red colour will make the jelly look richer.

APPLE PULP.

As a foundation for all cheap jams, no fruit is so useful as the apple. The pulp is the body of "Mixed Fruit Jams," Fruit Preserves and nearly all jams sold as flavoured "so and so." It would be impossible to give formulæ for all sorts of cheap jam because the mixing very much depends on what fruit the maker has available. Apple pulp tself makes a good wholesome jam, but is improved by the addition of plums, damsons, raspberries, &c., consequently, the mixing will be regulated according to the price at which the product is sold and the value of the different pulps in stock which vary every season. To make the pulp, fill the steam tub full of good cooking apples, put on

186

the cover and turn on the steam and let it boil for some twenty minutes then take off the cover and with a long spaddle, crush any that may remain whole against the side of the tub, then replace the cover and give another ten minutes steaming. The pulp is then ready for immediate use or storage.

N.B.—It may be necessary to put some heavy weights on top of the steam tub cover before turning the steam on as it is likely to be blown off.

APPLE JAM (by Steam.)

56-lbs. Apple Pulp.
54-lbs. White Sugar.

1-oz. Citric Acid.
Colouring.

Process.—Pass the pulp through a cane sieve fine enough to keep back the pips; put the ingredients in the pan with half a pailful of water; turn on the steam, stir till the sugar is dissolved and boil off in the usual way; tinge to a light pink.

MIXED FRUIT (by Steam, No. 1.)

40-lbs. Plums
40-lbs. Apple Pulp.

76-lbs. White Sugar.
$\frac{1}{2}$-Gallon Water.

Process.—Same as usual.

MIXED FRUIT JAM (by Steam), No. 2.

40-lbs. Plums.
40-lbs. Apple Pulp.

56-lbs. Sugar.
28-lbs. Glucose.

Process.—As usual.

RASPBERRY FLAVOURED JAM.

56-lbs. Apple Pulp.
14-lbs. Raspberries.

56-lbs. White Sugar.
$\frac{1}{2}$-lb. Gingelly (or Turkey) Seeds.
Colouring.

Process.—As usual. Black currant, red currant, and strawberry flavouring is made in the same way, excepting the gingelly (or Turkey) seeds—leave them out, of course.

CHEAP JAMS.

I have given four formulæ for cheap jams, but they are given as guides, and must not be taken as stereotyped. The nature of the apples and consistency of the pulp differ so much, that it would be impossible to be exact. However, I have given the principle on which jams are made. The chief difficulty with most people is to so manipulate and mix as to reduce the cost to the bottom. One of the principal ingredients necessary for this is a little common sense. Always calculate to have in the *finished* article at least half its bulk in sugar or sugar and glucose, or it will not keep. Jam, when well boiled, with proper proportions, should be bright, free, and congealed. If it is tough or syrupy, it contains too much sugar; if it is soft and watery, it lacks boiling, and, perhaps, a little sugar. For other cheap jams, see under.

DRIED FRUIT IN JAM.

DATES, figs, raisins, currants, and other dried fruits have all figured in "Fruit Preserves." They never make a good jam, but when sugar is much dearer, they are useful, because they are economical.

We do not now meet them so often, nor is it advisable to use them. Sugar is so cheap, that the difference in cost is very little, if any. Dates were generally selected in preference to the other fruits of this class, having a less distinctive flavour and more suitable for mixing. They are pulped in the same manner as apples, but take much longer to soften in the steam tub and require a few pailfuls of water added. When quite soft, they are rubbed through a coarse iron sieve to keep out the stones. This pulp is then mixed with the apples and other fruit pulps and boiled off in the ordinary way. About 6 to 10-lbs. sugar is allowed for each pailful of date pulp.

PULPING FOR STOCK (With Sulphur).

PULPING for stock is an important matter to jam makers, as the success of a winter trade depends very much upon the condition of the fruit pulp when required for use. Improper preserving or careless packing may lead to serious loss; and often ruin to a business; therefore, it is in the interest of proprietors to see this carried out personally in many cases. There are several methods. This one is perhaps the most popular with small makers but it is rather costly on account of the quantity of jars necessary. However, barrels may be substituted where circumstances make it necessary.

Break up some bar sulphur, put in an iron pot, and melt it by putting this pot on a furnace plate, or near a fire. Now get some unbleached cotton and cut it up into strips, about half a yard long and about $1\frac{1}{2}$-in. wide; dip one end of them in the melted sulphur; let them soak about half way up; separate them and lay them on a table to dry, when they will be ready for use. Have a number of clean jars with narrow necks, ready; light the sulphured end of the piece of cotton and put it in a jar, letting the whole of the sulphured part hang inside and the plain part outside; push in a bung in the neck, just tight enough to exclude the air. In a few minutes the air will be exhausted and the light go out. The rag must then be removed and the jar filled up quickly with the hot pulp, the bung driven in and waxed over. The same process exactly applies to casks, which must be sound and air-tight; have the sulphur rag larger, and see that the bung fits well. Where large quantities are put away, it is well to keep a lad sulphuring, then the operation is methodical and the supply continuous. Salicylic acid is used as a preservative in many establishments. For this method, dissolve 4-oz. of salicylic acid in 16-oz. of spirit of wine; pulp the fruit by boiling in a clean pan till quite soft, then add two ounces of this solution to each cwt. of fruit and well stir; store the fruit in air-tight casks or jars.

If casks are used in either case, it is well, after a day or two, to bore a hole with a gimlet. A little air will immediately escape. Have a wooden peg ready and drive in the hole directly.

GELATINE IN JAMS.

WE have before stated that jam made with fresh fruit, good sugar, and well boiled, requires no foreign matter to make it congeal. Sometimes when pulp has gone a bit wrong and no fresh fruit procurable, makers are in a fix to get a sloppy substance to set. In this case, soak a few sheets of good gelatine by covering with cold water for at least twenty hours. After the jam has been made, but while hot stir one or two sheets into the boil till dissolved; when the batch is cold, it will no doubt be stiff enough. Exact quantity cannot be given, as it will depend on the size of boil and condition of pulp. A little gelatine goes a long way.

MACHINES FOR MARMALADE MAKING.

Orange Clipping Machine.

Orange Slicing Machine.

UNTIL quite recently, marmalade makers had to content themselves with a machine for slicing the orange rinds in suitable thickness for marmalade making, while the quartering had to be done with a knife in the old style. There is now a new machine for this purpose, with which a boy or a girl can cut 22 oranges, any size, per minute. This is a great saving in time and labour, and well worth the attention of large makers.

MARMALADE.

To make good marmalade great care is necessary. Have everything connected with the process perfectly clean; not only the pans, tools, benches, and packages, but the ingredients also. Fruit, sugar, and water must be free from specks or dust, as any and every impurity shows in the bright transparent, and delicate tinge of the best article.

It is also necessary to use good, sound, heavy Seville or Malaga oranges, and the best Dutch crushed sugar. Notwithstanding the idiotic theory held by many ignorant people, that turnips, marrows, and, in fact, vegetables and fruits of any description or condition were some, if not the principal, ingredients of which this delicious preserve was composed there is a very fine quality of almost transparent marmalade now in the market, known as "home made," almost innocent of chips, consequently not so bitter and a great favourite with children. This sort is largely made up of orange pulp, known in the trade as "Dummies." Within the last few years, the rind only of the orange has been used by some firms for making essential oil, the whole pulp being repacked in boxes and selling at very low prices. The fruit is generally of good quality, and is a boon to marmalade people when pulp runs short or where the home made article is in demand.

TO PREPARE THE CHIPS AND PULP.

Put any quantity of oranges into a tub and cover them with boiling water, and let them soak for a few minutes, then pick them up one at a time and mark the rind with a sharp knife into four quarters ; now separate the pulp from the rind ; pack the rind cup shape into the boxes of the machine and cut into slices. When cold sort them over ; take out those imperfectly cut and put them through the machine again ; if well packed in the machine box in the first instance there will be few that require recutting. Now put the slices in the steam tub turn on the steam and let them cook until tender ; try them between the finger and thumb ; when you can nip them off short they are done, or they may be boiled in a steam pan by covering them with water, the steam turned on and allowed to cook for nearly two-and-a-half-hours ; when ready take them out and strain through a wicker sieve.

To prepare the pulp put any quantity into a steam pan cover them with water, turn on the steam and stir with a long flat stick until they are reduced to a mass of pulp ; now take them out and rub them through a cane sieve just large enough to keep back the pips or put them through a pulping machine with copper sieve eight holes to the inch. Dummies are treated in the same manner as pulp.

SUPERIOR ORANGE MARMALADE, No 1.

40-lbs. Orange Pulp. 20-lbs. Orange Chips.
60-lbs. Best White Sugar.

PROCESS.—Put the ingredients in a pan ; stir till the sugar is dissolved then occasionally till ready ; try it same as jam ; when it falls off the stick in flakes it is ready ; turn it into a cooler from which fill the packages.

ORANGE MARMALADE, No. 2.

40-lbs. Orange Pulp. 20-lbs. Orange Chips.
40-lbs. Best White Sugar. 20-lbs. Glucose.

PROCESS.—Put the sugar, pulp and chips in the pan ; boil as usual ; when almost ready add the glucose ; boil and stir in.

ORANGE MARMALADE.

35-lbs. Orange Pulp. 45-lbs. Sugar.
20-lbs. Chips. 20-lbs. Glucose.

PROCESS.—Put the sugar, pulp and chips in the pan ; boil as usual ; when almost ready, add the glucose ; stir well in and finish boiling.

HOME-MADE MARMALADE.

40-lbs. Orange Pulp, strained. 1 Gallon Best Apple Juice.
10-lbs. Orange Chips. 60-lbs. Dutch Crushed Sugar.

PROCESS.—Pass half the pulp while hot through a coarse hair sieve ; mix all the ingredients together in a pan and boil off in the ordinary way. The oranges for the home-made article should be specially heavy with a thinnish skin.

N.B.—When there is a superabundance of chips and no dummies to be had, work up the surplus chips in cheaper qualities, using apple juice and glucose. When preserving orange pulp for future use mix the pulp and chips together in the proportions for boiling.

CANDIED ORANGE AND LEMON PEELS.

YEAR by year the demand for candied peel increases. We find many of the large wholesale houses contracting for a supply of from twenty to forty thousand cases of oranges and lemons, besides a number of pipes of citron peel in brine for a season's consumption.

The process of preserving and candying is rather a long one. From the time the fruit arrives until ready for packing a clear month should elapse. It is possible to force through the operation in six or eight days but the result is unsatisfactory. The salt cannot be thoroughly extracted nor the peel perfectly permeated with syrup in this time. The oranges or lemons are first cut in half and the juice squeezed out. Small and effective machines are now used for this purpose. The lemon or orange is put in, a lever lifted, when it is cut, squeezed and thrown out by the one operation. The lemon juice should be saved as it has a market value.

Now put the peel in tubs and cover with brine; make the brine with salt and water strong enough to float an egg; let remain in soak for about ten days or until thoroughly penetrated; the next process is to strain out the peel and boil in water till tender; a good plan is to test them as you would potatoes; when the fork will penetrate without force they are done, then strain off the hot water and put the peel into cold water which will make it firm; now clear out the pulp with the thumb nail or a mussel shell and throw the peel again into cold water and let it remain for two or three hours. Afterwards, take it out and place loosely one in the other and pack into a vessel for syruping. Now make a thin syrup with best white sugar, sufficient to cover them; let this syrup be very thin, boil only to 215° by thermometer; pour it over the peel and let soak for three or four days then draw off, add more sugar and boil up again, this time a little thicker, say 230° by thermometer and pour over them and let stand again for three or four more days; again draw off the syrup add more sugar and boil a little thicker say 235° and repeat the operation; at the end of four days, throw out the peel on wicker sieves and allow to drain, bottoms upwards so that all the syrup will run out. The peel is now preserved and known in the trade as drain peel. Before the candying process the peel must be packed on wire sieves and put in the drying room for twelve hours, then taken out, packed one in the other and put into cases until required for the last operation.

Boil sugar and water in an ordinary boiling pan to make, say three gallons of syrup up to the degree of feather, 240°; then put in carefully half a bushel of peel ; let boil through and lift off the pan ; grain the sugar against the side of the pan by rubbing with a flat stick till it becomes cloudy ; now give the whole a stir round and commence to take out each piece separately with a fork and place it on its round part on a wire tray ; when cold it will have a grained sugar coating ; it is now finished, and only requires careful packing in dry boxes.

N.B.—The raw peel may be preserved for almost any length of time in the brine.

TO FROST FRUIT.

SELECT the finest plums, cherries, apricots, grapes or small pears ; leave on their stalks ; whisk the white of eggs to a stiff froth ; dip the fruit in the beaten eggs leaving the stalks out ; lift them, one at a time and cover them with finely powdered sugar ; cover a tray with white paper, lay the fruit on it, and place in a cooling oven ; when the icing becomes firm, pack and put in a cool place.

TO BOTTLE FRUIT.

RASPBERRIES.

THE raspberries must be fresh, whole and sound. Fill up the bottles gently not to crush ; colour some water red and cover the fruit with it ; now cork them tight with best corks and secure them by tying them down with wire or string ; place them upright in a boiling pan with a little hay between them ; fill the pan with cold water to the neck of the bottles and place on a moderate fire or a steam pan will answer the purpose ; raise the heat to 160 ; let them stand an hour, then increase the heat to 180 and let them remain another hour ; now take the pan from the fire, or turn off the steam and run off the water ; when the bottles are cold, pack them away on their sides.

GOOSEBERRIES, BLACK CURRANTS, CHERRIES, &c.

PROCEED as for raspberries, but of course the water in the bottles should be coloured according to the fruit.

PLUMS, DAMSONS, GREENGAGES.

PROCEED as for raspberries but raise the temperature in the first instance to 170° then to 185° degrees.

APPLES.

PARE and core the fruit and cut into quarters and proceed as for raspberries.

FRUITS IN SYRUP.

ANY of the above may be preserved in syrup by adding 5-lbs. of sugar to every gallon of water used for covering the fruit.

TO CRYSTALLIZE GINGER, FRUITS, &c.

WHEN nicely finished and well packed crystallized fruits make a tempting attraction. Though the process is simple, judgment is required to make it successful. Care must be taken that the different sorts are thoroughly saturated with syrup which it has penetrated right to the core before the finishing or crystallizing process is commenced or the goods will not keep—the larger the fruit the more time it will take to soak and the thinner the syrup must be for the first wettings. Attraction must be induced by packing the colours and shapes so that the blend may harmonise.

CRYSTALLIZED GINGER.

PROCESS.—Take any quantity of green ginger strained from the syrup and pack in a clean tub or pan. Make sufficient syrup to cover the bulk, in the proportion of 7-lbs. of sugar to each gallon of water and pour lukewarm on the ginger and allow to remain for twelve hours, then strain off. Now add one more pound of sugar to each gallon of syrup and reboil ; pour the syrup this time over the ginger while hot and let remain in soak two days and two nights, when it must be strained off again and reboiled with 1-lb. additional sugar to each gallon. Now pour the syrup again over the ginger and let remain for 24 hours longer ; again dry the ginger as much as possible from the syrup and stand in drying rooms for about three days, or until dry. Now make a boil of sugar with the usual quantity of water and a pinch of cream of tartar, to a soft ball ; remove the pan from the fire, and grain by rubbing a little of the syrup on side of pan (as directed for Grained Sugar Goods); now pass the dry ginger through the boil quickly; place on sieves and again in the drying room until hard. To finish, prepare a syrup with the usual proportion of sugar and water and boil to 220. Pack the ginger in crystallizing tins and cover them with this syrup when partly cool. Put them in a drying room for another 12 hours. Now drain off the goods, pack on trays, stand in a warm place; when dry, pack for sale.

CRYSTALLIZED FRUITS.

The fruits used for the purpose have generally been preserved in syrup till required. Drain the fruit from the syrup; clear them off by dipping slightly in hot water and pack them in trays; stand in drying room twelve hours to dry. Now pack them carefully in crystallizing tins and make sufficient syrup in the usual way boiling to 217°. Stand the syrup aside till coolish then cover the fruits with it; stand the tins in the drying room all night; drain off in the morning; when dry knock the goods out carefully, sort them out on trays, and when thoroughly dry, pack.

TO MAKE BAKING POWDER.

12-ozs. Tartaric Acid.   2-lbs. Cream of Tartar.
3-lbs. Bi-carbonate of Soda.

Process.—See that the ingredients are thoroughly dry. Now mix them together, first with the hands, then pass them two or three times through a fine sieve. Bottle off as quickly as possible, and cork air-tight.

PASTRY AND CAKE MAKING.

It would perhaps be difficult to define accurately the word *confectioner*, *ie.* where his art begins and where his function is supposed to end. The writer, without pretending to give even an opinion, may state that it is generally understood at least to include pastry and cake-making, if not the better sorts of fancy or small breads. The furnace and the oven are closely associated, and in many cases combined; the sugar boiler and pastry cook being one and the same person especially in small establishments; so much so, that the publishers have considered that the latest and best information in this department would be of service to many subscribers.

During recent years much progress and great developments have taken place in this as well as other branches of the business. Improved machinery and tools for almost every purpose connected with the craft have been introduced, also materials of greater variety and better quality.

Competition being keen, and transit quick, we are now within two or three days' reach of the largest and best markets of Europe; consequently goods are cheaper, as well as fresher. The up-to-date man must take advantage of every improvement by making himself thoroughly

The Oven.

conversant with the best markets and their products, as well as by testing and comparing the skill of the engineer in his endeavour to save labour and improve output.

Conservatism in business does not necessarily mean progress. Compare the window of a good confectioner's or pastry cook's shop of to-day with one of twenty years ago. Notice the selling lines, which are quite different, and note, too, that the old fashioned sweets and cakes are preserved in show glasses, while modern goods are uncovered and within easy reach. The successful tradesman is he who studies and provides for the wants of the public, keeping well abreast if not in front of them, but the *most* successful is he who creates or anticipates such acquirements and meets them with his own manufactures.

ON MAKING PASTRY.

THE quality of pastry not only depends upon the recipes from which the articles are made but also upon the materials which are used, and the manner in which they are prepared.

Best flour should be used, and the butter employed should be of good quality and "tough"; should it be hard, it must be worked with the hands until pliable, and of the same consistence as the dough before mixing with it. The paste should not be handled more than is necessary, nor rolled out oftener than three times. Mix the dough on a marble slab, in a cool place. When mixed, let it stand a short time before working up. Sweep off the extra flour which hangs to the paste when folding in.

It is essential that the oven be closely watched and the heat regulated according to the goods which are undergoing the process of baking. If pastry is well baked, it can be handled, and, with care, placed in clean tins or patty pans without their being greased or buttered.

On the other hand, should pastry be insufficiently baked, it is liable to be squashed when lifted from the patty pans, and, if not very tenderly handled, too soon gets out of shape. Light paste should be baked moderately quickly. If the oven is too cool, the goods will not come to perfection either in colour or size, if the oven is too hot, they become brown and puffy before ready, and when taken out, will fall flat. Again puff paste should not be baked in an oven with large goods which give off steam, or it will not rise nicely.

To determine the heat of the oven the old practice of opening the door should be abandoned in favour of the pyrometer which is much more simple and certain as well as a saver of fuel. By means of this instrument the heat of the oven can be ascertained in an instant, without causing trouble while the goods are undergoing the process of baking, and avoiding the risk of underdone or burnt batches.

PUFF PASTE, No. 1.

3-lbs. Flour.
3-lbs. Butter.

In preparing this paste best flour and good butter only should be used. Work the whole of the flour into ½-lb. of the butter using a little water to make a stiffish dough, roll it out, break up the remainder of the butter into small pieces and spread over the sheet. Fold up and roll out again, repeat this process two or three times, dredging a little flour over to prevent the paste from sticking to the rolling-pin. Brushing the sheet over, as often as it is rolled out, with the white of egg, encourages it to rise into flakes.

N. B.—A cheaper paste may be made by using 1½-lbs. of flour to each pound of butter.

PUFF PASTE, No. 2.

3-lbs. Flour.   3-lbs. Butter.
9 Egg Yolks.

Mix in the whole of the flour with 6 ozs. of the butter adding the egg yolks, a little water to form a dough then rolling out and spreading the remainder of the butter in small pieces over the surface; fold it up, dredge with flour, and roll out again very thin, repeat this process three or four times. To make a really good paste requires practice and skill; it should be touched as lightly as possible with cool hands and made in a cool place. This paste is used for the various kinds of raised or light pastry, covered tarts, fruit and other pies.

FRENCH OR SWISS PASTE.

This paste is made exactly as puff paste the only difference being the cutting and baking.

Take the paste and roll it out about half an inch thick, cut into strips about three inches long and half an inch wide, lay these strips on a baking plate with the cut side uppermost about three inches apart, bake in a moderately quick oven. While baking, instead of rising they will spread out like a fan, now take them out and dust over with fine powdered sugar, put them again in the oven for one minute to glaze, when done form a sandwich by spreading some raspberry jam between two pieces. Iced goods, tarts and puffs, which have been washed over with powdered sugar and egg must have a cooler oven otherwise the icing will be liable to catch.

BANBURY PUFFS.

Puff Paste. Mince Meat.

Roll out the puff paste and cut to size required with a cake cutter, form an oval with the hand, put some meat in the centre, then take another piece of paste shape it in the same way and lay it on top, dust over with powdered sugar and bake in moderate oven. The meat for Banbury puffs is generally mixed from ingredients at command, the following for example—chop some apples, cut some candied peel fine, bruise some currants, crumble some stale sweet cake and mix with a little treacle or moist sugar, shaking mixed spice over the lot.

THREE CORNERED PUFFS.

Puff Paste. Raspberry Jam.
Egg Whites.

Roll out a thin sheet of puff paste and cut to size with a cake cutter, put a teaspoonful of raspberry jam in the middle, turn up the sides in three places forming a peak at the top and place them on a board, side by side, fitting in closely together, whisk the white of egg and wash them all over laying it on with a brush, then dredge them with powdered sugar, just before putting into the oven sprinkle a little water over them.

N.B. The richer the paste the hotter the oven ought to be. Patty pans, tart tins, moulds and cake dishes should be buttered before being used, although good puff paste is generally too greasy to stick if even the vessel is unbuttered. Goods to be baked on sheets should be placed on greased paper. Raised pie paste should be baked in moderate oven with steady heat till quite done. Glazed goods require a coolish oven so that the icing may not be discoloured. Tarts should be iced when they are three parts baked.

BLOCK CAKES.

These goods are now very popular and the demand is increasing. For some reason not very obvious, the genuine pastry cook and baker seems to have treated this important want in such an indifferent manner as to allow it to drift into the hands of outsiders who have more quickly recognised the position and prepared to encourage and cater for it. It must be admitted that large and flourishing businesses have lately been built up practically for the manufacture of this class of goods alone and that other channels than the confectioner and pastry cook have been found for distribution.

It is hardly conceivable that when a manufacturer can make, sell, deliver and collect, with the expenses attached to each of these items and then make a profit, and leave one for the grocer or other retailer, that a pastry cook or baker, with every facility at hand, could not make these goods and sell them remuneratively. Grocers as a class are estimable men of business, but when they interest themselves in sweets and cakes they do the confectioner and pastry-cook no good. The margin which they can accept as a working profit will certainly not pay those who have to rely on this trade alone for expenses. When a grocer handles these goods, the manufacturer's profit and expenses must be paid before he gets them, and a margin however small for himself when he sells them. The baker should be well able to produce as good, if not better articles which would pay him to sell at as low a price as his competitor, since he saves the profit and expenses of both manufacturer and retailer. Besides, other things being equal, the public will prefer to purchase their cakes where they are made, and where the surroundings should be more tempting.

The following mixings will be found suitable for nearly all purposes, the instructions should be carefully followed, the ingredients weighed and the result tested. The formulæ given are the result of experience and experiment and are the best for the various qualities indicated. However individual taste may differ, and what may be a favourite in one locality may not be popular in another. When the finished article is produced, examined, cost reckoned, and tested thoroughly, then will it be time for variation or improvement at the discretion of those chiefly concerned and not before.

BLOCK CAKES.

Method of Preparing and General Instructions.

PREPARE the fruit by rubbing through sieves, washing and drying carefully, sorting over, removing all stones, stalks and foreign matter. This is important to the success of cake making ; nothing is more objectionable or even dangerous than to have one's teeth suddenly bite a stone, and it is anything but pleasant to rub one's tongue against a quantity of grit. The process of cleaning the tools and machines for the purpose is, or ought to be, known by every apprentice before he has been three months in the bake house. Weigh the ingredients and stand them in little heaps, break up the eggs dropping them one at a time into a small dish, pass under the nose then empty into a larger receptacle. Everyone knows the importance of the nose in this process. Now commence to cream the butter and sugar by beating them well together until a white creamy mass is the result ; add a small portion of the eggs and continue to beat up, adding further portions of the egg each time the butter creams, until all the eggs are used up, although care must be exercised not to splash the batter every time fresh moisture is added in the shape of eggs ; elbow grease is the chief item for the perfection of this "creaming," on which depends the success of practically all cakes, more especially the better sorts, as they contain but a small portion of *blow*. Do not spare labour which will be amply repaid by the appearance of the cakes. During the process of creaming, if the butter be not good and genuine or has too much salt, two things may happen. First, the batter may become curdy after a portion of the eggs has been added. In this case add a handful of the flour weighed for the mixture and beat up well with the batter, continue to add a little flour with each fresh lot of eggs ; by this method you will be able to save your batter and turn out fairly decent goods. The second awkward predicament is the batter turning oily and sloppy, into which you cannot beat the eggs ; this state of affairs is caused through over heating, generally by warming the butter carelessly. In this case it is better to turn the whole lot back and commence again, if you continue with it, gelatine must be used to stiffen but is no improvement to the finished article.

To avoid these pitfalls, use good butter which should be washed if too salt, and, with care in the manipulation, a good cake batter should be a certainty. Having the batter properly prepared, work in the flour and fruit small quantities at a time, keeping it moist with milk as required. Be careful not to add too much milk at a time, the appearance of the cake depends a good deal on this.

RICH GENOA BLOCK CAKE (to sell at 1/- to 1/4 per lb.)

2¾-lbs. Flour.	2-lbs. Sultanas.
2-lbs. Butter.	1½-lbs. Glacé Cherries.
2-lbs. Sugar.	1½-lbs. Peel.
2-lbs. Currants.	20 Eggs.

Essence of Lemon, Grated Nutmeg and Blanched Almonds.

PROCESS.—Weigh up the ingredients, line the frame with a few sheets of paper, with a sheet of good white paper on top. Put butter and sugar into a bowl and set in warm place to soften (be careful not to over-heat it), blanch the almonds, shred the peel fine, prepare the eggs, sieve the flour and grate the nutmeg. Commence to cream the sugar and butter as already directed adding the eggs from time to time and beating well up between each addition; when well creamed and the whole of the eggs are used up, add a few drops of essence of lemon and a $\frac{1}{4}$-oz. of Grated Nutmeg. When well mixed into the batter, add the other ingredients carefully, thoroughly mixing them during the process; then turn the lot into the prepared frames, and cover with blanched almonds. Bake in a moderate oven, covering the cake with three or four sheets of paper as soon as it is set. Time, about $2\frac{1}{2}$ hours.

GENOA BLOCK CAKE (to sell at 10d. to 1/- per lb.)

2¾-lbs. Flour.	1¾-lbs. Currants.
1½-lbs. Butter.	1-lb. Mixed Peel.
1¾-lbs. Sugar.	12 Eggs.
1¼-lbs. Sultanas.	1¼-oz. Baking powder.

Essence of Lemon, Blanched Almonds.

PROCESS.—Mix the Baking powder with the flour by passing them together through a sieve two or three times, then proceed in the same manner as for last; if necessary, moisten the batter with a little milk when adding the flour and fruit, cover top with blanched almonds, bake in moderate oven.

GENOA BLOCK CAKE (to sell at 8d. per lb.)

2-lbs. Plain Flour.	2-lbs. Sugar.
1-lb. Soda Flour.	1-lb. Sultanas.
1¼-lbs. Butter.	1¼-lbs. Currants.
¾-lb. Mixed Peel.	10 Eggs.

Egg Colouring. Milk. Almonds.

PROCESS.—As before, using just sufficient colour to give it rich tinge. Chop the almonds and sprinkle on top.

GENOA BLOCK CAKE (to sell at 6d. per lb.)

2¼-lbs. Plain Flour.	1-lb. Sultanas.
2¼-lbs. Soda Flour.	4-lbs. Currants.
1-lb. Butter.	1 Mixed Peel.
1¾-lbs. Sugar.	6 Eggs.
Egg Colouring.	Milk.

PROCESS.—As before, a few almonds or nuts chopped fine lightly sprinkled over the top; use the colouring with discretion.

GENOA BLOCK CAKE (to sell at 4d. per lb.)

2½-lbs. Plain Flour.	½-lb. Sultanas.
2½-lbs. Soda Flour.	2½-lbs. Currants.
1-lb. Good Margarine.	½-lb Peel.
1¼-lbs. Sugar.	4 Eggs.
Egg Colouring.	Milk.

PROCESS.—Mix up in pan as usual adding eggs and colouring, this mixing will require more colouring than the others, moisten with milk or milk and water, add the flour and fruit making a good batter; turn the whole into a frame and bake in a moderately hot oven.

GENOA SEED CAKE (to sell at 1/- per lb.)

2¾-lbs. Plain Flour.	1-lb. Lemon Peel.
1¼-lb. Soda Flour.	22 Eggs.
2½-lbs. Butter.	½-oz. Carraway Seeds.
2¾-lbs. Sugar.	
Essence of Lemon.	Milk.

PROCESS.—Pass the flours two or three times through the sieve to well mix, beat up the cream as before directed, paper the frame with two or three layers; when the mixing has been turned into the frame, cover the top with chopped almonds. See that the batter is stiffish and bake carefully in a moderate oven.

GENOA SEED BLOCK CAKE (to sell at 8d. per lb.)

2¼-lbs. Plain Flour.	½-lb. Mixed Peel.
1-lb. Soda Flour.	7 Eggs.
1¼-lbs. Butter.	¼-oz. Seeds.
1½-lbs. Sugar.	
Essence of Lemon.	Chopped Almonds. Milk.

PROCESS.—As before. See that the batter is well and properly mixed up as already directed; moderate oven. Sprinkle the almonds lightly on the top.

GENOA SEED CAKE (to sell at 6d. per lb.)

2¼-lbs. Plain Flour. 2-lbs. Sugar.
1¾-lbs. Soda Flour. ½-lb. Mixed Peel.
1½-lbs. Butter. 6 Eggs.
Essence of Lemon. Seeds. Milk. Egg Colour.

PROCESS.—As before, bake carefully in moderate oven. Many leave out the chopped nuts in the cheaper cakes, this is a matter of discretion, if none are used brush the top over with lard.

GENOA SEED CAKE (to sell at 4d. per lb.)

3-lbs. Plain Flour. 1 lb. Mixed Peel.
3-lbs. Soda Flour 4 Eggs.
¾-lb. Butter. 1-oz. Caraway Seeds.
1½-lbs. Sugar.
Egg Colouring. Milk.

PROCESS.—As before, beat up the mixture, using the colour carefully, have your frames of a proper size and papered; glaze the top with melted lard, bake in moderate oven.

SULTANA BLOCK CAKE (to sell at 10d. per lb.)

4-lbs. Flour. 3½-lbs Sultanas.
2¼-lbs. Butter. 16 Eggs.
2½-lbs. Sugar. ¾-oz. Baking Powder
Essence of Lemon. Milk.

PROCESS.—See that the fruit is well cleaned and quite free from strings. Sift the flour and baking powder together to well mix. Prepare the frame and cream the butter and sugar, adding the eggs, and using just sufficient milk to make a nice, not sloppy, batter. When the flour and fruit have been added, flavour with Essence of Lemon and turn into frame. Bake in moderate oven.

CHERRY BLOCK CAKE (to sell at 1/-)

2-lbs. Flour. 1¼-lbs. Glacé Cherries.
1¼-lbs. Soda Flour. ¾-lb. Citron Peel.
2-lbs. Butter. 18 Eggs.
2-lbs. Sugar.
Essence of Lemon. Milk. Colouring.

PROCESS.—Line your frame with 3 layers of papers at bottom, then a thick white paper on top to cover both bottom and sides. Cream the butter adding sugar with the eggs, tinge to a bright pink with liquid cochineal or carmine, add the fruits and flour, making a nice batter with a little milk, then flavour with essence of lemon. Turn the whole into a frame and bake in moderate oven. Ice the cake with orange coloured almond icing. When set finish with layer of white water icing on top.

ALMOND BLOCK CAKE (to sell at 8d. per. lb.)

2¾-lbs. Flour.	¾-lb. Orange Peel.
1¼-lbs. Ground Rice.	1¼-oz. Baking Power.
1¼-lbs. Butter.	8 Eggs.
1½-lbs. Sugar.	

Almond Essence. Milk.

PROCESS.—Shred the peel and line the frame with paper. Mix the flour, rice and baking powder and pass through sieve 3 or 4 times; then cream the butter and sugar, using up the eggs by degrees, as before; mix in the flour and peel with a few drops of almond essence, and sufficient milk to make a good batter; then turn it out into the frame making the sheet about $1\frac{1}{2}$ inches thick, cover with blanched or chopped almonds, bake carefully in moderate oven.

COCOANUT BLOCK CAKE (to sell at 1/- per lb.)

4-lbs. Flour.	1½-lbs. Fine Desiccated Cocoa-nut.
2-lbs. Butter.	¾-oz. Baking Powder.
2¼-lbs. Sugar.	18 Eggs.

Essence of Vanilla. Milk.

PROCESS.—Prepare the frame by carefully lining with paper. Mix the baking powder with flour and pass three times through sieves. Cream the butter sugar and eggs as before, add the flour and cocoa-nut and moisten with milk to make good batter, turn out into the frame and bake in moderate oven. When finished, ice the cake over with almond icing with which half its weight of fine desiccated cocoa-nut has been incorporated.

CURRANT BLOCK CAKE (to sell at 4d. per lb.)

12-lbs. Flour.	2-lbs. Margarine fat.
7-lbs. Currants.	¾-lb. Peel.
5-lbs. Sugar.	8 Eggs.

Colouring. Milk.

PROCESS.—Beat well up the fat and sugar until well creamed, add the eggs from time to time with colouring, then the fruit and flour using milk or milk and water to make batter; bake in rather hot oven.

POPULAR CHEAP CAKES FOR READY SALE.

These goods together with the cheap block varieties, are the cakes for the million; they are cheap, wholesome and tasty, and just what suit the majority, hence the big demand and large sale. The better and more expensive cakes will always have a sale at good prices in good neighbourhoods, but they have their limit as luxuries, while the substantial economical cake has become almost a necessity, and, as such, the sale is unlimited and universal. In their own interests and that of the trade bakers and pastry cooks, they should not quietly stand aside and see important branches of the business slip through their fingers without making an effort to retake them. All the advantages are in their favour; it is worth thinking over.

BAKING FLOUR.

The mixings for cheap cakes which follow may be abbreviated both in details of ingredients and simplicity of working, by having the flour previously prepared, in preference to using baking powder in each batch, as the same preparation will be suitable for all the recipes and the mixing will be more thorough.

> 3 oz. Tartaric Acid.
> 4½-oz. Cream of Tartar.
> 6-oz. Bi-carbonate of Soda.
> 30-lbs. Flour.

PROCESS.—If the tartaric acid is hard and lumpy (which it usually is) rub it down to a fine powder with a heavy bottle. Then pass it through a fine wire or hair sieve, together with the Cream of Tartar and Bi-carbonate of Soda, mix the chemicals with the flour, which must be quite dry, pass the whole at least four times through sieve. Store in cool dry place till required.

MADEIRA CAKE (popular price.)

> 12-lbs. Baking Flour.   3-lbs. Fat.
> 4-lbs. Fine Sugar.   10 Eggs.
> Essence of Lemon.   Buttermilk.   Egg Colouring.

PROCESS.—Place the flour in a heap on the board, make a bay in the middle into which place the fat and sugar together with some egg colouring and a few drops of essence of lemon. Break the eggs into a bowl testing each before letting it drop. Rub the fat and sugar well together until quite smooth, then add some eggs from time to time, rubbing well between each addition till all are used up, mix in the flour using sufficient milk (buttermilk for preference) to make a good batter, not too soft. Weigh out into lined hoops or tins, (cut up some long slices of citron peel, lay two on top of each cake and dust with powdered sugar), about $1\frac{1}{2}$ lbs. in each; flatten the top and bake in fairly hot oven. These cakes sell at 6d.

COCOANUT CAKE (popular price.)

12-lbs. Baking Flour.	2-lbs. Desiccated Cocoanut fine.
2-lbs. Fat.	8 Eggs.
4-lbs. Sugar.	
Colour. Essence of Lemon.	

PROCESS.—As last. Sprinkle quantity of shredded cocoanut over top before putting into the oven. Weigh $1\frac{1}{2}$-lbs. Sell at 6d.

SULTANA CAKE (popular price).

12-lbs. Baking Flour.	2-lbs. Sultanas.
$2\frac{3}{4}$-lbs. Fat.	$\frac{1}{2}$-lb. Mixed Peel.
4-lbs. Sugar.	8 Eggs.
Colour. Milk. Essence of Lemon.	

PROCESS.—As before. See the fruit is well picked over. Weigh $1\frac{1}{2}$ lbs. Sell at 6d.

CURRANT CAKE (popular price).

14-lbs. Baking Flour.	3-lbs. Currants.
$2\frac{1}{2}$-lbs. Fat.	$\frac{1}{2}$-lb. Mixed Peel.
4-lbs. Sugar.	10 Eggs.
Egg Colouring. Milk. Essence of Lemon.	

PROCESS.—Proceed as before. See the fruit is well cleaned, and mix in carefully not to break it; do not make batter too soft. Weigh $1\frac{1}{2}$ lbs. Sell at 6d.

ALMOND CAKE (popular price).

12-lbs. Baking Flour.	$3\frac{1}{2}$-lbs Sugar.
$2\frac{1}{2}$-lbs. Fat.	12 Eggs.
Egg Colouring. Milk. Essence of Almonds.	

PROCESS.—As before. Flavour with a few drops of essence of almond. Cover the top with almonds or with almonds and nuts mixed, blanched and chopped. Bake in moderately hot oven. Weigh $1\frac{1}{2}$ lbs. Sell at 6d.

RICE CAKE (popular price).

5-lbs. Baking Flour.   1¼-lbs. Fat.
1-lb. Ground Rice.   5 Eggs.
2-lbs. Fine Sugar.

Essence of Lemon. Milk. Egg Colouring.

PROCESS.—Prepare as before, dredge over the top a sprinkling of semolina. Weigh 1½-lbs. Sell at 6d.

SEED CAKE (popular price).

12-lbs. Baking Flour.   ½-lb. Peel.
2-lbs. Fat.   8 Eggs.
4-lbs. Fine Sugar.   1-oz. Caraways.

Egg Colouring. Milk.

PROCESS.—Prepare your mixing as before, chop up the peel very fine and mix it in together with the seeds; sprinkle a few seeds over the top.

SCOTCH PASTRY.

Scotland is perhaps better known for its whiskey than its pastry, but in the latter as well as in the former there is that peculiar something which appeals to the palate of a great many who probably never saw a kilt. For the 4th Edition of the "Confectioner's Handbook" a noted pastry cook from ayont the Tweed sent me his 30 years' experience in the bake-house in the shape of formulæ for small goods which were good selling lines in the North. They are here reprinted exactly as the writer received them, of the genuineness of which there can be no question.

SCOTCH SHORTBREAD, No. 1.

Eight pounds of flour, 2 lbs. of butter, 2 lbs of lard, 2 lbs. of sugar, 1 oz. volatile salts, four drops of oil of cinnamon, two gills of water. Rub the flour, butter, and lard together, then add the sugar and oil of cinnamon, and make a dough, bake in round frames. Sold in cakes from one penny upwards.

SCOTCH SHORT BREAD, No. 2.

Eight pounds of flour, 4 lbs. of butter, 2 lbs. of sugar, and one gill of water. Rub the flour, butter, and sugar together, and add the water to make a dough, bake in a moderate oven.

SCOTCH SHORT BREAD, No. 3.

Eight pounds of flour, 4 lbs. butter, 2 lbs. of sugar, 8 ozs. of ground rice, three eggs. Beat up the eggs with the sugar, rub the flour and butter with the hands, then mix all together, making a dough.

SCOTCH SPONGE CAKES.

Twelve ounces of sugar, twelve eggs, 12 ozs. of flour. Whisk up the eggs and sugar lightly, then mix the flour, put in round or square tins and bake.

SCOTCH SEED CAKES.

One pound of butter, 1 lb. of sugar. $1\frac{1}{2}$ lbs. of flour, twelve eggs, $1\frac{1}{2}$ lbs. of orange peel. Beat the butter and sugar to a cream, then add the eggs three at a time, then put in the flour with $\frac{1}{2}$ oz. of caraway seeds, bake in round hoops.

SCOTCH PLUM CAKES, No. 1.

One pound of butter, 1 lb. of sugar, ten eggs, $\frac{1}{2}$ lb. of currants, $\frac{1}{2}$ lb of candied peel, 2 ozs. of almonds, 18 ozs. of flour. Made in the same manner as seed cakes.

SCOTCH PLUM CAKES, No. 2 (Cheap).

Six pounds of flour, $1\frac{1}{2}$ lbs. of lard, $1\frac{1}{2}$ lbs. of sugar, 2 ozs. of bi-carbonate of soda, 2 ozs. of volatile salts, $1\frac{1}{2}$ ozs. of tartaric acid, 5 lbs of currants, caraway seeds, mix with butter milk, spread out on buttered tins. Sold at sixpence per pound.

SCOTCH SODA SCONES.

Four pounds of flour, 1 oz. of bi-carbonate of soda, 2 ozs. of cream of tartar, mix these ingredients by sifting them through the flour sieve three times, then rub 8 ozs. of butter with the mixture, make a dough with buttermilk, adding 8 ozs. of sugar, form them into round two-penny cakes and bake. These cakes are afterwards cut into four pieces, selling at a halfpenny each.

14

LOCH KATHERINE CAKES (Scotch).

Four pounds of flour, $\frac{1}{2}$ lb. of lard, 1 lb. of sugar, 6 ozs. of currants, 1 oz. of bi-carbonate of soda, $1\frac{1}{2}$ ozs. of cream of tartar, make a dough with buttermilk, flavour with essence of lemon, spread on buttered tins and bake. Sold at one penny each.

SCOTCH CREAM CAKES.

Two pounds of flour, $2\frac{1}{2}$ ozs. of lard, 10 ozs. of sugar, $\frac{1}{2}$ oz. of volatile salts, two eggs, form a dough with buttermilk, flavour with essence of lemon.

INVERNESS CAKES.

Four pounds of flour, 2 ozs. of lard, 2 lbs. of sugar, 2 ozs. of volatile salts, three eggs, mix with buttermilk, cut with small cutter, loaf sugar on top. Sold at four a penny.

PERKINS BISCUITS (Scotch).

One-and-a-half pounds of flour, $1\frac{1}{2}$ lbs. of oatmeal, 8 ozs. of lard, 9 ozs. of sugar, 2 ozs. bi-carbonate of soda, 2 ozs. mixed spices, 2 lbs. of treacle, one gill new milk, washed with eggs, almonds on top, sold at four ozs. a penny.

PARIS BUNS (Scotch).

Four pounds of flour, 1 lb. of lard, 2 lbs. of sugar, four eggs, 1 oz. bi-carbonate of soda, $\frac{1}{2}$ oz. tartaric acid, mix the soda and acid together, add sugar, etc., buttermilk to make dough, wash with eggs, rough pounded loaf sugar on top, baked on buttered tins in steady oven, sold at three a penny.

GARIBALDI SCONES (Scotch).

" Two pounds of flour, 5 ozs. of lard, 8 ozs. of sugar, 1 oz. cream of tartar, $\frac{1}{4}$ oz. bi-carbonate of soda, pass the flour, soda, and cream of tartar through the sieve, add the other ingredients, and make dough with butter milk, sold at four ounces for one penny.

SULTANS CAKES (Scotch).

Four ounces butter, five eggs, 6 ozs. sugar, 1 lb. flour, 14 ozs. sultana raisins, a pinch of volatile salts, bake in hoops, papered.

KING'S BISCUITS (Scotch).

One pound flour, 1 lb. butter, 1 lb. sugar, six eggs, drop on buttered tins, put ground sugar on top, flavour with lemon.

GERMAN WIGS (Scotch).

One pound flour, $\frac{1}{2}$ lb sugar, 6 ozs. butter, $\frac{1}{2}$ oz. volatile salts, dust sugar on top, flavour lemon.

JUDGE'S BISCUITS (Scotch).

Twelve eggs, 2 lbs. sugar, $\frac{1}{2}$ oz. volatile salts, 1 lb flour, and a few caraway seeds, bake on buttered tins.

HONEY CAKES (Scotch).

"One pound flour, 5-ozs. butter, 6-ozs. sugar, 1-oz. almonds, $\frac{1}{2}$-oz. volatile salts.

BRIGHTON BISCUITS (Scotch).

"Rub $\frac{1}{2}$-lb. butter, $\frac{1}{2}$-lb. flour, $\frac{1}{2}$-lb. powdered sugar, $\frac{1}{2}$-oz. volatile salts, two drops lemon, three eggs, roll out and put cut almonds and sugar on the top.

LEMON BISCUITS.

"Half pound flour, 4-ozs. butter, $\frac{1}{2}$-lb. sugar, $\frac{1}{4}$-oz. volatile salts, flavour with essence of lemon, and cut."

INDIAN GINGER BREAD (Scotch).

"Fourteen pounds golden syrup or treacle, 4-lbs. moist sugar, 10-ozs. pearlash, 10-ozs. ground alum, 7-lbs. oatmeal, nine gills of water, put the pearlash with the water, and let it stand one night to dissolve, mix the sugar and alum together, then mix in the oatmeal, afterwards add the syrup or treacle to set sponge, take fine flour to make dough; the third day this gingerbread stands the weather. Spice, peel, or almonds may be added to taste.

BRANDY WAFERS (Scotch).

"Half pound flour, 14-ozs. sugar, 8-ozs. butter, 1-oz. ground ginger, buttered tins.

COMMON GINGER BREAD (Scotch).

"Twenty-one pounds flour, 12-ozs. bi-carbonate of soda, 6-ozs. of alum, 14-lbs. treacle, $1\frac{1}{2}$-pints of water, sift the flour and soda together through a fine sieve, boil the alum and water. Mix the whole together and make a dough. Bake in large or small cakes, add spices, seeds, or peel, sold at sixpence per pound.

BRQWN BISCUITS (Scotch).

"Eight pounds of flour, 2-lbs. of lard, $1\frac{1}{2}$-lbs. of sugar, 2-ozs. of bi-carbonate of soda, 1-oz. tartaric acid, mix with butter milk to make dough.

PRINCE'S BISCUITS (Scotch).

"Two pounds of flour, 6-ozs. of sugar, 8-ozs. of butter, three eggs, $\frac{1}{2}$-oz. of volatile salts, flavour with lemon.

RICE CAKES (Scotch).

"One pound of flour, 1-lb. of sugar, $\frac{1}{2}$-lb of ground rice, fourteen eggs, make the same as sponge cakes, but drop on buttered tins, bake in cool oven.

THE PURITY OF CONFECTIONERY.

SUGAR, the principal ingredient used in all kinds of sweets, has now become so cheap that confectionery made in any part of Great Britain may be considered comparatively pure, No doubt isolated cases may occur where resort may have been made to increase the bulk by the substitution of something even cheaper than sugar, but happily these cases are few and far between. When the writer first entered the trade, and during his apprenticeship, things were different, sugar was much dearer, and the confectioner's knowledge of colours did not seem to be fully developed, and in many cases ingredients, of which to say the least were questionable, were used for this purpose, Sugar was mixed with foreign matter, in the shape of an article called terra alba (ground Derby stone), and made into lozenges, and other matters all more or less deleterious were used to increase the bulk when manufactured. However, things are altered, sugar is cheap, colours are now specially manufactured for the trade, and generally speaking every article used in the manufacture of sweets, especially by large houses, is strictly wholesome. The very small amount to be gained by resort to adulteration of any kind is not now tempting enough to induce even those who otherwise might entertain the idea, besides the Adulteration Act of 1872 holds out a very wholesome dread to unprincipled manufacturers, as its penalties are very severe upon the adulterater. The offender in England renders himself liable on conviction for the first offence to a penalty of £50, and for the second goes to jail for six months with hard labour. These facts, coupled with the small amount of gain which would be derived from such practices, render the buying and consuming of confectionery a matter of comparative safety. However, should the reader wish to test the purity of any article of confectionery, he may do so as follows :—Put a few of the sweets you wish to test into a glass vessel and pour over them some hot water, and let stand for twelve hours, after which time the sweets, if pure, should be dissolved and amalgamated with the water, as sugar is perfectly soluble in water. In the case of comfits and lozenges, a little wheaten flour or starch powder is necessary to be used in making therefore a small sediment would fall to the bottom ; this, if required, could be easily dried and examined with a microscope for foreign matter.

E. S.

INDEX

Acid Drops and Tablets	...	40
Acid Sticks	...	46
Almonds, Burnt ...	...	73
Almond Cake (Popular price)		207
Almond Hardbake ...	...	27
Almond Ice Cream ...	...	169
Almond Rock	...	27
Almond Tablets ...	...	40
Almonds, Imitation ...	...	45
Almonds, Sugared ...	...	138
Almonds to blanch ...	...	28
American Cream Sticks	...	50
American Fruit Toffee	...	28
American Gum Pastilles	...	117
American Hash ...	...	29
American Honeycomb Sticks		49
American Ice Cream ...	...	167
Aniseed Balls	...	135
Aniseed Lozenges ...	...	147
Anti-Acid Lozenges ...	...	148
Anti-Bilious Lozenges	...	148
Apple and Goose-berry Juice in		
Jams	...	174
Apple Jam (Steam Power)		186
Apple Jelly	...	179
Apple Jelly (Steam Power)		185
Apple Pulp (Steam Power)		185
Apricot Candy ...	...	30
Apricots, Crystallized (Gelatine		
Work)	...	105
Artificial Figures ...	...	128
Bacon and Eggs ...	...	26
Baking Powder ...	195,	206
Balls, Aniseed	...	135
Balls, Rifle	...	134
Balls, Round (Hand made) ...		52
Balls, Round (Machine made)		53
Banbury Puffs ...	...	199
Barcelona Cream Candy	...	34
Barcelona Toffee ...	...	25

Barley Sugar Drops ...	...	38
Barley Sugar Sticks, Twisted		
(Hand made) ...	...	50
Barley Sugar Sticks, Twisted		
(Machine made) ...	...	51
Bars, Cocoanut Cream	...	77
Bars, Cream	...	76
Bars, Raspberry or Rose Cream		77
Bars, Vanilla Cream ...	...	76
Bath Pipe	...	158
Beginners, Hints to ...	...	14
Birds' Eggs	...	135
Biscuits, Brighton (Scotch)		211
Biscuits, Brown (Scotch)	...	212
Biscuits, German Wigs (Scotch)		211
Biscuits, Judge's (Scotch)	...	211
Biscuits, Lemon ...	...	211
Biscuits, Prince's (Scotch)	...	212
Biscuit's Perkin's (Scotch)	...	210
Blackcurrant Jam ...	...	177
Blackcurrant Jam, Nos. 1 and 2		
(Steam Power) ...	...	184
Blackcurrant Jellies ...	...	109
Blackcurrant Jelly ...	...	178
Blackcurrant Lozenges	...	157
Block Cakes	...	199
Almond	...	205
Cherry	...	204
Cocoanut	...	205
Currant	...	205
Genoa, Rich ...	...	202
Genoa No. 1 ...	...	202
,, No. 2 ...	...	202
,, No. 3 ...	...	203
,, No. 4 ...	...	203
,, Seed No. 1 ...	...	203
,, ,, No. 2 ...	...	203
,, ,, No. 3 ...	...	204
,, ,, No. 4 ..	...	204
Block Cakes, Method of Pre-		
paring	...	200

215

Boiled Sugar Goods, To crystallize 57
Bon Bons 127
Bottled Fruits 193
Bottled Gooseberries, Black-
currants, etc. 193
Bottled Plums, Damson, Green-
gages and Apples 194
Bottled Raspberries 193
Brandy Wafers (Scotch) ... 211
Brighton Biscuits (Scotch) ... 211
British Pharmacopœia Recipes 149
Bull's Eyes, Peppermint ... 51
Bull's Eyes, Various 52
Buns, King's Scotch) 211
Buns, Paris (Scotch) 210
Burnt Almonds 73
Burnt Almond Chocolate ... 127
Butternut Creams 126
Butter Scotch... 24

Cake, Almond (Popular price) 207
Cake and Pastry Making ... 195
Cake, Cocoanut (Popular price) 207
Cakes, Honey (Scotch) ... 211
Cake, Currant (Popular price) 207
Cake, Maderia (Popular price) 206
Cake, Seed (Popular price) ... 208
Cake, Sultana (Popular price) 207
Cakes, Block 199
Cakes, Inverness 210
Cakes, Loch Katherine (Scotch) 210
Cakes, Popular, for ready sale 206
Cakes, Rice (Popular price) ... 208
Cakes, Rice (Scotch) 212
Cakes, Scotch Cream 210
Cakes, Sultan's (Scotch) ... 210
Candied Nuts 81
Candies 29
Candies, Cream 34
Candies, Peels, Orange & Lemon 191
Candy, Apricot 30
Candy, Barcelona Cream ... 34
Candy, Cherry Cream ... 35
Candy, Chocolate 32
Candy, Chocolate Cream ... 36
Candy, Cocoanut (Brown) ... 31
Candy, Cocoanut Cream Ice ... 37
Candy, Cocoanut (White) ... 31
Candy, Cough 30
Candy, Cream Chips 36

Candy, Cream Pats 37
Candy, Cream White 37
Candy, Devonshire Cream ... 35
Candy, Fruit 32
Candy, Indian Cream ... 35
Candy, Lemon 29
Candy, Raspberry 30
Candy, Sponge (Lemon) ... 32
Candy, Sponge (Rose) ... 33
Candy, Sugar (Pink & White) 79
Candy, Vanilla Cream ... 37
Candy, Walnut Cream ... 34
Caramels 67
Caramels, American 69
Caramels, Chocolate 69
Caramels, Chocolate (No. 1) ... 71
Caramels, Chocolate (No. 2) ... 71
Caramels, Cocoanut 68
Caramels, Maple 70
Caramels, Opera Cream ... 73
Caramels, Raspberry 68
Caramels, Raspberry and Straw-
berry 70
Caramels, Unwrapped ... 71
Caramels, Vanilla 68
Caramels, Vanilla No. 1 ... 70
Caramels, Vanilla No. 2 ... 70
Caramels, Walnut 69
Caraway Comfits 136
Cased Goods 54
Cayenne Lozenges 146
Chalk Lozenges 148
Cheap Ice Cream 105
Cheap Lozenges, Mixings for ... 153
Cherry Cream Candy 35
Cherry Water Ice 170
Ching-Changs 135
Chocolate, Burnt Almonds ... 127
Chocolate Buttered Creams ... 126
Chocolate Cocoanut Sticks ... 45
Chocolate Creams (by hand) ... 92
Chocolate Creams (by ma-
chinery) 93
Chocolate Cream Bars, No. 1 88
Chocolate Cream Bars, No. 2 89
Chocolate Cream Bars or Tab-
lets, Moulded (by hand) ... 90
Chocolate Cream Bars or Tab-
lets, Moulded (by machinery) 90
Chocolate Cream Buns and Cakes 88

Chocolate Cream Candy	...	36	Comfits, with Boiled Centres 137
Chocolate Cream Lozenges	...	155	Confectionery, The purity of 212
Chocolate Cream Roll (Thick)		88	Coral Beads and Green Peas ... 134
Chocolate Cream Sticks, Imita-			Coriander Comfits 136
tion	...	44	Cough Candy 30
Chocolate Drops, Plain	...	92	Cough Drops (Brown) ... 41
Chocolate, for Dipping	...	95	Cough Drops (Light) 41
Chocolate Ice Cream ...	...	66	Cough Lozenges 146
Chocolate Ice Cream ...	...	168	Cream Bars, etc., ... 76
Chocolate Making	...	84	Cream, Butternut 126
Chocolate, Milk	...	94	Cream Cakes (Scotch) ... 210
Chocolate Nibs	...	39	Cream Candies 33
Chocolate Nougatines	...	65	Cream Candies 34
Chocolate, Parisian Bon-Bons		127	Cream Candy (White) ... 37
Chocolate Patties	...	128	Cream Chips 36
Chocolate Paste, Sweet	...	91	Cream, Chocolate Buttered ... 126
Chocolate Roast Almonds	...	126	Cream for Chocolate Cream or
Chocolate, Sweet	...	87	Bars 87
Chocolates, Sweet	...	91	Cream Lozenge Paste ... 154
Chocolate, The quality of,	...	94	Cream Lozenges 154
Christmas Pudding, Imitation		80	Cream Lozenges, Mixed ... 156
Cinnamon Comfits	...	136	Cream Pats 37
Cinnamon Lozenges	...	147	Crystallize, Best way to (Gum
Cinnamon Sticks	...	48	Goods) 116
Clove Sticks	...	48	Crystallize, Ginger Fruit, etc.,
Cocoanut Bars, Gelatine (Yellow)		105	To 194
Cocoanut Cake (Popular price)		207	Crystallize, To 57
Cocoanut Candy (Brown)	...	31	Crystallized Apricots 105
Cocoanut Candy (White)	...	31	Crystallized Cocoanut Chips ... 78
Cocoanut Chips, Crystallized		79	Crystallized Fruits 195
Cocoanut (Chocolate)	...	32	Crystallized Ginger 194
Combination Cream Bars	...	89	Crystallized Jubes 102
Cocoanut Cream Ice ...	...	37	Crystallizing, Coloured Sugar
Cocoanut Cream Lozenges	...	156	for 79
Cocoanut Cream Rolls	...	126	Currant Cake (Popular price) 207
Cocoanut Cream Rolls	...	157	Custard Ice Cream (No. 1) ... 164
Cocoanut Ice Cream ...	..	168	Custard Ice Cream (Nos. 2 and
Cocoanut Perfections ...	...	137	3) 165
Colours, Poisonous	...	19	Cutting the Grain, Lowering or
Cocoanut Quarters (Imitation)		157	Greasing 13
Cocoanut Tablets	...	40	
Cocoanut Toffee	...	26	Damson Jam No. 1 (Steam
Cocoanut Toffee or Stickjaw		26	Power) 184
Coloured Sugar for Dry Crystal-			Damson Jam No. 2 (Steam
lizing	...	79	Power) 185
Colours and Flavours	...	16	Dandies, for Mixtures (Ameri-
Coltsfoot Rock	...	158	can) 125
Comfits, Caraway	...	136	Dates, Clear Gum 116
Comfits, Cinnamon	...	136	Decorate Fancies, To 129
Comfits, Coriander	...	136	Delight, English 107

217

Dessert Ice Cream	 167	French or Swiss Paste ...	198
Dessert Ices	... 167	Fruit Candy	32
Devonshire Cream Candy	... 35	Fruit Preserving, etc.	171
Directions, General ...	... 143	Fruit, To bottle	193
Drops (Machine made)	... 38	Fruit, To frost	193
Drops, Almond Tablets (Machine made)	40	Fruits, Crystallized	195
Drops, and Tablets, Acid (Machine made)	40	Fruits, Ginger, etc., To Crystallize	194
Drops, Barley Sugar (Machine made)	39	Fruits, in Syrup	194
Drops, Brown Cough (Machine made)	41	Garabaldi Scones (Scotch) ...	210
		Gelatine Cocoanut Bars (Yellow)	105
Drops, Chocolate (Nonpariel)	92	Gelatine Work	101
Drops, Chocolate Nibs (Machine made)	39	General Directions	143
		German Wigs (Scotch) ...	211
Drops, Chocolate, Plain ...	92	Ginger Bread, Common (Scotch)	212
Drops, Cocoanut Tablets (Machine made)	40	Ginger Bread, Indian (Scotch)	211
		Ginger, Crystallized	194
Drops, Light Cough (Machine made)	41	Ginger Lozenges, ...	146
		Ginger, To Crystallize ...	194
Drops, Pear (Machine made)	39	Glaces	66
Drops, Pineapple (Machine made)	40	Glazing Pan Goods	138
		Glucose in Jams	174
Drops, Raspberry (Machine made	39	Glycerine Pastilles	116
		Gooseberries, ... 182,	193
Drying Room	98	Gooseberry Jam	179
		Gooseberry Jam No. 1 (Steam Power)	182
Eggs and Bacon	26	Gooseberry Jam No. 2 (Steam Power)	183
English Delight	107	
Everton Toffee	24	Green Peas and Coral Beads	134
		Gum Dates, Clear	116
Fancies, To decorate	129	Gum Goods	113
Farthing and Halfpenny Sticks	45	Gum Goods, Imitation ...	117
Fig Toffee	25	Gum Goods, To Crystallize ...	116
Figure Piping	130	Gum Pastilles, American ...	117
Figures, Artificial	128	Gum Pastilles, French ...	117
Flavours and Colours ...	16	
Fondant Cream for Centres ...	121	Hardbake, Almond	27
Fondant Cream Work ...	120	Hash, American	29
Fondant, Making by Machinery	123	Hints to Beginners	14
Fondants Cherry	123	Honey Cakes (Scotch) ...	211
Fondants, Chocolate and Vanilla	122	How to make Ice Cream ...	164
		Hundreds and Thousands (Nonpareil, ...	133
Fondants, Cokernut	122	
Fondants for Mixture ...	125	
Fondants, Raspberry and Vanilla	121	Ice Cream, Almond	169
		Ice Cream, American	167
Fondants, Strawberry ...	122	Ice Cream (Cheap)	165
French Almond Rock ...	27	Ice Cream, Chocolate 66,	168

218

Ice Cream Cocoanut 168
Ice Cream Confectionery ... 65
Ice Cream, Custard No. 1 ... 164
Ice Cream Custard, No. 2 ... 165
Ice Cream Custard, No. 3 ... 165
Ice Cream, Dessert 167
Ice Cream, How to make ... 164
Ice Cream, Lemon 166
Ice Cream Making 160
Ice Cream, Neapolitan ... 169
Ice Cream, Noyeau 169
Ice Cream, Parisian Coffee ... 168
Ice Cream, Pineapple... ... 168
Ice Cream, Raspberry 166, 168
Ice Cream, Raspberry and ...
  Strawberry Confectionery ... 66
Ice Cream, Strawberry ... 168
Ice Cream, Tea 168
Ice Moulds 171
Ice Pudding or Nesselrode ... 170
Ices, Cherry Water 170
Ices, Dessert 167
Ices from Jams, ... 170
Ices, Lemon Water 169
Ices, Lemon Water (Best) ... 170
Ices, Raspberry Water ... 170
Ices, Strawberry Water ... 170
Ices, To mould 171
Imitation Almonds 45
Imitation Indian Corn ... 57
Indian Corn, Imitation ... 57
Indian Cream Candy 35
Indian Ginger Bread (Scotch) 211
Inverness Cakes, ... 210
Ipecacuanha Lozenges ... 147

Jam, Blackcurrant 177
Jam, Blackcurrant No. 1 (Steam
  power) 184
Jam, Blackcurrant No. 2 (Steam
  power) 184
Jam, Cheap (Steam power) ... 186
Jam, Damson No. 1 (Steam
  power) 184
Jam, Damson No. 2 (Steam
  power) 185
Jam, Dried fruit in Jams (Steam
  power) 187
Jam, Gelatine in 188
Jam, Gooseberry 179

Jam, Gooseberry No. 1 (Steam
  power) 182
Jam, Gooseberry No. 2 (Steam
  power) 183
Jams, Apple and Gooseberry
  Juice in 174
Jams, Jellies and Marmalade 172
Jam, Mixed Fruit Jam No. 1
  (Steam power) 186
Jam, Mixed Fruit Jam No. 2
  (Steam power) 186
Jam, Plum 178
Jam, Plum (Steam power) ... 184
Jam, Pulping for stock (Steam
  power) 187
Jam, Raspberry Flavoured
  (Steam power) 186
Jams, Raspberry (No. 1) ... 175
Jam, Raspberry (No. 2) ... 176
Jam, Raspberry No. 1 (Steam
  power) 183
Jam, Raspberry No. 2 (Steam
  power) 183
Jam, Redcurrant (Steam power) 184
Jam, Redcurrant No. 1 ... 178
Jam, Redcurrant No. 2 ... 178
Jam, Roley Poley 107
Jam, Strawberry (Steam power) 183
Jam, Strawberry No. 1 ... 176
Jam, Strawberry No. 2 ... 176
Jams, Various 180
Jam, Whole Fruit Strawberry
  No. 1 176
Jam, Whole Fruit Strawberry
  No. 2 177
Jam, Whole Fruit Strawberry
  (Steam power) 183
Jap Nuggets 59
Jap Nuggets No. 1 60
Jap Nuggets No. 2 60
Jap Nuggets No. 3 61
Jap Nuggets No. 4 (American) 61
Jellies, Jams and Marmalades 172
Jellies, Raspberry 108
Jelly, Apple 179
Jelly, Blackcurrant 178
Jelly Fancies, ... 107
Jelly Goods (Cheap) 106
Jelly, Raspberry 176
Jubes, Blackcurrant 104

Jubes, Clear Licorice ...	... 104	Lozenges, Lavender ...	... 147
Jubes, Clear Pineapple	... 104	Lozenges, Lettuce ...	... 148
Jubes, Clear Pink (Imitation Gum)	... 103	Lozenges, Long-Life ...	... 149
		Lozenges, Magnesia ...	... 147
Jubes, Crystallized, Rose and Lemon	... 102	Lozenge Making ...	... 139
		Lozenges, Mixed Cream	... 156
Jubes, Licorice ...	... 114	Lozenges, Musk ...	... 145
Jubes, Wedding Cake	... 106	Lozenges, Nitre ...	... 148
Judge's Biscuits (Scotch)	... 211	Lozenges of the British Phar-	
Jujubes, Clear Pine (Gum)	... 114	macopœia	... 149
Jujubes, Clear Pink (Gum)	... 114	Lozenges, Paregoric ...	... 148
		Lozenges, Peppermint	... 144
King's Biscuits (Scotch)	... 211	Lozenges, Peppermint (Extra)	145
		Lozenges, Peppermint (Cheap)	153
Lemon Biscuits (Scotch)	.. 211	Lozenges, Quinine ...	... 148
Lemon Candy	... 29	Lozenges, Raspberry Cream ...	155
Lemon Cream Patties	... 128	Lozenges, Rose ...	... 146
Lemon Fruit Bon Bons	... 127	Lozenges, Tolu ...	... 147
Lemon Ice Cream ...	... 166	Lozenges, Vanilla Cream	... 155
Lemon Pipe	... 158		
Lemon Sticks	... 47	Maderia Cake (Popular price)	206
Lemon Toffee	... 23	Magnesia Lozenges ...	... 147
Lemon Water Ice (Best)	... 170	Marmalade, Jellies and Jams	172
Lemon Water Ices ...	... 169	Marmalade, To prepare Chips	
Lettuce Lozenges ...	... 148	and Pulp (Steam Power) ...	190
Liqueurs	... 117	Marmalade ... 179, 189,	191
,, Brandy, Rum or Gin		Marshmallows, American ...	67
Almonds ...	... 118	Milk Chocolate ...	... 94
,, for Mixture ...	... 119	Mixed Fruit Jams (Nos. 1 and	
,, Orange and Lemon		2)	... 186
Slices ...	... 119	Mixtures, Dandies for	... 125
,, Wedding Rings	... 119	Mixtures, Fondants for	... 125
Liquorice Goods ...	... 159	Mixings for cheap Lozenges	153
Loch Katherine Cakes (Scotch)	210	Motto Rock	... 55
Long-Life Lozenges ...	... 149	Moulds for Ices ...	... 171
Lowering or Creasing, Cutting		Moulds, To make (for Pastilles,	
the grain	... 13	Creams, etc.) ...	... 100
Lozenges, Aniseed ...	... 147	Musk Lozenges ...	... 145
Lozenges, Anti-Acid ...	... 148		
Lozenges, Anti-Bilious	... 148	Neapolitan Ice Cream	... 169
Lozenges, Blackcurrant	... 157	Nesselrode, or Ice Pudding ...	170
Lozenges, Cayenne ...	... 146	Nibs, Chocolate ...	... 39
Lozenges, Chalk ...	... 148	Nitre Lozenges, ...	... 148
Lozenges, Cheap Mixings for	153	Nonpareils, Hundreds and	
Lozenges, Chocolate Cream ...	155	Thousands	... 133
Lozenges, Cinnamon ...	... 147	Nougat, Bulgarian ...	... 62
Lozenges, Cocoanut Cream ...	156	,, ,, (No. 1 best)	62
Lozenges, Cough ...	... 146	,, ,, (No. 2 cheap)	62
Lozenges, Cream ...	... 154	Nougat, Vanilla (Best) ...	63
Lozenges, Ipecacuanha	... 147	,, ,, (Cheap) ...	64

220

Nougats, Various	...	...	63
Nougatines	...	...	65
„ Chocolate	...	...	65
Noyeau	...	...	81
Noyeau Ice Cream	...	...	169
Noyeau, Raspberry (Old method)	...	...	81
Noyeau, Raspberry, No. 2	...	82
Nuts, Candied	...	...	81
Official Recipes, British Pharmacopœia	...	...	149
Orange Fruit Bon Bons	...	127
Orange Marmalade	...	...	179
Orange Sticks	...	...	48
Pan Goods, Glazing	...	...	138
Pan Goods, with Lozenge Bottoms	...	...	138
Pan Room	...	...	130
Paregoric Lozenges	...	...	148
Paris Buns (Scotch)	...	...	210
Parisian Chocolate Bon Bons		127
Parisian Coffee Ice Cream	...	168
Paste, Cream Lozenge	...	154
Paste, French or Swiss	...	198
Pastilles, French Gum	...	117
Pastilles, Glycerine	...	116
Pastilles, Gum (Lemon)	...	115
Pastilles, Gum (Rose)	...	115
Pastry and Cake Making	...	195
Pastry, on Making	...	...	197
Pastry, Scotch	...	...	208
Patties	...	...	128
Pear Drops	...	...	39
Peels, Candied Orange and Lemon	...	...	191
Peppermint Cream Patties	...	128
Peppermint Lozenges	...	144
Peppermint Lozenges (Cheap)		153
„ „ (Extra Strong)		145
Peppermint Pipe	...	...	158
Peppermint Rock	...	...	42
Peppermint Sticks	...	...	47
Perkins, Scotch Biscuits	...	210
Pineapple Drops	...	...	40
Pineapple Ice Cream	...	...	168
Pineapple Jellies	...	...	109
Pineapple Rock	...	...	43
Pipe, Bath	...	...	158
Pipe, Lemon	...	...	158

Pipe, Peppermint	...	...	158
Pipe, Regent	...	...	158
Pipe, Rose	...	...	158
Piping, Figure	...	...	130
Plain Toffee	...	...	22
Plaited Rock	...	...	44
Plum Cakes (Scotch)	...	...	209
Plum Jam	...	...	178
Plum Jam (Steam Power)	...	184
Poisonous Colours	...	...	19
Pop Corn	...	...	58
Pop Corn Balls	...	...	58
Pop Corn Bricks	...	...	58
Pop Corn Cakes	...	...	58
Popular Cakes, for ready sale		206
Pralines, Blackcurrant	...	75
„ Cocoanut	...	...	75
„ Raspberry and Cocoanut	...	...	75
„ Satin	...	...	74
„ Vanilla	...	...	74
Preserves by Steam Power	...	180
Apple Jam	...	...	186
Apple Jelly	...	...	185
Apple Pulp	...	...	185
Blackcurrant Jams (Nos. 1 and 2	...	...	184
Cheap Jams	...	...	186
Damson Jam (No. 1)	...	184
Damson Jam (No. 2)	...	185
Dried Fruit in Jams	...	187
Gelatine in Jams	...	188
Gooseberries	...	...	182
Gooseberry Jam (No. 1)		182
Gooseberry Jam (No. 2)		183
Home made Marmalade		191
Marmalade	...	...	189
Mixed Fruit Jam (Nos. 1 & 2)		186
Orange Marmalade (Nos. 1, 2 and 3)	...	...	191
Plum Jam	...	...	184
Pulping for Stock	...	187
Raspberry Flavoured Jam		186
Raspberry Jam (Nos. 1 & 2)		183
Preserves by Steam Power—		
Red Currant Jam	...	184
Strawberry Jam	...	...	183
To prepare the Chips and Pulp	...	...	190
Whole Fruit Strawberry		183

221

Preserving Fruit 171
Prince's Biscuits (Scotch) ... 212
Pudding, Brown Cream ... 80
Pudding, Imitation Christmas 80
Puff Paste (Nos. 1 and 2) ... 198
Puffs, Banbury 199
Puffs, Three-Cornered ... 199
Pulled Sugars 41
Purity of Confectionery ... 212

Quality of Chocolate 94

Raspberries 193
Raspberries, Clear (Gelatine work) 103
Raspberry Candy 30
Raspberry Cream Lozenges ... 155
Raspberry Drops 39
Raspberry Jam (No. 1) ... 175
Raspberry Jam (No. 2) ... 176
Raspberry Ice Cream 166, 168
Raspberry Jam Nos. 1 and 2 (Steam Power) 183
Raspberry and Strawberry Ice Cream Confectionery ... 66
Raspberry Jellies 108
Raspberry Jelly 176
Raspberry Sticks 49
Raspberry Toffee 25
Raspberry Flavoured Jam (Steam power) 186
Raspberry Water Ice ... 170
Recipes, British Pharmacopœia 149
Red Currant Jam (Steam Power) 184
Red Currant Jam (No. 1) ... 178
Red Currant Jam (No. 2) ... 178
Regent Pipe 158
Requisites for Sugar Boiling 4
Rice Cake (Popular Price) ... 208
Rice Cakes (Scotch) 212
Rifle Balls 134
Ripe Pears 54
Roast Almond Chocolates ... 126
Rock, Almond 27
Rock, Coltsfoot 158
Rock, French Almond ... 27
Rock, Motto 55
Rock, Peppermint 42
Rock, Pineapple 43

Rock, Plaited 44
Rock, Rose 44
Rock, Star, or Rock Varieties 56
Roley Poley Jam 107
Rolls, Cocoanut Cream ... 157
Rose Buds 54
Rose Lozenges 146
Rose Pipe 158
Rose Rock 44

Scones, Garibaldi (Scotch) ... 210
Scones, Scotch Soda 209
Scotch Cream Cakes 210
Scotch Pastry 208
Scotch Plum Cakes (No. 1) ... 209
Scotch Plum Cakes (No. 2) ... 209
Scotch Seed Cakes 209
Scotch Shortbread ... 208, 209
Scotch Soda Scones 209
Scraps and Siftings, What to do with 82
Seed Cake (Popular price) ... 208
Seed Cakes (Scotch) 209
Sherbet, Lemon 83
Sherbet, Persian 83
Sherbet, Raspberry 84
Sherbet Sticks 43
Shortbread, Scotch 208, 209
Sponge Candy (Lemon) ... 32
Sponge Candy (Rose) ... 33
Star Rock, or Rock Varieties 56
Starch Room 95
Starch Room, Tools used in ... 97
Stickjaw or Cocoanut Toffee ... 26
Sticks, Sugar 51
Sticky Sweets 21
Strawberry Ice Cream ... 168
Strawberry Ice Cream Confectionery 66
Strawberry Jam (Nos. 1 and 2) 176
Strawberry Jam (Steam power) 183
Strawberry Jam, Whole Fruit (Steam power) 183
Strawberry Water Ice ... 170
Sugar, Coloured for Dry Crystallizing 79
Sugar Boiling 1
Sugar Boiling, Method of ... 11
Sugar Boiling, Wrinkles on ... 19
Sugar Candy, Pink and White 79

Sugared Almonds 138
Sultana Cake (Popular price) 207
Sultan's Cakes (Scotch) ... 210
Sweet Chocolate 87
Sweet Chocolate Paste ... 91
Sweet Chocolates, ... 91
Swiss or French Paste ... 198

Table Jellies, Concentrated ... 110
Blackcurrant ... 112
Lemon 111
Raspberry ... 110
Strawberry ... 111
Tablets, Almond 40
Tablets, Cocoanut 40
Tea Ice Cream 168
Three Cornered Puffs ... 199
Toffee, American Fruit ... 28
Toffee Apples 29
Toffee, Barcelona 25
Toffee, Cocoanut 26
Toffee, Everton 24

Toffee, Fig 25
Toffee, Lemon 23
Toffee, Plain 22
Toffee, Raspberry 25
Toffee, Walnut 25
Tolu Lozenges 147
Toys, Boiled Sugar 56
Turkish Delight (Lemon) ... 112
Turkish Delight (Raspberry) 113
Twisted Barley Sugar Sticks 50, 51

Vanilla Cream 37
Vanilla Cream Lozenges ... 155

Wafers, Brandy (Scotch) ... 211
Walnut Cream Candy ... 34
Walnut Toffee 25
Whole Fruit Strawberry
Jams 176, 177
Workshop, with Sugar Boiling
requisites 4
Wrinkles on Sugar Boiling ... 19

CPSIA information can be obtained
at www.ICGtesting.com
Printed in the USA
BVHW041926231118
533673BV00008B/40/P